Women of Komala

"An epistemic intervention addressing the neglect of Kurdish women's experiences from Western and Middle Eastern feminist studies, as well as from Kurdish and Iranian studies, fields that have historically overlooked both women and Kurdish perspectives. Drawing on extensive interviews yet written with the immersive depth of longstanding ethnography, Fatemeh Karimi reveals how these women's military, intellectual, and everyday contributions in the post-revolutionary era were essential to the organization and challenged traditional hierarchies, both in society and within the organization."

—Fataneh Farahani, Professor in Ethnology, Stockholm University

"*Women of Komala* is a groundbreaking contribution in the field of Kurdish studies. It brilliantly provides meticulous research that intertwines gender, class, national, and political struggle in Kurdistan, centering on women's role through the political turmoil leading up to and after the 1979 revolution in Iran."

—Pedram Baldari, Assistant Professor of Interdisciplinary Art and Design, University of Michigan

"Caught between the murderous onslaught of the Islamic Republic, the Iran-Iraq War (1980–88), and their highly traditional families, a generation of brave Kurdish women joined Komala in the villages and mountains of Kurdistan to fight for both autonomy and gender equality. Yet despite all these sacrifices, they have never received equal recognition, not even in death. This is a remarkable story, beautifully translated from French. Fatemeh Karimi should be commended for her outstanding telling of it, which together with the many anecdotes and interviews she brings, provide a vivid real-life texture to this story."

—Janet Afary, Distinguished Professor, author of *Sexual Politics in Modern Iran*

"A fascinating book which brings timely insights into Kurdish Iranian women's political activism and struggles. Karimi's in-depth research and thoughtful analysis shine new light on how gender shapes political movements and revolutions in Iran."

—Jane Freedman, Professor, Université Paris 8 and co-editor of *Gender-Based Violence in Migration*

Women of Komala

Gender and Revolution in Iranian Kurdistan

Fatemeh Karimi

Translated by
Katharine Hodgkin with Janet Biehl

PLUTO PRESS

Originally published in French as *Genre et militantisme au Kurdistan d'Iran: Les femmes kurdes du Komala 1979–1991* by L'Harmattan, 2022.
First published 2025 by Pluto Press
New Wing, Somerset House, Strand, London WC2R 1LA
and Pluto Press, Inc.
1930 Village Center Circle, 3-834, Las Vegas, NV 89134

www.plutobooks.com

British Library Cataloguing in Publication Data
A catalogue record for this book is available from the British Library

ISBN 978 0 7453 5082 0 Paperback
ISBN 978 0 7453 5081 3 PDF
ISBN 978 0 7453 5083 7 EPUB

Typeset by Stanford DTP Services, Northampton, England

Simultaneously printed in the United Kingdom and United States of America

EU GPSR Authorised Representative
LOGOS EUROPE, 9 rue Nicolas Poussin, 17000, LA ROCHELLE, France
Email: Contact@logoseurope.eu

Contents

Contents

Introduction

At the height of the Woman, Life, Freedom uprising, in November 2022, an incredibly powerful video, less than one minute long, began circulating on social media.[1] The video captured a remarkable scene: ordinary men and women had taken control of parts of the Kurdish city of Mahabad, sitting behind makeshift barricades and singing the old revolutionary Kurdish song, "*Rey Xabatman*" (Our Way of Struggle).[2] This song, which dates back to the Kurdish leftist struggles following the 1979 Revolution, resonated deeply within the uprising. Its prevalence—alongside other symbols and collective memories from that era—demonstrates the enduring political impact of those historical struggles, offering inspiration and continuity to ongoing Kurdish social movements.

The Kurdish leftist struggles in Iran that are the focus of this book have become even more politically relevant today than when it was originally published in French in 2020. To grasp why this is the case, I would like to detour to the Woman, Life, Freedom uprising, which occurred almost two years after the publication of the French edition.

The Woman, Life, Freedom uprising was ignited by the killing of 22-year-old Kurdish woman, Jina (Mahsa) Amini. Arrested by the Morality Police in Tehran in September 2022 for allegedly violating Iran's compulsory hijab laws, Jina's death became a catalyst for widespread popular outrage and protest. During her funeral at the Aychi cemetery in Saqqez, her hometown in Iranian Kurdistan, women protesters chanted in Kurdish: "Jin, Jiyan, Azadi" (Woman, Life, Freedom). This powerful slogan quickly became the rallying cry of a wave of revolutionary protests that spread like wildfire to over 160 cities across Iran, challenging the very foundations of the regime for more than three months. The uprising had the markings of a feminist revolution, driven by radical and intersectional aspirations. Its main agency was a de facto coalition of women and ethnic, racialized, and minoritized populations of

Iran concentrated in the peripheral regions, particularly Kurdistan and Baluchistan. Additionally, the central slogan of the uprising, "Woman, Life, Freedom," was originally articulated in the Kurdish freedom movement in Bakur (Turkish Kurdistan) and Rojava (Syrian Kurdistan) in the context of women's struggles against authoritarian states and gender hierarchies within Kurdish communities. The journey of this slogan to Iranian Kurdistan sets the stage for both recalling the histories of Kurdish political parties and elevating the voices of Kurdish women, whose critical contributions are now being recognized in feminist studies.[3]

This book focuses on Kurdish women's struggles during the 1979 Revolution and its aftermath until the end of the 1980s. Unlike the dominant historiographies marked by nationalist and patriarchal undertones, this book seeks to render visible the historical struggles of women, highlighting neglected contributions on their own terms. The efforts of many of these women in the 1979 Revolution established a political tradition that continues to influence contemporary social movements in profound ways.

Along with the majority of Iranians, Kurdish women participated in huge numbers in the 1979 Revolution, which led to the passing of power from the Pahlavi monarchical system to the Islamic Republic of Iran.[4] Neither the patriarchy, which had confined most women to the private sphere, nor the years of discrimination by the Pahlavi regime, which had deliberately excluded the Kurdish regions from socio-economic development, could prevent them. Nor was this participation limited to the revolutionary period itself, but lasted until the end of the 1980s. In the years immediately after the fall of the Pahlavi regime, when the weakness of the new government opened up a greater space for the free expression of political opinions, numerous political organizations officially launched their activities in the Kurdish regions and elsewhere. In this environment, the activism of Kurdish women increasingly shifted from individual activities to involvement in an organization, something few of them had previously experienced.

Komala, a Kurdish political organization with Maoist tendencies, officially appeared on the Kurdish political scene on February 15, 1979, and quickly attracted women's attention. As Komala activists, women would not only participate in its social and political campaigns in urban centers but also, from 1982 until the late 1980s, engage in armed struggle against the government forces in the rural and mountainous areas. During this period a new type of Kurdish woman emerged in Iran, Iraq, Syria, and Turkey: the woman fighter ("peshmerga" in Kurdish) who took up arms and fought alongside men.*

At the end of the 1980s, Komala was defeated politically and militarily, whereupon it withdrew its forces to Iraqi Kurdistan. Many activists went into exile, particularly to European countries. Komala's defeat, however, should not overshadow the significance of women's large-scale involvement in the organization in the 1980s. It profoundly transformed the lives of these Kurdish women, the vast majority of whom would traditionally have been confined to the role of wives and mothers. It made possible a reconfiguration of the sexual division of labor at the heart of Kurdish society, causing a major upheaval in the socio-cultural structure of the Kurdish community not only in Iran, but also in Turkey, Syria, and Iraq. The figure of the politically active woman, and still more that of the armed female fighter, overturned the traditional gender stereotypes that saw women as "weak" and "fragile," in need of "protection," in contrast to the "strong," "brave" and "warrior" man.[5] The deaths of dozens of Komala women, either killed in combat (48 women) or murdered in prison (41 women), during the 1980s demonstrated that Kurdish women were equally capable of fighting and dying for their political beliefs—a significant break in dominant Kurdish gender norms.[6]

Drawing on seven years of sociological research, this book offers an analysis of Kurdish women's political participation in Komala between 1979 and 1991, a social phenomenon structured by the interweaving of gender and ethnicity in the lives of Komala militants. Their participation can be divided into two periods. The first, from 1979 (the date of the Iranian revolution and also the

* The word "peshmerga," which means "one who faces death," was first used in the political literature of Iranian Kurdistan in 1946. Within Komala, it refers not only to the fighters but to all of its members based in rural or mountainous areas or in the camp during the armed struggle, regardless of their field of activity (armed or not). While the PKK (the Kurdistan Workers' Party, formed in 1978 in Kurdistan, Turkey) chose to use the non-Kurdish word "guerrilla," the word "peshmerga" is used more by Kurds in Iran and Iraq.

foundation of Komala) to 1981, saw hundreds of Kurdish women from urban areas join the socio-political activities of Komala. The second period covers the years from 1981, when women peshmergas officially joined the armed struggle in the organization in rural and mountainous areas,* to 1991, when the organization suffered its political and military defeat, along with its first split and the exile of most of its members. In order to understand what drove Kurdish women's participation, it is essential to analyze their situation before the 1979 Revolution.

THE INVISIBLE WOMEN OF KOMALA

Shahrzad Mojab, an Iranian Marxist feminist revolutionary, observed the post-revolutionary socio-political events in the Kurdish regions. In her view, it is Komala's break with traditional gender relations that distinguishes it from other Kurdish political organizations: "With the exception of Komala, other organizations fighting for autonomy have at the same time pursued conservative gender policies."[7] The French sociologist Olivier Grojean similarly notes, "Gender relations have been a legitimate issue since the founding of the party in 1969. Inspired by Maoism, it attacks the 'traditional' structures (and in particular, the tribes), which embody both feudalism and patriarchy."[8] The significance of women both in theoretical discourse and in practice within Komala has not been as widely recognized as it should be.

The reasons for this are several. First, Komala's archives themselves offer little trace of women's presence in the early years. They contain an incomplete list of women from the organization who disappeared in the 1980s, along with a video made by Komala that shows the first group of armed women, but they contain very little information on the subject of women's participation.[9] For example, the exact date of the arming of women is mentioned only in a book published in 2023 by one of Komala's former peshmerga women.[10]

The names of Komala women remain unknown to the public, even among most Kurds in Iran. By contrast, two female revo-

* Women were able to become official members or peshmergas in 1981, and from the following year they were able to bear arms.

lutionaries from Iraqi Kurdistan—Laila Qasim, a young activist hanged by the Baath regime in Baghdad on May 12, 1974, and Margaret George Shello, the first peshmerga of Assyrian origin in the armed struggle against the Baath regime in the 1960s—have remained alive in the collective memory of the Kurds, especially those in Iraq.[11] The women fighters of the PKK in Turkish and Syrian Kurdistan also occupy a special place: Western media see them as revolutionaries, liberated and liberating, promising freedom not only for Kurdish women but for women all over the world.[12] However, Komala's female activists, including the dozens of women who fell in battle or were imprisoned, remain marginalized and unknown. Even though I had devoted years to researching Kurdish women, it wasn't until this study that I became aware of Komala's female members. My research thus offers insights not only about Komala in general but specifically the peshmerga women who are mostly absent from the collective memory of this struggle.

Little work has been done on Komala itself, and still less on the political presence of women within it. Farideh Koohi-Kamali, for example, has carried out valuable research on Kurdish political movements in Iran in the 1980s, and does not address women's engagement.[13] Kurdish political theorist Abbas Vali, in his study of Kurdish political movements in Iran in the 1980s, is similarly silent on women's political activity. While he notes the centrality of their participation in Komala, referring to "the younger generation of the Kurdish men and women who . . . were soon to form the backbone" of the organization, he does not mention women's involvement again.[14]

Women's invisibility in the social and political history of Komala is intertwined with the issue of ethnicity. In much analysis, the socio-political history of middle-class Iranian women in the central regions is generalized to apply to all Iranian women, notwithstanding their heterogeneity in ethnicity, religion, language, and class.[15] Given this, the political participation of female minorities such as the women of Komala, who were mostly based in peripheral regions, remains invisible. Shahrzad Mojab accurately summarizes the lack of data on Kurdish women, who belong to a stateless, ethnic group and are spread across four countries in the Middle East (Turkey, Iran, Iraq, and Syria). In her view, Middle Eastern studies programs clearly exemplify the exclusion of Kurdish women from academic research. Such programs, she notes, are "primarily focused on Turkish, Arabic, Persian, and Hebrew studies, some with strong ties to Middle Eastern states. Thus, there is a double exclusion; Kurds are excluded from Middle Eastern studies institutions and Kurdish women are excluded from Middle Eastern women's studies."[16] This underlines the point that, as Mojab puts it, "engaging in a study of Kurdish women is in itself a form of resistance against intellectual repression."[17]

ORAL HISTORY: MAKING VISIBLE THE WOMEN OF KOMALA

My principal challenge in writing this book has been the absence of written sources, both on the Kurds in general and on the women of Komala in particular. The organization's archives, moreover, published in the 1980s (in three magazines: *Communist*, *Peshro*, and *Peshang*) are scattered and difficult to access due to the exile of activists and the organization's recurrent internal divisions. The available sources make very little mention of women. *Communist* magazine, Komala's propaganda organ, published from 1983 to 1990, devotes only four articles to the question of women in its 63 issues. As such, this book draws primarily on two sources: first, the memoirs and other writings by 25 former Komala peshmergas that have been published in recent years (22 by men and five by women),[18] and second, my own extended interviews with former Komala activists and fighters, mostly women (37 women and 10 men), between 2014 and 2018.* These interviews took place in various European cities, mostly in Sweden and Germany, where former activists have settled as political refugees since the 1990s.†

Interviews with former Komala activists are vital tools "to express again, after a time of silence, the urge to bear witness,"[19]

* In terms of research ethics, I have provided little information about the interviewees, using pseudonyms to preserve their identities, and mostly not specifying their hometowns or villages. See Appendix 2 for the profile of the interviewees.

† The interviews that form the heart of this book were conducted only with exiles so as not to endanger non-exiled former Komala peshmerga.

and to give a hearing to voices that have been absent from other sources. Analyzed using a life-history approach,[20] these oral histories make it possible to uncover "low-intensity events" that are invisible in the dominant accounts, so as to reinsert the transformations affecting Kurdish women activists into the center of the narrative. Arlette Farge, a historian specializing in the voices of the marginalized, has demonstrated how what we think of as "events" are created by the "most miniscule elements, such as silences, utterances, emotions, low intensities, and the ordinary course of things."[21] Events that appear to be minor, unimportant, chaotic, or contradictory can in fact illuminate specific conjunctures and the material and historical forces at play. A low-intensity event "creates light because it can instantaneously illuminate mechanisms that had up until then been invisible."[22]

The aim of this study is thus both to investigate the place of Kurdish women as historical subjects of post-revolutionary Iran and to reread this context from their perspective: What can the low-intensity events experienced by individual Kurdish women tell us about Kurdish political organization in this period? How does the sexual division of militant labor[23] shape the political decisions of the organization? Attending to low-intensity events enables us to decenter the dominant ideological narrative of the organization. The chronology of the struggle from the perspective of women's experience makes visible the gendered dimension of the boundaries between sympathizers, activists, and peshmergas. This analysis aims ultimately, as political sociologist Olivier Fillieule puts it, to "redefine the boundaries of militancy and thus of the intentions and goals of social movements through a rejection of the usual divisions between private and public, political and domestic, resistance and political action."[24]

THE KURDS OF IRAN

The Kurds are one of the largest of the world's stateless peoples. In 1639, the territory of Kurdistan was "divided" between the Persian and Ottoman empires. After the First World War, the Ottoman Empire fell and its Kurdish regions were again divided, this time between Turkey, Iraq, and Syria. "Iranian Kurdistan" (Rojhelat in

Kurdish),* which constitutes the eastern part of the geo-cultural space of "Greater Kurdistan," is located in Iran's western and northwestern sector, bordering the Kurdish territories in Iraq and Turkey.[25] Kurds are one of several ethnic groups in Iran, along with Persians, Turks (or Azeris), Baluchis, Arabs, Turkmen, and others. There are no statistics relating to ethnicity in Iran, and differentiating between ethnicities is forbidden on the grounds that all are considered "Iranians."[26] According to various estimates, Kurds are the country's third-largest ethnic group, after Persians and Turks. It is estimated that Persians make up less than 50 percent of the total Iranian population, Turks 20–30 percent, Kurds 9–10 percent, Baluchis 3 percent, Arabs 2.5 percent, and Turkmens 1.5 percent.[27]

The Persian community, located predominantly in the central regions of Iran, has benefited most substantially from state socio-economic policies since the beginning of the twentieth century, and Persian identity and language have been recognized as symbols of the central Iranian state. This prioritization of the Persian community in government policy was reinforced during the Pahlavi dynasty (1925–79), and it has continued since the establishment of the Islamic Republic of Iran in 1979 to the present. The non-Persian ethnic communities are mostly settled in the borderlands or outlying areas.[28] Some of them, such as Kurds, Baluchis, and Turkmens, suffer further discrimination as a result of not only ethnic but also religious difference: most Kurds, Baluchis, and Turkmen, are Sunni, while the majority of Iranians are Shia. As Abbas Vali points out, "the concepts of core and periphery here do not denote specific geographical or demographic entities, but rather they are discursive constructs referring to the conditions of the constitution of these communities, in particular their 'constitutive outsides' that account for their constitutive difference from their 'other' communities at any specific time."[29]

* Some Kurds, who reject this imposed division, use the term "Eastern Kurdistan" or Rojhalat (which means "East" in Kurdish) to refer to Kurdistan in Iran. They use the term Bakur or "North" for Kurdistan in Turkey, Bashur or "South" for Iraqi Kurdistan, and Rojava or "West" for Kurdistan in Syria. These are not internationally recognized terms.

The areas inhabited by Kurds are estimated to encompass 125,000 square kilometers.[30] However, as Vali notes, Kurdistan of Iran does not "have a juridical-political unity as a cohesive provincial administrative entity. It lacks the authority to issue uniform administrative and social and cultural processes and practices. Modern nation-state and sovereign power have deprived Kurdistan of its territorial and political unity as a single contiguous province within Iran."[31] Although only one province is called "Kurdistan," the geographical area occupied by Kurds is much larger. Under the Pahlavi dynasty, this geographical area was divided into four administrative units, overriding ethnic and linguistic identifications. Bordering the province of Kurdistan, three other administrative provinces, namely West Azerbaijan, Kermanshah, and Ilam, are also populated by Kurds. At a considerable distance from these four provinces, as a result of forced population displacements in the nineteenth century, communities of Kurds are also found in the Khorasan provinces of northeastern Iran, in the provinces bordering the Caspian Sea in the north of the country, and on the border with Turkmenistan. In this book, references to "Iranian Kurdistan" thus use a "broad" definition that includes these four provinces and the Kurdish population living there.

The territorial division of the Kurdish community, despite some differences in dialect, economy, and religion, does not affect its ethnic and linguistic unity or its cultural cohesion. Before the twentieth century, the Kurds of Iran were a tribal mountain people leading a nomadic or seminomadic life; subsequently they became sedentary farmers. From the 1950s, changes in state policies led to an increase in their numbers in urban areas, where they became teachers, public employees, and shopkeepers. The Kurdish rural areas, neglected by the socio-economic policies of the central government, have remained poor despite their natural mineral resources (coal, copper, gold, silver, uranium). Notably, Kermanshah is an oil-producing province, but the rate of oil extraction is negligible.[32]

While the Kurds of Kermanshah and Ilam are predominantly Shiite, the majority of Kurds in West Azerbaijan and Kurdistan are Sunni. There are also minority groups who practice other religions such as Yarsanism, Zoroastrianism, Christianity, and Judaism.[33]

Map 1 The four Kurdish provinces in Iran[34]

The Kurdish language, which is part of the Indo-European language family, is made up of several dialects. The Kurds of West Azerbaijan speak Kurmanji and Sorani, those of Kurdistan province speak Sorani and Hawrami, and the majority of Kurds in Kermanshah and Ilam speak Gorani or Kalhori. However, despite the considerable linguistic and cultural heterogeneity of the Kurdish community and its territorial division, the Kurds of Iran have a strong sense of cultural coherence, due in part to a desire to distance themselves from the dominant Persian identity.[35]

KOMALA: FROM EMERGENCE TO DEFEAT

During the twentieth century, Marxism emerged as the most radical emancipation strategy to resolve major social contradictions—notably class conflict, colonization, and imperialist intervention—in China, Latin America, Vietnam, and the Middle East. Kurdish society was no exception. As land reforms in the 1960s led to greater urbanization, improved means of communication, and an increase in the number of university graduates, new generations of Kurdish activists were attracted to Marxism.[36] In the countries where Kurds were living, Marxist parties marginalized the Kurdish cause,[37] and so from the 1970s, Kurdish Marxists increasingly sought to establish their own political organizations as a more comprehensive response to their social challenges.[38] Several political organizations with Marxist tendencies emerged in the various regions of Kurdistan, such as the Patriotic Union of Kurdistan (PUK) in Iraqi Kurdistan in 1975, the Kurdistan Workers' Party (PKK) in Turkish Kurdistan in 1978, and Komala in Iranian Kurdistan in 1979.

Komala, or the Revolutionary Organization of the Working Masses of Kurdistan of Iran (*sâzemân-e enghelâbi-ye zahmatkeshân-e kordestan-e iran*), a group influenced by Maoism, officially appeared on the political scene on February 15, 1979, just four days after the victory of the revolution.[39] It was the second-largest Kurdish political organization in Iran after the Democratic Party of Kurdistan of Iran (DPKI).* A small group of young Kurdish students, reacting to political oppression by the Pahlavi regime, formed the nucleus of Komala clandestinely in Tehran in 1969, inspired by the Iranian Marxist movement and the PUK.[40] Although this clandestine group did not publish any statement on its political positions before the revolution, it advocated revolutionary socialism and was committed to the liberation struggle of Iranian workers and peasants, oppressed by capitalist exploitation and imperialist domination.

This discourse was compatible with the desire to eradicate national oppression in Iran; the group also asserted that "socialist revolution in Iran is the means and condition for the democratic

* The DPKI was founded in 1945. The following year, as international forces occupied Iran, it established the Republic of Kurdistan in Mahabad, which lasted just eleven months. Currently based in several camps in Iraqi Kurdistan, the DPKI is divided into two branches that are not very active on the Iranian political scene.

resolution of the Kurdish question."[41] The partisans based their program on militancy and aimed their activities at the popular masses. Initially the group focused on workers in urban areas, but under the influence of Maoism, it subsequently expanded into the Kurdish rural areas.[42] Although there were no women among the founders of this group, young Kurdish women began to work with them as teachers in rural areas even before the revolution. The group members engaged in a campaign of clandestine propaganda, which led many activists to be imprisoned in 1975 during a crackdown.

After the revolution of 1979, this small and previously anonymous group gradually came into public view as a popular organization, with numerous activists and sympathizers in cities in the Kurdish regions, particularly the provinces of Kurdistan and West Azerbaijan. Most of the members, and even the leaders, were young and inexperienced. Nonetheless, with its revolutionary goals and politics, Komala succeeded in attracting the attention of many young people, including women. For this reason, Komala, along with the DPKI, actively participated in negotiations with the new Iranian government in order to resolve the Kurdish issue. These negotiations were not successful, however, giving way to armed conflict from May 1980 until the end of the decade.

Komala's presence as an independent Kurdish organization was short-lived. Withdrawing completely to rural areas in order to mount resistance to government forces, it formed an alliance with some non-Kurdish Marxist groups such as the Union of Communist Fighters to found the Communist Party of Iran (CPI) on September 3, 1983.* Komala's strategy was to draw on this group's theoretical consciousness; to bring together Iranian Marxists, now more divided than ever on the strategy to adopt against the Islamic

* Non-Kurds had been members of Komala since its inception, and with the wave of repression in 1981, many non-Kurdish Marxists went to live in the Kurdish regions, and some joined the organization. However, the number of non-Kurdish Komala members is not mentioned anywhere. According to interviewees, non-Kurdish members of Komala represented only 3 or 4 percent. Among them were around 30 members of the Union of Communist Fighters, several of whom took a high position within the organization. The CPI is generally known as Komala by most of its members, researchers, and Kurds, and this is the usage followed here.

Republic of Iran; and to find allies outside the Kurdish regions. Thereafter Komala would appear as the Kurdish branch of the CPI, focusing on the organization's practical aspects, in particular on armed struggle, while the small non-Kurdish group concentrated on developing the CPI's theoretical framework.[43]

While Komala became part of the new party (CPI), it nevertheless retained autonomy by preserving its central committee and leadership. Additionally, Komala maintained control over its own publications and retained the right to make internal decisions independently. Nevertheless, Maoist theoretical discourse yielded to revolutionary Marxist discourse. Komala changed from a popular regional Kurdish organization (that is to say, a mass organization that in addition to emphasizing the Kurdish question defended all oppressed groups—peasants, workers, women) into a nationwide Iranian party that aimed to defend the interests of the working class. While Komala's popular Marxism, following Maoist doctrine, had emphasized the fight against imperialism, its new revolutionary Marxist discourse foregrounded overthrowing capitalism through the struggle of the Iranian working class.

The CPI advocated a return to the principles of original Marxism and an in-depth rereading of the works of Marx, Engels, and Lenin. The workers and the struggle for their emancipation were at the heart of the party's thought.[44] The enemy was identified as international capitalism, and the only way to annihilate it was to bring the working class to power under the leadership of a communist party, which would inevitably lead to the emancipation of all the oppressed, particularly ethnic minorities and women. The organization's resolutions expressed their commitment to the self-determination of ethnic minorities, albeit in a reductionist spirit. Thus, the ethnic question was subordinated to the question of class, and the question of ethnic minorities was bound up with the victory of socialism in Iran.[45]

In the mid-1980s, as government forces advanced, Komala gradually withdrew to camps in Iraqi Kurdistan. Its activities from then on would be limited to scattered armed assaults. Following a string of defeats, the alliance among its members gave way to rivalry and enmity. This resulted in the organization's first split in 1991. Insecurity and frustration led many members to go into exile. Today, there are at least eight political groupings stemming from Komala. They are currently not active on the political scene of Iranian Kurdistan except in name. Their members, for the most part, are political refugees in Europe, while only a few activists remain in the camps of Iraqi Kurdistan.

This book is divided into three parts, which trace a historical-sociological chronology. Part I investigates the status of Kurdish women in Iran during the Pahlavi regime (1925–79), providing an overview of the social conditions that influenced Kurdish women's participation in the 1979 Revolution. It offers an analysis of the social conditions of Iranian Kurds in general, giving specific focus to Kurdish women and to the regime's cultural, political, and economic practices that shaped their lives, as well as the situation of women specifically within Kurdish society, particularly within family structures.

Part II focuses on the immediate aftermath of the revolution, from 1979 to 1981. It examines the political engagement of Kurdish women in urban areas as supporters of Komala, elucidating their motivations for joining the organization. I analyze their preference for Komala among the various organizations of the time, the challenges hindering their political involvement, their socio-political activities, and ultimately, the factors that would drive them to become peshmergas in rural and mountainous areas from 1981.

Finally, Part III delves into the lives of women activists from 1981 to 1991, with a focus on their participation as peshmergas in armed struggle in rural and mountainous areas. Here I analyze the arming of women, the imposition of disciplinary orders, aspects of family life, and the status of female peshmergas within Komala's hierarchy.

PART I

Kurdish Women in Revolution: The Path to Engagement

One of the most remarkable features of the 1979 Revolution was the historically unprecedented mass participation of women.[1] Although government policies had improved the socio-economic situation of Iranian women during the 1960s and 1970s, most women—like other revolutionaries—were convinced that the overthrow of the Shah's regime was the only way to improve the position of Iranian women. Whatever their socio-economic or ideological differences, women participated in the revolution both individually and as members of clandestine organizations. These underground activists, largely from middle-class backgrounds, were the pioneers of the 1979 Revolution.

Women joined a range of clandestine political organizations—nationalist, Islamist, and Marxist—and participated fully in political activities, including the armed struggle against the Pahlavi regime. Among the 341 opponents of the regime who were involved in armed struggle and were killed between 1971 and 1977, 39 were women.[2] The term *zan-e cherik* (woman combatant) entered Iranian political discourse for the first time. Female political prisoners (323 women were given prison sentences, ranging from one week to life or the execution of women (three women were sentenced to death in 1974),[3] a penalty previously applied exclusively to men. As Mohammad Reza Shah, the last Pahlavi monarch, commented, "Their determination and will in battle is incredible. Even the women continue to fight to the last breath."[4]

Women's participation in the revolution was not limited to those from major cities in the central regions, nor to those from the middle class. Women living in peripheral regions and from ethnic minorities, including Kurdish women, actively participated in street demonstrations and strikes, joining the ranks of the revolutionaries.

Why and when did Kurdish women, especially those who later continued their political involvement as members of Komala, became involved in the revolution? The answers to this question, as my interviews with some of them elucidate, depend on social context. The repressive policies of the Pahlavi regime toward Kurdish women, in cultural, political and socio-economic terms, motivated many to mobilize. As we will see, the socially determined constraints of gender relations in large part explain why

Kurdish women joined the revolution only in its final months, when participation in small-scale union protests developed into to large-scale demonstrations.[5]

1

Between Repression and Deprivation: Women Under the Pahlavi Dynasty

Under the reign of Reza Shah (1925–41), the Pahlavi dynasty sought to transform Iran from a multiethnic, multilingual, multireligious, precapitalist, and decentralized country into a homogeneous and industrialized one, governed by a centralized state.[1] It developed a secular public education system, a banking system, roads, railways and other communication networks, health and information centers, and modern administrative and judicial systems. In 1936, the first modern university was founded in Tehran. The regime reduced the power of the clergy, strengthened the armed forces, and made military service compulsory.

Reza Shah's eldest son Mohammad Reza Shah followed his father in his determination to drive Iran forward on the path of development and modernization during his rule (1941–79). His major development program, implemented in 1963 and known as the White Revolution, or the Revolution of the Shah and the People, was intended to fundamentally reform society, primarily politically. It was based on six pillars which together would strengthen the capitalist system in both urban and rural areas and develop the agricultural and industrial sectors: agrarian reform, nationalization of the forests, the sale of state-owned factories to private entrepreneurs, profit-sharing for industrial workers, extension of the right to vote to women, and the establishment of a "knowledge army" to spread literacy in the country's rural areas.[2]

Improving the situation of women was a key objective of these policies.* Nationalist aspirations to be a modern state led to an

* The reforms benefiting women were not the result solely of the government's will to present Iran as a modern country, but were also due to the efforts of women activists. See

expansion of citizenship rights that clearly benefited women, allowing some to go beyond the limitations set by institutions and customs that confined them within the particular traditions of their ethnic and religious communities.[3] State policies thus facilitated the regulated access of educated and "modern" women to the public sphere.[4]

For the first time in Iran's history, girls' education was institutionalized and legitimized. Women were encouraged to acquire a university education, and they also became eligible for some civil service jobs and professions from which they had previously been excluded, including that of judge. In 1963, Iranian women obtained the right to vote; that same year women entered parliament. A woman even served as minister of education between 1968 and 1976. The Protection of the Family Law (as it was known), passed in 1967, set stricter limitations on polygamy, raised the age of marriage for girls to 15, and placed divorce under the jurisdiction of family courts. In 1975, new family laws gave women the right to custody of their children, reduced penalties for abortion, and in certain cases offered free abortion on demand.[5]

Women were seen as pivotal to a more unified and stable state: a modern nation, with a healthier, better educated, and more productive population, alongside a family system that not only preserved national honor but also produced better wives and mothers, "civilized" partners, and responsible members of the nation. Notwithstanding this vision, the process of modernization varied according to class, religion, ethnicity, and geographical location (peripheral, central, urban, or village). The experience of women from ethnic minorities, including Kurdish women residing mostly in the periphery, was inevitably quite different from that of the Persian women living in the center of Iran who found themselves at the heart of the state's political and socio-economic ambitions.

WOMEN AND CULTURAL REPRESSION

One of the key reasons that some Iranian women, above all Kurds, opposed the policies of the Pahlavi dynasty was essentially

---

Eliz Sanasarian, *The Women's Rights Movement in Iran: Mutiny, Appeasement, and Repression from 1900 to Khomeini* (New York: Praeger, 1982).

cultural. Modernization sought to impose a culturally homogeneous Iranian national identity on a heterogeneous society.[6] To establish its "imagined community"[7] and "civilize" the Iranian nation, state nationalism demanded two measures: the Europeanization of dress, in an Iranian society with a Muslim majority, and the imposition of Farsi as the country's official language, regardless of people's mother tongue.

As was the case in many other countries in the region (Turkey, Egypt, Afghanistan, the Caucasus, the Balkans), the state's drive to impose European-style dress was seen as a defining component of its modernist and nationalist project.[8] In its attempt to eliminate cultural diversity of dress, the Iranian state asserted an equivalence between national unity and uniformity of appearance. A law passed by parliament in 1935 instituted mandatory European dress for all Iranians, men and women alike.[9] This phase of homogenization was more significant for women than men. On January 7, 1936, the wearing of the veil was forbidden.[10] From this date, identified by the state as the "day of women's liberation," women could no longer wear the veil in any public space, and those who did risked assault and harassment by the gendarmes.[11] According to Azadeh

Figure 1.1 The first anniversary of the ban on the hijab at Saadat School in Mahabad, January 7, 1937. (Personal archive of Hassan Ghazi, a Kurdish writer and researcher originally from Mahabad.)

Kian, "for the overwhelming majority of women, not wearing the veil amounted to nakedness and the loss of honor."[12] This law, which aimed to homogenize and de-Islamicize the country, clearly affected urban women more than women residing in rural areas, who, working in agriculture and husbandry, did not usually veil in the way that urban women did.

Kurdish women in Iran thus no longer had the right to appear in public places wearing either their traditional clothes or a hijab. Sayran, a former Komala activist, recalls her grandmother's account of these changes in Sanandaj, the capital of Kurdistan province:

> My grandmother used to tell me about the period during the time of Reza Pahlavi when women in Sanandaj were not allowed to leave their homes in hijab. There were gendarmes everywhere to tear it off them. It was a very difficult situation for women. My grandmother, who had previously worn Kurdish clothing with the veil, was forced to dress differently when she went out of the house, which was at first very strange for her. She was lucky because her family was not very conservative, but some families were opposed to this new way of dressing, and would not let their wives and daughters leave the house. So, they were forced to stay at home most of the time, unless they could leave the house secretly or at night without being seen by the gendarmes.

Such women took refuge in their homes and went out only when they had to, such as for their weekly visit to the public baths. They went out at night wearing a chador, going by circuitous routes or through dark, narrow, and frightening alleys, so as not to be spotted by the police. Some older Kurdish women refused to accompany their husbands in public, sending their daughters in their place. Others wore a coat and hat over their chador, so as to appear to be wearing European clothes.[13] Kobra Azimi, who grew up in Mahabad, writes in her autobiography: "We, who used to go to school in Kurdish clothes and chadors, had to go to school in hats and coats. For this reason, some parents forbade their daughters from going to school. My parents also banned me from going to school for two years under social pressure exercised by those around us."[14]

An official letter from the interior minister in 1940 (Figure 1.2) asserted that "the state of education for women in Mahabad is unsatisfactory, and although the matter of hijab may not be a major concern for the Kurds, they nevertheless intentionally choose to stay within their homes."

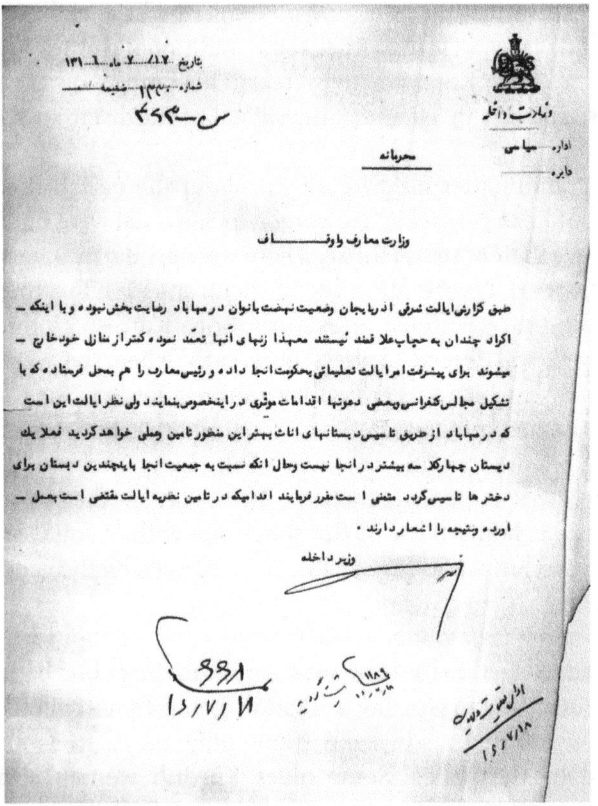

وزارت داخله

اداره سیاسی

دایره

بتاریخ ۲/۱۷/۷ ماه ۶ ۱۳۱

شماره ۲۳۳۱ ضمیمه

محرمانه

وزارت معارف و اوقاف

طبق گزارش ایالت شرقی آذربایجان وضعیت نهضت بانوان در مهاباد رضایت بخش نبوده و با اینکه اکراد چندان به حجاب علاقمند نیستند معهذا زنهای آنها تعمّد نموده کمتر از منازل خود خارج میشوند برای پیشرفت امر ایالت تعلیماتی بحکومت انجا داده و رئیس معارف را هم بمحل فرستاده که با تشکیل مجالس کنفرانس و بعضی دعوتها اقدامات موثری در اینخصوص بنمایند ولی نظر ایالت این است که در مهاباد از طریق تاسیس دبستانهای اناث بهتر این منظور تامین و عملی خواهد گردید فعلا یک دبستان چهارکلاسه بیشتر در انجا نیست وحال انکه نسبت به جمعیت انجا بایدچندین دبستان برای دخترها تاسیس گردد متمنی است مقرر فرمایند اقدامیکه در تامین نظریه ایالت مقتضی است بعمل اورده ونتیجه را اشعار دارند.

وزیر داخله

Figure 1.2 Official letter from the interior minister, 1940. (Source: Personal archive of Hassan Ghazi.)

Although Mohammad Reza Shah withdrew the ban on the hijab in 1941, the media and the education system popularized Western styles of dress, and this supposedly "modern" appearance became a requirement for urban women in order to access education and employment.[15] Gradually the rejection of the veil in favor of

Western dress styles gained favor not only among educated women in the cities of the central region, but also among women in other regions and across social classes. Religious and traditional clothing was increasingly looked down upon, regarded as a sign of cultural backwardness and unrefined attitudes. Thus, traditional Kurdish dress was considered "ugly" and "dirty," a mark of "poverty" or "illiteracy."[16] It implied a premodern rurality that had to be progressively eliminated, either through direct violence or through humiliation. Marjan, a former Komala activist, recalls:

> I remember very well a time when we led a demonstration in support of a hunger strike by political prisoners in front of the Sanandaj courthouse. To keep us quiet, one of the officials of the courthouse approached us and asked to speak to our spokesperson. Two people were appointed. The government official was angry, and said, "I asked you for educated people, and you dare give me two village men?" In fact, these two people were high school teachers, but they were in Kurdish clothes.

The other component of Iranian collective identity relates to language. In 1923, Farsi was designated the official language of all the peoples of Iran, although nearly half the population spoke a different language.[17] The first constitution of Iran, adopted in 1906, had identified Farsi as the national language, but only with the rise to power of the Pahlavi dynasty in the 1920s did the central government impose it as the language of education, administration, and media. Unlike Turkey, where even speaking languages other than Turkish was forbidden, in Iran minority languages were not entirely banned. Farsi became the sole official language in the domain of the state,[18] and writing and publishing in other languages was declared illegal and punishable by law. In the words of Hemin, a contemporary Kurdish poet (1921–86): "Thousands of Kurds, in schools, offices and even on the street, were arrested, tortured and disgraced on the charge of speaking Kurdish."[19] Another contemporary Kurdish poet, Hazhar (1921–91), put his "few Kurdish books in a metal box and buried them in the courtyard of their village house, which was far from the city." He read "the books only at night, and then buried them again."[20]

Although in official documents Reza Shah replaced Persia with Iran as the name of the country as a gesture toward national unity, the imposition of a single language ran directly counter to this goal, by denying the country's national, linguistic, and cultural diversity. Languages such as Turkish, Kurdish, and Arabic were described as "local dialects." In the later years of his rule, Mohammad Reza Shah would authorize the broadcasting of cultural programs in Kurdish, though only on the radio, in order to show himself to be more democratic than his Iraqi counterpart, Saddam Hussein, who brutally repressed the Kurdish revolts in the 1970s. Cultural repression remained in force, however. Thus, while speaking Kurdish was never forbidden in Iran, anyone possessing a book in Kurdish risked imprisonment.*

During this period, the education system played a central role in nation building. Anne-Marie Thiesse emphasizes the importance of education systems for national projects generally: "At school one learns not only the language, history or geography of the nation, but also how to be and to think nationally."[21] Kurdish girls who entered the education system were required to attend school unveiled, to wear modern clothes, and to sit through classes conducted in a language that was not their mother tongue.[22] A former peshmerga, Diana Nammi, writes about her experience on her first day of school in Saqqez in 1969:

> Our teacher, Miss Nastaran, was tall and dressed in a stylish modern skirt and top with high heels. Her hair was piled up on her head. She started to talk to the class in Farsi, the official language of Iran. This took me and my classmates by surprise. We only spoke Kurdish at home. When we replied in Kurdish, we quickly found out what the sticks were for. Miss Nastaran took them off the window ledge and started to beat us. This is the last time you speak Kurdish, Miss Nastaran said, continuing to strike us on the palms of our hands and also on our legs. It was so terrifying that a couple of my classmates wet themselves.[23]

---

* According to the memoir of a former member of Komala, his older brother was imprisoned for two years in the 1970s for carrying a book in Kurdish. Marouf Ka'abi, *Dashti Daré* (Plain of Daré) (Aweneh, 2010), 20.

This requirement was particularly sensitive in rural areas, where few girls had access to elementary school. As Marjan, who taught in the villages in 1978–9, describes it:

> At that time, almost all parents in the villages were illiterate. Moreover, most families had no access to the radio, which was the only way to listen to Farsi at that time. Little Kurdish children from these backgrounds were forced to study in Farsi, a language they had never heard, and which was very strange to them. That is why these children had difficulties keeping up at school and adapting to the school environment.

The central government successfully promoted the idea that Farsi was superior to all other ethnic languages, and so most Iranians—Persians and non-Persians alike—came to perceive the ability to speak the language as indicating prestigious status.[24] The objective was to achieve cultural homogenization and, at the same time, to ensure the wide diffusion of an Iranian–Persian national identity. Under the educational system that the government imposed, non-Persian-speaking women thus found themselves split off from their native culture and language. Persianization represented a cultural risk, and as a result women were under social pressures to be vigilant in socializing their children, culturally and linguistically.

WOMEN, CENTRALIZATION, AND AUTHORITARIANISM

The centralization of Iran went hand in hand with the stifling of all political dissent, until the overthrow of the Pahlavi dynasty in 1979. The Iranian state tolerated no oppositional voices. Except in the period between the abdication of Reza Shah in 1941 and the consolidation of power by Mohammad Reza Shah in 1953, repression became ubiquitous in the lives of Iranians, in both the central and peripheral regions. Secular and intellectual forces opposing the state and calling for political freedom and the establishment of political parties and independent newspapers were silenced.

All legislative institutions (parliament, ministries, the government cabinet, parties, and elections) remained under government control, while opposition leaders and political forces were killed, imprisoned, or exiled.

In the mid-1950s, the regime deemed it politically necessary to maintain the facade of a participatory parliamentary system, and established two political parties: the ruling Melliyun (Nationalist) party and the opposition Mardom (Popular) party. However, in 1975, when Mohammad Reza Shah declared that in the interests of national development all political disputes should be eliminated, these two parties were replaced by a single party entirely dependent on the monarch, Rastakhiz (Resurrection), which dominated the political scene throughout the country.[25] Reza Shah and his son after him ruled the state delegating very little authority; even minor decisions rested with them. The Pahlavi regime imposed a "brutal iron cage of modernity" on Iran, and national sovereignty was based on coercion rather than consensus.[26]

During the reign of Reza Shah (1925–41), the state considered the peripheral regions, populated largely by tribes and ethnic groups that were socio-economically and militarily autonomous, not only to be backward but a source of political instability. These "non-national elements" became synonymous with "national disunity" and as such became targets for repression.[27] Numerous tribal uprisings throughout the country, especially in the Kurdish regions, were suppressed.* Subsequently the populations of these regions were subjected to forced sedentarization, confiscation of landed properties, execution, imprisonment, internal exile, the subjugation of chiefs, and deportation of some tribal members.[28] The destruction of the socio-economic self-sufficiency of the tribes also led to considerable impoverishment of the Kurdish rural areas.

After Reza Shah's gradual rapprochement with Germany, he was compelled by Allied pressure to abdicate in 1941. In the power vacuum that followed, a number of socio-political movements in

---

* Hassan Arfa, who led some of the state expeditions to the Kurdish regions during the reign of Reza Shah, later wrote that the main goal of the state in relation to the Kurds was to prevent them from getting involved in armed tribal insurrections. See Hassan Arfa, *The Kurds: An Historical and Political Study* (London: Oxford University Press, 1966), 65–6.

both central and peripheral regions resumed their political activities. For a brief period, political parties and independent women's associations reemerged, and Kurdish nationalism asserted itself openly.

The Kurdish political party, the Democratic Party of Kurdistan of Iran (DPKI), emerged on the Iranian political scene in 1945. The following year, members of the DPKI succeeded in establishing the short-lived Republic of Kurdistan in Mahabad, at which point we see some of the first records of Kurdish women's participation in politics.* After the fall of the Kurdistan Republic in late 1946 and the execution of its leader in March 1947, many DPKI members were imprisoned or forced to leave Iran.

The authoritarianism of the state under the rule of Mohammad Reza Shah became more extreme in the 1950s, particularly with the establishment of Savak (the National Intelligence and Security Organization) in 1957. Henceforth the state relied not only on the army but also on this powerful police apparatus.† While possession of a modern army was effective in controlling the peripheral regions, Savak came to be a central element in the repression of dissidents.[29] During the 1960s and 1970s, through mass murder, torture, and detention, it played a key part in spreading "a deep sense of fear, mistrust, disbelief and apathy throughout the country" forcing Iranians into submission.[30] It was largely due to the activ-

* The objective of the Republic of Kurdistan was the autonomy of the Kurds within the territorial boundaries of Iran and the administration of Kurdish affairs in their own language. See William Eagleton, *The Kurdish Republic of 1946* (London: Oxford University Press, 1963). One remarkable feature of the Republic of Kurdistan was that the Kurdish nationalists included women as part of the people, encouraging them to take part in public activities in support of their cause; some women from well-known Mahabad families answered their call. According to DPKI's ideology, Kurdish women, who were oppressed by the enemy as much as men, should participate in liberating the homeland as symbols of a modernizing nation. Great interest was thus taken in the education of women. On this topic, see Shahrzad Mojab, "Women and Nationalism in the Kurdish Republic of 1946," in *Women of a Non-State Nation: The Kurds*, ed. Shahrzad Mojab (Costa Mesa, CA: Mazda, 2001), 71–91.

† As Ervand Abrahamian notes, "In 1977, Iran had the largest navy in the Gulf, the most modern air force in the Middle East and the fifth largest military force in the world." Ervand Abrahamian, *Iran Between Two Revolutions* (Princeton, NJ: Princeton University Press, 1982), 435–6. Savak was created in 1957 with help from the CIA, FBI, and Mossad to carry out domestic repression and social control. This organization had 60,000 full and part-time staff. See Robert Graham, *Iran: The Illusion of Power* (London: Croom Helm, 1978), 146.

ities of Savak during this period that, according to Amnesty International, "no country in the world has a worse human rights record than Iran."[31]

The Kurdish regions were among the major targets of the state's repressive policies. Following the fall of the Kurdistan Republic in 1946, government forces acted swiftly to prevent further revolts, ensuring that the Kurds were no longer in a position to threaten the regime's political sovereignty.[32] The armed forces and Savak controlled the Kurdish regions in small towns and rural areas more closely than ever, generating a climate of fear and distrust even at the heart of the family. Shirin, a former Komala activist, describes this pervasive fear:

> I grew up in a fairly political family. Throughout my childhood, my family, especially my brother, always had a close relationship with the Iraqi Kurds. The Iraqi peshmergas used to come and visit us, and we would help one another. But once I got married, I was very scared to talk with my husband about my family's ideological past and my own political views. I didn't want to take any chances, even though I was pretty sure that my husband had the same political views as us. Then I realized that he was listening to banned radio stations whenever I was asleep. The brutality of the repression meant that I did not dare to talk about my ideas to my husband. It took us a long time to be able to trust each other.

Nasrin, also a former Komala member, similarly captures this atmosphere of fear and repression in her narrative. Nasrin grew up not knowing that her father had been an important figure in the Kurdistan Republic in 1946; in order to avoid endangering his children, he had hidden his political past from them. She discovered his role only when she stumbled upon his name in a long-hidden document.

For Kurdish women, largely confined to the family space as wives and mothers, this repression weighed more heavily on them than on men, and made their access to political life very difficult. As a former DPKI activist wrote in his memoir: "A young man who had grown up in a small town, if he did not go to university, would go to the big cities to do military service or to look for work so as to see the world in new ways, and come to a new understanding and knowledge of the difficulties of life and its contradictions."[33] But this was not the case for most Kurdish women. While Komala women often had brothers who were politically involved—Nasrin and Shirin had brothers who lost their lives as a result of their political activism, while those of Marjan and Fatima spent years in prison before the revolution—almost all these women remained involuntarily removed from the world of politics. For most, knowledge of the political world came only through their family ties, especially their brothers, who through their studies, work or, compulsory military service in cities, were able to engage in political activity.

Throughout the period from the Kurdistan Republic in 1946 until the revolution of 1979, then, the vast majority of young Kurdish women effectively had no possibility of participating in political life. Even as the revolution reached its zenith in the central regions, protesters in Kurdish areas found it necessary to frame their initial protests in terms of trade union problems. With this strategy, they aimed to shield themselves from state repression. According to Marjan:

> From the first months of the demonstrations, when the security forces oppressed the demonstrators by arresting or even killing them, it was mainly the young people who were joining in the revolution. Our first anti-regime demonstrations started with the pretext of problems with the teachers' union. But a bit later, when the control of the security forces had weakened, all generations, even the very old mothers, joined the demonstrators with the slogan of "Down with the Shah."

THE EXCLUSION OF WOMEN FROM SOCIO-ECONOMIC DEVELOPMENT

In its efforts to modernize the country through rapid industrialization, the nationalist state initiated a radical transformation of Iranian society. Financed by the rising price of oil,[34] the government constructed and improved infrastructure, and developed the public service sector (education, health, media, cultural centers), in both the central regions and the peripheries, the latter largely populated by ethnic minorities. Women, taking advantage of these improvements, were able for the first time to access public and secular education, higher education, and paid employment outside the domestic space.

Although the peripheral regions of Iran saw positive changes, and the Pahlavi modernization policies led to improvements in the daily lives of many Iranians, the distribution of economic resources, especially during the reign of the second Shah, was extremely unequal.[35] Notwithstanding the land reform of 1963,* state industrial and urban development was focused primarily on the central regions of the country, where the largest share of national budget and foreign investment was spent.[36] Inhabitants of the rural and agricultural peripheral regions were thus increasingly dependent on the central areas, both economically and politically.[37] A significant proportion of ethnic minorities, including Kurds, Baluchis, Turks, and Arabs, became even more impoverished.[38] The agricultural sector continued to employ over half of the population, especially in a peripheral region like Kurdistan, but the contribution of agriculture to GNP (Gross National Product) declined sharply in the 1970s, making Iran one of the largest importers of food and agricultural products in the Middle East.[39]

The impact of the government's policies was disastrous for the rural population, particularly women. As making a living through agriculture became increasingly unviable, men sought temporary

* One of the main reasons for land reforms was the concentration of land in the hands of large landowners, which translated not only into the exploitation of farmers and reduced incentives for production but also widespread poverty in rural areas. Mohammad Reza Shah, under both domestic and international pressure—especially from the United States to curb the spread of leftist ideologies and strengthen his regime—pursued land reform as a means to reduce class disparities and modernize the agricultural system. However, the outcomes of the reforms largely failed to align with these objectives. In many rural areas, the land distributed to farmers was too small to sustain a viable livelihood, forcing many farmers to sell their plots. Moreover, the lack of adequate infrastructure, support services, and modern technology led to a decline in agricultural productivity. As a result, many rural inhabitants migrated to urban areas, exacerbating the inequality between rural and urban regions. Instead of reducing class disparities, these policies destabilized the social and economic structure of rural areas, increasing poverty and triggering widespread migration. See: Keith Mc Lachlan, *The Neglected Garden: The Politics and Ecology of Agriculture in Iran*, (London: I. B. Tauris, 1998).

or permanent salaried work, whether in their own villages or in industry. As men migrated to the towns in search of work, women gained greater authority at home,[40] although this was offset by their diminishing financial contribution as the family economy became ever more dependent on the income of men working in the towns. As Erika Friedl notes: "The home [was] no longer centered on the productivity of the woman, but on the economic success of her husband."[41]

To address dwindling family incomes, some Kurdish women in rural areas took to weaving for the carpet market.[42] This additional daily task intensified their exploitation. In 1972, an estimated 70 percent of labor in this sector was to be found in these regions. Between 1965 and 1971, more than 90 percent of carpet weavers were women and young girls, 40 percent of them less than 15 years old.[43] According to a report published by Komala in 1986, many women living in villages and even small Kurdish towns were involved in the industry:

> Carpet weaving is one of the most common areas of domestic production, often involving women and young girls, especially in the villages and towns of southern Kurdistan. This is the main source of income for the women workers. In addition to undertaking household tasks, mothers weave carpets. Altogether these tasks take over 14 hours [a day].[44]

The extent to which Iranian women benefited from socio-economic improvements was largely determined by their social class, their geographical location, and their ethnicity. In practice, the mostly Farsi-speaking elite and urban middle classes in the central regions benefited much more from modernization than did others. While the urban middle class in the central regions enjoyed dramatically better access to education, healthcare, and modern leisure activities during the 1960s and 1970s, the majority of the population living in the peripheries, including urban areas, saw considerably less change in their standard of living.[45] These regions continued to be characterized by poverty, illiteracy, unemployment, inadequate public health infrastructure, and lack of access to electricity and clean water. Medicine was unknown to many Kurdish village women, and the gap was filled by superstition and powerful religious figures.[46]

The lack of elementary schools in rural areas, and of secondary and vocational schools in small towns, along with socio-cultural restrictions on women's education, was a major obstacle to the literacy of women, especially Kurds. Statistics from 1976 show the extent to which women were disadvantaged. While 74.8 percent of men and 56.6 percent of women in the central regions were literate, the literacy rates in other provinces were significantly lower: 43.8 percent of men and 15 percent of women in Kurdistan province; 51.1 percent of men and 21.7 percent of women in East Azerbaijan; and 39.1 percent of men and 19.4 percent of women in Sistan-Baluchistan.[47] Amineh Kakabaveh, a former Komala activist from a poor village family, recalls in her autobiography, "In our village, there was only primary school. To carry on their education, students had to go to the nearby big cities like Saqqez or Bukan. And this was an option only for the rich, especially their sons."[48]

This situation was worse at the level of secondary education, as many girls from the peripheral regions were obliged to abandon their studies. This was not the case for Sara, a former Komala activist, who recounts: "Although I started my education in my hometown, I had to go to a neighboring town for high school. My family, especially on my father's side, encouraged me to continue my education even in another town, but many of my friends were forced to give it up."

The effects of modernization were thus double-edged. Mass media such as radio, as well as the new educational programs, fueled the Kurds' resentment of regime authorities. In a context of increasing inequality, Kurds felt more marginalized than ever, and their growing awareness of the injustice of their situation pushed them to demand a better standard of living. As Zara, a former Komala activist, testifies:

> I lost one of my sisters, who died while giving birth to her first child. At the time we accepted this tragedy, attributing it to the will of God, as our elders did. Then in the last years of the Shah's regime, everything changed. Schools and medical centers

opened in the towns. We discovered that such things had already existed, and that if we had been able to access them, our lives would undoubtedly have been different. While before we had justified everything as God's will, now we understood that our unhappy fate was due above all to the cruel policies of the Shah.

2

Women's Subordination in Kurdish Society

While the Pahlavis' modernizing policies—industrialization, socio-economic reforms, urbanization, education, and public services— improved the status of women, especially in the central regions, they failed to bring about significant change within the Iranian family, or indeed in most socio-cultural norms. The reasons are numerous. As sociologist William F. Ogburn explains, lifestyle, values, and socio-cultural norms generally undergo transformation at a slower rate than do technology or the economy.[1] Moreover the inadequate scale of socio-economic change, and the authoritarian, contradictory, and discriminatory way the Pahlavi regime implemented modernization, contributed to the lack of significant change in gender relations within the family. By comparison with other developing countries in the region, Iran recorded the lowest increase in rates of urbanization, industrialization, and education during the 1960s and 1970s.*

Despite numerous modifications in family law to the advantage of women, the framework of male domination was maintained. For example, Articles 1042–3 of the Civil Code, ratified in 1931, required the consent of the father or grandfather for a woman to enter into a first marriage. Article 1105 specified that the husband was the head of the household and was responsible for providing for it. Nor did systems put in place to implement the government's

---

* While urbanization had the effect of increased employment and greater family mobility, reducing the sexual division of labor, Iran's total population in 1966 was only 39 percent urban. In 1971, Iran lagged behind Turkey, Egypt, and six other nations in the region in modernization, as measured by the degree of urbanization, industrialization, and education. See the figures cited in James F. Keller and Lloyd Mendelson, "Changing Family Patterns in Iran: A Comparative Study," *International Journal of Sociology of the Family* 1, no. 1 (1971): 10–20.

socio-economic and cultural policies improve the position of women. As a result of regulations requiring women to abandon traditional dress for European clothes, traditional and/or religious families kept their daughters away from school or refused to allow them to participate in after-school activities.[2] Even families that were not religious, as well as oppositional groups across a range of ideological positions, from Marxist to Islamist, targeted the image of the modern woman promoted by the government. The Iranian historian Afsaneh Najmabadi summarized this in the following way: "The *Gharbzadeh* [westoxificated] woman came to embody at once all social ills: she was a super-consumer of imperialist/dependent-capitalist/foreign goods; she was a propagator of the corrupt culture of the West; she was undermining the moral fabric of society; she was a parasite, beyond any type of redemption."[3]

The Kurds of Iran, as part of a predominantly illiterate rural population, were among the most politically, economically, and culturally oppressed in the population; patriarchal norms that lay at the heart of this population's way of life were maintained with greater force than in the central regions of the country. The delayed emergence of Kurdish women into political life is the consequence of this social context.

WOMEN'S PRIMARY SOCIAL ROLE: THE WIFE

Religious and heterosexual marriage, as the founding act of the family, represented a crucial stage in the life of each member of the Kurdish community. Every human being was expected to marry. Only within marriage was it possible to live as a sexual being and to have legitimate children. Sexual relations outside marriage were forbidden. Marriage was more essential for women than for men: while men might establish identities in the public domain, women's primary role was in private life, within the family. Although young people in Iran across ethnic groups faced moral and religious pressures to marry, a number of specific features characterized marriage in the Kurdish community in the 1960s and 1970s.

Age gaps between couples were common. Most girls married at a younger age than men, which was associated with early or forced marriage. Although such unions were more common in traditional or lower-income families, whether in rural or urban areas, for various reasons (notably poverty), middle-class girls were not immune. Under the Pahlavi modernization policies, civil law imposed a minimum age of 15 for girls, but this new law did not succeed in suppressing customary practice, and in some families, in order to maintain traditional values, daughters were encouraged or even compelled to marry very young. Such families would readily falsify a daughter's date of birth, or avoid official registration of the marriage, especially in rural areas where these traditions were strongest. Early and forced marriage thus remained the fate of many women in the peripheries.[4] The sisters of Nasrin, despite their upper-class background, were married at aged 12 and 13. According to their father's logic, "This kind of marriage could be a way of protecting family honor, which might be threatened at any moment by unmarried daughters."

The virginity of the bride-to-be was essential. It was to be confirmed by the husband after the first act of sexual intercourse, which had to take place during the wedding night. Traditionally a woman, the *barbuk* or *pâ-khasû* (literally, "in front of the bride"), would accompany the bride through her new house, from the threshold to the bridal room as night fell. The following day the *barbuk* would be responsible for retrieving the bloodstained sheet that was taken as the irrefutable proof of virginity. A single act of sexual intercourse transformed a girl (whatever her age) into a woman (one who was no longer a virgin). By proving her chastity, she protected the honor of her parental family. If she turned out not to be a virgin, she might be sent home or killed by her male relatives. Under these social conditions, the best thing to wish for a Kurdish girl was *Bexti sur bi*, or "may her luck be red," that is, may she be married with an unbroken hymen.[5]

Polygamy was permitted for Kurdish men, although it was uncommon. According to Thomas Bois, in his 1950s study of the family in Kurdistan of Iraq and Turkey—where the same conditions pertained most likely as in Kurdistan of Iran—observed:

> The Kurds, being Muslims on the whole, are therefore religiously permitted to be polygamous. In the past, often for political purposes, chiefs in particular married several wives and had

many children. Today, this is no longer the case. Polygamy is in fact increasingly dying out. It still exists in the uneducated urban environment, but never with more than two wives. Among the peasantry, monogamy is dominant, for economic reasons, and the average number of husbands with more than one wife does not exceed 2 percent. The common people thus avoid the difficulties of complex households, keeping in mind the proverb, "The man who marries two wives must become a doorkeeper."[6]

Although endogamous unions between first cousins were favored among Kurds, not all marriages followed this pattern.[7] Before the revolution, endogamous marriages were the majority: cousin marriages were seen as a way of strengthening the relationships between relatives, especially between brothers. This was the case even in the urban areas of the central regions, where high levels of public education and employment might have encouraged social mobility and exogamous marriages.[8] In the absence of a first cousin, other members of a family's lineage offered themselves as suitors. As the Dutch anthropologist Martin van Bruinessen writes concerning the importance of endogamous marriage in Kurdish tribes before the 1970s:

> There is a clear preference for marriage to the father's brother's daughter (real or classificatory). In fact, a daughter's father's brother's son has the theoretical right to refuse his cousin's marriage to someone else. If her father wishes to marry her to a stranger, he must in theory ask his nephews for permission, unless they have already waived their right of the first proposal. I have never witnessed a concrete case in which this has happened, but I have heard of this custom in several places in Kurdistan. And if a father's brother's son wants to marry the daughter, it is difficult, if not impossible, for the girl's father to refuse.[9]

Marriage in the Kurdish community, as in the rest of Iran, was not primarily an individual act. Its purpose was to unite two families rather than two individuals. Indeed, the union of the two sexes was possible exclusively through religious marriage, which was an obligation rather than a personal choice for the two parties. The choice of spouse was thus in general a family affair, imposed with little interest in the individual's wishes, especially that of a girl or woman. Parental permission remained an important factor in the stability of the marriage; parents often refused to give support to a union that had met with disapproval at the outset. My interviews with former Komala activists indicate that before the revolution, as a rule, families of any socio-economic status arranged the marriage of their children in line with family interests. Of course, men were freer than women to choose their wives, even though some women may have done so as well; but in all cases, the permission of the family, particularly the father, appeared necessary. As Roonak, a former Komala activist, explains:

> In my family, it was my father alone who determined the life of all his children. He would not let us continue our studies and wanted to marry us while we were very young to a husband of his choice. My sisters were married at the ages of 12, 13, and 14. But I resisted my father's intentions. I carried on with my studies, and at 17 I married a man of my own choice. It was very difficult, but in the end my father accepted my decision.

Whether endogamous or exogamous, marriage—even with the consent of the woman herself— freed the woman from the authority of her father only to deliver her to that of her husband. Amir Hassanpour, in his valuable research on the Kurdish language, examines the verbs applied to marriage. His analysis of an extensive list of verbs demonstrates that it was always men who have the right to initiate the marriage proposal. Women could at most express their views: yes or no.[10] This is clearly signified in verbs such as *xuwazbeni kirdin*, which means "to send an intermediary to the girl's parents to ask her to marry" or "to ask a girl to become a wife."

However, this vocabulary does not indicate that women had no form of resistance. The emergence of a practice in some Kurdish regions, *radûkavtin* (the flight of lovers), is an example. In order to marry the man of their choice, at the risk of their lives, some women secretly eloped with their lovers, seeking refuge with a respected or powerful person so as to avoid being caught and killed. Once the couple was safe, the parties would usually reach a compromise in which all received their share in the political economy of marriage.[11] Marriage was fundamentally a commercial transaction in which the woman was exchanged for the dowry (*mârayî* in Kurdish), varying in value according to the social class of the future husband. The dowry, given to the bride and accompanied by jewels and gifts, is a safeguard in case of divorce or the death of her husband. In some cases, the dowry may be reduced, as in a union between cousins, or in the Kurdish tradition known as *jin ba jiné* (exchange of women).[12] In the latter case, which is now rarely used, two families, generally poor, agree to exchange their daughters, bypassing the material aspects of the transaction.

Despite the socio-economic changes within the Kurdish community, the financial aspect of marriage continues to be very important today, especially for women who lack economic independence. To a certain extent, this allowed women a modicum of power, particularly in relation to divorce. In a situation where the right to divorce was reserved for men, women who were unhappy in their marriages could decide to give up their dowry in order to encourage their husbands to agree to a divorce.

Following marriage and the establishment of a new family, the kinship group would make every effort to maintain this new covenant, overseeing the various stages of the marriage, as it would be directly affected if any problems arose in the newly formed family leading to conflict or divorce.[13] Kurdish proverbs such as "One must enter the husband's family in white and leave it in white" (leave after death in a white shroud, according to Muslim ritual), and "Women know only three houses: their father's, their husband's, and the grave," illustrate this family anxiety, especially for women. Women were not only denied freedom of choice in marrying; they were also denied the right to divorce. The husband, meanwhile, could decide to leave his wife for no particular reason or to remarry as he wished. A Sunni man could easily terminate married life, at any time and for any reason, by the "triple *talaq*" (i.e., repeating the declaration of *talaq* or divorce three times) or by uttering a different formula such as "You are haram to me." While Shiite jurisprudence does not recognize this type of divorce, Sunnis validate it, giving men absolute power in marital life.[14]

The negative impact of divorce was felt more by a woman than by a man. Traditionally, a divorced woman had to return to her parents, had lower social status, and her actions and behavior were constantly maligned. It was to minimize the risk of separation that the woman's family tried to impose a high bride-price on their future son-in-law. Most women also tried to maintain the family circle, doing everything possible to maintain the union, even in the face of domestic violence, humiliation, insults, and sexual unhappiness.[15] Mahrokh, a former Komala activist, describes her divorce in 1981 following a forced marriage:

> My family forced me to marry one of my relatives, but a year later I was divorced with a child. Although I had been freed from my husband, my family's behavior became unbearable. They interfered with everything in my personal life, even the color of my clothes.

THE REPRODUCTIVE ROLE OF WOMEN AS MOTHERS

In the 1970s, Iranian women had an average of seven children.[16] Women in rural areas often had more children due to the family's greater need for labor in agriculture and animal husbandry. Providing children was women's primary contribution to the community; a woman's entire being was defined by motherhood, the enlargement of the family, and the maintenance of the lineage. Motherhood was imposed on young women after marriage, not only through dominant cultural norms but also the state programs of the Pahlavi regime, which presented it as a national duty. As Azadeh Kian states: "The nation is certainly gendered, but it is also sexualized. If in the nation's imagination, women were primarily chaste and loving mothers, women's femininity would be associated with women's fertility."[17]

Bearing many children for one's husband was the essential criterion for being a good wife. The Kurdish proverb "The wife who cannot give birth is no more than a stranger" captured the reality that a bride would not be fully accepted by her in-laws until bearing children. A childless couple was considered a "house without light," and an infertile woman was to be cast aside, as another proverb advised: "If the tree is not fruitful, it will have to be cut down." A woman who could not give birth was sent back to her parents or had to accept her husband taking another wife. Rosemary Gillespie argues that in patriarchal social orders, "motherhood has been perceived primarily as natural for women, their desire for it inevitable, unquestionable and central to constructions of normal femininity."[18] No woman could exempt herself from this responsibility. It was only through childbearing, as a rite of passage, that women gained a valued status in family and social life. Women who did not bear children for whatever reason were considered abnormal or deviant. In Kurdistan, as in many other regions of the world, "the young girl acquires the status of womanhood only at the moment when she conceives, and the infertile woman is not considered a real woman."[19] In so far as the woman's body was perceived as an instrument of biological reproduction, her sterility could be seen as a disability.[20] Similarly, the birth of a child served to confirm the husband's virility, and a husband who did not father children was seen as weak and feeble. To avoid this stigma, men would choose polygamy or divorce. Taking an additional wife was an option primarily for rich men, while others divorced their wives and remarried.[21]

A further requirement for a woman to win the respect of the family was to give birth to a son.[22] The prestige men acquired through having a large number of children was enhanced when those children were boys, and the social status of women was largely linked to bearing sons. Women would enter into endless cycle of pregnancies and childbirths, and if they did not have at least one boy, they were expected to accept that their husband would take another wife in order to ensure male offspring. According to research carried out in 2014, among 19 Kurdish polygamous men from different social strata who had taken a second wife at least 30 years earlier, it was the lack of sons from their first marriage that drove four of them (all from the urban middle class) to remarry. (One of these polygamous families failed to achieve its goal, with seven daughters born after the second marriage.)[23]

A woman who gave birth only to daughters was almost as stigmatized as one who was infertile, and her husband would be regarded as having a "house without light," that is, having no one to provide him with money or food. The birth of a boy was therefore welcomed with joy and pride: "numerous gifts are offered to the young mother on the occasion of a birth, especially if she has given birth to a son, often more desired than a daughter."[24] Some of the names that used to be given to girls show very clearly the importance of having a son; names such as Kafiye (enough) or Basiye (sufficient), sometimes found in families who had several daughters in a row without a son, sent the message that they did not want any more.[25] A mother who could not give birth to a boy often suffered from guilt, fueled by the attitude of the husband's family and wider kin: giving birth to girls was bad luck. Nonetheless, the kinship group would celebrate and honor a daughter if, after her, one or more sons are born. Narmin, a former Komala activist, explains:

> I was always very much respected in my family, especially by my parents. They always called me Golden Feet or *Paçké Zeriné*, because after my birth, several boys were born. They thought that I brought luck and happiness to the family.

WOMEN AND THE REPRODUCTION OF THE SOCIAL ORDER

As a mother, the role of the Kurdish woman in the family was central, while as in most patriarchal cultures, public life was the domain of men. This sexual division of space and labor is founded on biological determinism in relation to social roles: motherhood is regarded as biologically instinctive and universal for all women independently of socio-cultural pressures and structures. Housework (cleaning, cooking, and caring for children and for the sick or elderly family) and childrearing were seen as the natural responsibilities of women, who had to strive to be seen as "good" mothers. As Maria O'Shea points out in her work on Sanandaj (the capital of Kurdistan province) between 1992 and 1996, "The family is the central institution for healthcare in Sanandaj. Families care for sick relatives, with women being primarily responsible for that care. Women are considered to be generally responsible for domestic harmony and good health, especially of small children."[26] The slightest failure to fulfill these duties, or anxiety over the difficulty of balancing family and social life, could lead to a deep sense of guilt. Neither the entry of some Kurdish urban women into the labor market following the socio economic changes of the 1960s and 1970s nor the agricultural work performed by rural women could break this sexual division of labor. Women's primary domestic role remained unchallenged. As Sayran describes it:

> It was always my mother, one of the first women to work as a teacher in town, who took care of everything, inside and outside the house. She never got tired. She did her best to take care of all our daily needs.

Women's exclusive responsibility for household tasks was still more marked in rural areas, where most of them worked in agriculture, enduring harsher conditions than urban women as well as more total subordination. Thomas Bois, writing in 1956 about Kurdish women in villages, observed:

> They are on their feet from five in the morning to eleven at night. It is certain that all the heavy work of the household falls on her. In addition to milking the sheep, making butter and cheese . . . she is also responsible for baking bread. . . . It is also the woman's duty to fetch water from the village spring, sometimes half an hour's walk away, and to gather fuel, collecting dead wood or kneading dung cakes that are then dried in the sun by sticking them to the walls of the houses. Cooking is of course also the woman's prerogative. . . . The weekly wash, with board, beater and soap, done at the communal fountain and often in groups, is also the responsibility of the Kurdish housewife. In almost every corner of Kurdistan, women spin wool as they come and go. As soon as any other work stops, the spindle turns in their skillful hands. Some also weave on looms.[27]

Another significant role for the "good" Kurdish mother was the transmission of socio-cultural heritage to the next generation. This reflects a sexual division of responsibilities based on the assumption of male superiority. As in many languages, the words for "woman" (*jin*) and "man" (*piyaw*) in Kurdish are respectively associated with a set of generally opposing qualities, values, and emotional connotations, that are constructed and reinforced in proverbs and folk sayings. While the word *piyaw* is used in the sense of "human being," it also implies positive character traits such as courage, power, intelligence, and humanity. The meanings associated with the word *jin* are diametrically opposed; it is associated with "weakness" (*ze'ife*) and "feebleness" both in reasoning capacity and in practical skill. It also connotes the evil and cunning of those who, through their seductive powers, can lead men astray.[28]

"Good" mothers were also responsible for educating the young within this value system, communicating to future generations their gendered roles and places in society. For example, while the Kurdish political world was predominantly male, women played the role of narrators, mourning the victims and passing on stories of the past to their children. Christine Allison writes,

> A Kurdish child would hear and learn a whole range of songs and stories from his/her mother, aunts and grandmother. . . . In modern times, when so many fathers and uncles have been "in the mountains" (i.e., as guerrilla fighters), in exile, in prison, or dead, women have had a crucial role in passing on not only traditional forms of folklore, but also a distinctively Kurdish world view, which has helped to shape the national consciousness of the younger generation.[29]

Allison adds, "As with lamentations for the dead, it seems to be up to women more than men to express their emotions of anxiety, vulnerability, loss, and grief."[30]

In line with these distinctions of gender, the socialization of children would take two different paths, as Bois observed in the 1950s: "The little boy spends his first years with women. But as soon as he knows how to run, he will spend all his time in the streets with his friends, while his little sister will be gradually initiated into all the labors of a good housewife."[31] Within a few years, the boy would begin to identify with the father, to whom respect and obedience were due; and this sense of superiority, along with the preference shown for him, would be reinforced at every stage of his life, leading him to believe himself to be essentially superior to the female members of the household. His personality would be largely based on the role he was expected to play, which was organized around characteristics such as autonomy, decisiveness, authority, and inflexibility. Representing through these qualities the future security of his parents, he was considered the heir of the material and symbolic capital of the family.

The mother's duty to her daughter, meanwhile, was the opposite: it was to prepare her to become a housewife. Identifying herself with the world of the household, the daughter would imitate what she saw, learning to share the cares, anxieties, secrets, and rituals of mothers. Thus, her mind would be gradually shaped by the mentality of women, especially that of her mother, from whom she learned her conduct. In the words of a Kurdish proverb: "To choose a wife, instead of paying attention to house and possessions, look at the mother and then marry her daughter." Daughters usually had no role models to learn from but their mother and close relations.

The boundaries separating the world of women from that of men were not to be crossed, but since men's behavior was positively valued, it was more acceptable for women to adopt some masculine characteristics. In this vein, Ziba, a 31-year-old Kurdish woman from a middle-class Sanandaj family, and a university-educated divorcee working as a hairdresser, is quoted in a 2012 study commenting: "My sister and I have been working since we were young, and we are economically independent. That's why those around us regard us as men, and they let us know it."[32]

Despite the important responsibility assigned to women for children and family tasks, most women were kept in a position of economic dependence, and their labor in the domestic space was exploited, depriving them of power and social recognition. This distinction between private and public spheres stemmed from an entrenched social hierarchy. Even in the private sphere, men were considered more important than women. Women were no more than men's property, as were their children, who belonged to the father and his family from birth, taking the first name of the father and grandfather in order to perpetuate the lineage. Children were frequently removed from the mother's care by the husband's family if the couple divorced or the father died. A widowed daughter-in-law would be allowed to retain custody of the children subject to two conditions: either she would not remarry or she agreed to marry a relative of the deceased husband. The husband of Miriam, a 43-year-old housewife from a middle-class family in the Kurdish city of Marivan with three children and educated to elementary level, married his brother's wife after his death. Miriam explained in a 2014 study that "despite the fact that my husband loved me, and our love was mutual, the death of my brother-in-law [my husband's brother] changed everything. My husband did not want to see his nieces and nephews under the guardianship of another man [his sister-in-law's potential new husband]. So he married her."[33]

NAMÛS: THE IDEOLOGY BEHIND THE CONTROL OF WOMEN'S BODIES

Since the social mores of Kurdish community of Iran were little affected by the reformist drive of the Pahlavi regime, the question of honor continued to occupy a predominant place. Control over women's bodies and over their sexuality was maintained in the name of *namûs* (honor), a fixed system rooted in custom, culture, and religion. While culturalist perspectives often overlook the material conditions in which dominant norms operate, these norms are equally shaped by the objective conditions that govern the society's political and socio-economic structures.[34]

Kurdish women, regardless of their marital status (married, single, or widowed), were considered the embodiment of family honor; only the elderly were exempted. They were accepted as members of their family and community only if they maintained their *namûs* by controlling their sexuality. It was women's primary responsibility to respect and uphold the codes of honor, while male family or community members were the guarantors of women's sexuality; men's honor was directly related to their ability to control women's sexuality. The sexual harassment of a woman would send a message to the men in her family that they had failed in their role as protectors, and the woman would be seen as dishonored rather than violated.

The many codes governing women's behavior went beyond sexuality to forbid any conduct perceived as a threat to family honor. As Nazand Begikhani and Gill Hague point out, women could bring dishonor and shame to their families by crossing a range of social and sexual boundaries: smoking, leaving the house too often, laughing, dressing too revealingly, talking with strangers, for example.[35] Any change in their lives could represent a threat to the dominant social norms. Marjan was one of the first girls in her village to go to school in the 1950s. She explains that her father was not against girls' education, but it was a struggle to convince people to let them study:

> We lived in a village near Marivan where no girls could go to school. My sisters and I were the first to go to school. But this was not an easy decision, neither for us nor for my parents, especially my father. Although he was well known and respected in the area, he was criticized and mocked for allowing his daughters to be educated. The very conservative society considered an educated girl a danger to the honor of her family. Once educated, she could seduce men without thinking about her family's reputation.

Facing a threat to their honor, sometimes families would seek to avoid scandal and find a peaceful solution to repair it. As Shirin explains:

> Having an extramarital relationship was particularly frowned upon for women. I heard it said that some women, or even men, were killed in the name of honor. However, most families did not react in this way, and often preferred to remain silent. And sometimes, in the case of extramarital sex between two young unmarried people, the families would force them to marry instead of killing them.

In her memoir, Diana Nammi tells the story of a bride who was not a virgin. Nammi's own father intervened, and the groom accepted the bride. She writes that her father said to Ahmed, the groom, "If you send this woman back to her family then you have to leave the city too. This matter is not more important than her life. You must accept her as your bride." Nammi continues: "With these words, the tension dissipated. Everyone fell silent. My father was a respected member of the community. I don't know how long we all waited in silence but eventually Ahmed said to my father: 'I respect you and your words. I will accept her. I will not send her back to her family.'"[36]

Nonetheless some families, in both rural and urban areas, violently punished those who crossed the red line of honor. While men were not immune to such treatment, it was generally women, considered as the source of evil and the main agent of men's misconduct, who were severely punished. Those lucky enough to escape murder may have had their ears or noses cut off or their hair shaved as punishment.[37] Writing on the subject of honor-based violence, a Kurdish writer in 1963 commented that women "knew . . . that they would be killed if they engaged in 'bad deeds,'" that is, premarital or extramarital sex. "The threat of murder struck fear into the hearts of women, and it was only this fear that kept them from committing 'bad deeds.'"[38] Women were expected to demonstrate reserve, modesty, silence, and obedience. Like Christiane Chaulet-Achour observes in the case of Algerian women,[39] most Kurdish families raised their children to observe these dominant norms, insisting on the duty of little boys to control their sister's sexuality, and that of little girls to be the "guardian of the family's honor."[40] The aim was to "preserve virginity" at all costs and to control the everyday behavior of female family members in a variety of ways, by restricting their freedom of movement, requiring early or forced marriage, or even subjecting them to female genital mutilation (FGM).*

In terms of freedom of movement in public space and also of everyday relations with men, the experience of Kurdish women varied according to class and whether they lived in a town or village. Village women's involvement in agricultural activities meant that they normally had more freedom than urban women, who were mostly housewives. Zara, a village woman, explains:

---

* Although FGM is less frequent today, it was still practiced until very recently among different social strata in some Iranian Kurdish regions. Fatemeh Karimi, "Teragedi-y-é Tan" (Tragedy of the Body), in *Entesharat-é Roshangaran va Motal'éaté Zanan* (Tehran, 2010).

> Although we always tried to behave according to rules of society and family, this did not mean that we were locked up in a cage. So long as we respected the rules, there was no strict segregation between women and men. We were often together for farming activities, talking and joking.

Living in a city like Sanandaj, the capital of Kurdistan province, may also have provided more freedom for women than living in small towns in the provinces, such as Bukan, Marivan, or Baneh. Some of the former middle-class women activists of Komala in Sanandaj (nine interviewees) said they were more or less able to move around in public. Most were able to continue their education up to high school level, go to the cinema, or take part in sports or music classes. However, girls from poorer urban families, whether in big cities or small towns, were seldom able to continue their secondary education due to lack of appropriate schools or family restrictions. Shilan, a former Komala activist from a poor family in Sanandaj, comments:

> I used to hear some of my former Komala comrades (from the middle class) saying that they could go to the cinema or other places. This was really surprising, because it wasn't at all the case for my sisters and me. We were never allowed to go anywhere except to school (single-sex) or to our relatives' homes.

Nasrin, the daughter of a large landowner in a small Kurdish town, similarly stated that:

> Although I come from a rich and well-known family in our region, my father was not at all in favor of educating his daughters. While my brothers were never kept back from education, and could carry on studying until they finished university, he allowed my younger sisters and me only to finish elementary school.

When urban women, who were usually confined to the private sphere, did appear in public space, they were expected to present a good image of their group, family, or community, and to comply with certain norms of dress and comportment. As a number of interviewees testified, the movement of women in public space was restricted; to differing degrees, they all faced limitations on social activities in public space. They were not allowed to walk alone on the street after dark, and indeed they were preferably accompanied at all times by a man of the family. They had to avoid unnecessary outings, wear appropriate clothing, walk in a "decent" manner, and not mix with men who were not their relatives. Any violation, no matter how small, could result in punishment. If they went out too often, or if their outings were seen to be ill-defined and without a concrete purpose, they would be quickly singled out for criticism. Everything about the behavior of young women was minutely observed by their families and members of the wider community who had some connection to them, whether near or distant. This scrutiny was relatively common among conservative families in urban areas, regardless of class. Shirin, who married a teacher from a town in Kurdistan, reports:

> I saw women who had more freedom than us who often walked around alone, but some families, like my in-laws, were very cautious about the women of their families. I never went out alone. When my husband was away, another man from my family-in-law always accompanied me.

In such a society, women tended to compensate for their lack of social legitimacy by cooperating with the patriarchal system. All women, especially young women and girls, would be concerned about what people said about them. Almost all women accepted these constant controls imposed on them since childhood, and most internalized them as something unquestionable and in their own best interests. This perpetual control of women as the source of evil also led women to have negative views of their bodies and everything related to them. As a consequence, many young women were alienated from the first signs of femininity their body showed, such as menstruation and breasts. Mehri, a former Komala activist, confides: "As soon as my breasts started to grow and I got my period, I tried to hide it as much as possible from those around me, especially my brothers."

Kurdish women faced dual discrimination based on their gender and ethnic identity, resulting in limited political engagement. In the period leading to the 1979 Revolution, most Kurdish women became politicized relatively late compared to other social groups. Non-Kurdish Iranian women from middle-class backgrounds and young Kurdish men were more actively involved in politics, despite paying a heavy price. Before the revolution, for instance, Nasrin and Shirin's brothers lost their lives for political reasons, while Marjan and Fatima's brothers spent several years in prison. The majority of Kurdish women did not leave the Kurdish regions, and so remained distant from the emerging political landscape in the rest of Iran.

While a few Kurdish women, like Marjan and Sayran, became teachers in villages before the revolution to serve the underprivileged—considered a cultural-political act by the small Maoist group that later became Komala—most women remained uninvolved in politics. These circumstances partly elucidate why Kurdish women joined the revolution only in the last months before victory. However, their participation proved more significant than that of Kurdish men in the sense that through their involvement, they not only expressed discontent with the oppressive policies of the Pahlavi regime, but also challenged gender norms in Kurdish society, particularly familial constraints. As we will see in Part II, one reason for women's participation in the political life of the time, initially in the revolution and later within Komala, stemmed from their desire to escape routine and monotony.

The gender division of labor could not be disrupted without a significant transformative event. The 1979 Revolution shattered the repetitive rhythm of Kurdish women's lives, allowing them to move prominently to the forefront of political life. After the revolution, the transformed political landscape led to increased active participation of Kurdish women in subsequent events. It created an opportunity for them to take a leading role in the political and public spheres during the 1980s. Kurdish women embarked on a transformative journey beyond imposed social and political constraints to reshape their lives and identities within the revolutionary movement. In the following chapters, we will delve into the narratives that trace their compelling stories.

Kurdish women faced dual discrimination based on their gender and [illegible], resulting in limited political engagement. In [illegible]

[illegible]

[illegible] the majority of Kurdish women [illegible]

[illegible]

the repressive position of Kurdish women [illegible], allowing them to [illegible]

[illegible]

[illegible] Kurdish women embarked [illegible] and [illegible] social and political conditions to reshape [illegible] and [illegible] [illegible] compelling stories.

PART II

Militant Trajectories Within Komala from the Revolution to 1981

Doubly discriminated against, as women and as members of an ethnic minority, Kurdish women did not restrict their political activism to the overthrow of the Pahlavi regime. They also aimed to play a role in the building of a new society as members of political organizations, including Komala. These women's narratives highlight a significant turning point in their political involvement. In the early post-revolutionary period, between February 1979 and March 1981, women contributed to Komala as sympathizers, joining in socio-political activism in the urban areas. From March 1981, however, following the outbreak of armed conflict between Kurdish political forces and government forces in May 1980, increasing numbers of women gradually joined the ranks of Komala as official members or peshmergas.

THE POLITICAL SITUATION OF THE KURDISH REGIONS FOLLOWING THE 1979 REVOLUTION

The occupation of Iran during the Second World War had given Kurdish political forces the opportunity to establish the Republic of Kurdistan in 1946. Similarly, the 1979 Revolution opened a space in which Kurds could make their political demands heard. The overthrow of the monarchy in February 1979 saw the emergence of a number of political organizations, Kurdish and others, taking advantage of the weakening of central power.* Among the Kurdish groups, three types of political orientation can be distinguished: Islamism, nationalism (KDPI), and Marxism (Komala).†

Although Kurdish revolutionaries shared the same primary goal as others during the 1979 Revolution—the overthrow of the Pahlavi regime—in the aftermath of the revolution, the ideological and programmatic differences between groups became apparent. After the victory of the revolution, a coalition of Kurdish political forces including the KDPI and Komala, demanded political and cultural rights specifying several points, including:

* The non-Kurdish political organizations were the Iranian People's Fedayeen Guerrilla Organization, the Tudeh Party, the Paykar, and the People's Mojahedin Organization of Iran. While the first three were Marxist in tendency, the last was Islamist and most active in the Shiite regions of Kurdistan such as Ilam and Kermanshah.

† For Kurdish Islamists, the religious cause took primacy over the Kurdish cause.

- The boundaries of Kurdistan would be determined by the Kurdish people, taking into consideration their historical, economic, and geographical situation;
- On matters of defense, foreign affairs, and long-term economic planning, Kurdistan would follow the decisions of the central government, and the Central Bank of Iran would control the currency;
- There would be a Kurdish parliament, whose members would be popularly elected. It would be the highest legislative power in the province;
- All government departments in the province would be run locally rather than from the capital;
- There would be a people's army; the police and gendarmerie would be abolished and replaced by a national guard;
- The Kurdish language would be the official language of the provincial government and would be taught in all schools. Farsi would also continue to be an official language;
- All ethnic minorities in Kurdistan would enjoy equal rights, be allowed to use their own language and to have their own traditions respected;
- Freedom of speech and of the press, rights of association, and trade union activities would be guaranteed.[1]

Notwithstanding some negotiations with the post-revolutionary provisional government, these demands were interpreted from the outset by the new authority in Tehran as a desire for independence and separatism.[2]

The priority of the new authorities was to hold a referendum to determine the new political system, which took place on March 30–1, 1979. Offering no details about the character of the new government, the pro-Khomeini Islamists asked only a single question in the referendum: yes or no to an Islamic Republic in Iran. The Kurdish political forces, with the exception of the Islamists, boycotted the referendum because of the ambiguous content of the Islamic Republic's program and the unknown fate of the question of their autonomy.[3] Komala announced, as reported, in the daily newspaper *Kayhan** on March 27, 1979:[4]

> In so far as the programs of the Islamic Republic do not clearly recognize the democratic demands of the Iranian revolution or the Kurdish political forces, based on the autonomy of Kurdistan in a democratic Iran, we consider participation in such a referendum to be ignoring the demands of all the Iranian people. We are therefore not willing to take part in this referendum.

The Khomeinist seizure of power through the referendum was consolidated by elections to the Assembly of Experts that took place on August 3, 1979. The purpose of this assembly was to draft a new constitution and this time Kurdish political forces participated. The Khomeini Islamists won a substantial victory in the elections.† The election results sparked numerous protests, which Khomeini's forces suppressed, while the authorities closed down dozens of newspapers and magazines.[5]

The Kurdish political forces increasingly directed their energies toward consolidating control over their own regions and making concrete demands through daily demonstrations. In response, the new revolutionary authorities chose to make an example of them, attacking the Kurdish resistance as comprised of traitors and anti-revolutionaries. Under the pretext of maintaining security, Ayatollah Khomeini attempted to extinguish this political threat, launching an attack on Kurdish political forces with a decree of jihad on August 19, 1979.‡ During this armed conflict, which

* The Kayhan newspaper has been published in Persian in Tehran since February 1943. Before and after the revolution, the newspaper's editorial line was usually close to government policy. Published in Iran as well as in London, .

† Abdolrahman Ghassemlou (1930–89), the charismatic leader of the KDPI, was elected as the only secular representative. However, he never attended assembly sessions because of threats by Ayatollah Khomeini.

‡ This attack was not the first. On March 18, 1979, three days before the Kurdish New Year, Nowruz, the new regime had already bombed the city of Sanandaj (the capital of the province of Kurdistan) ostensibly to put an end to tensions between certain revolutionary groups there. This first attack, which lasted several days, resulted in many victims. In the collective memory of the Kurds, it is known as the "bloody Nowruz" of Sanandaj. See David Romano, *The Kurdish Nationalist Movement: Opportunity, Mobilization and Identity* (Cambridge: Cambridge University Press, 2006), 236.

lasted only three months (from August to November 1979), the main Kurdish political organizations were banned, starting with the KDPI, which was more well known than Komala at that time.[6] Ayatollah Khomeini publicly called for a holy war against the Kurdish political forces, urging his Kurdish Muslim "brothers" to fulfil their Islamic duty against what he described as corrupt tendencies. On August 20, 1979 he announced in *Kayhan* that all those who supported these forces were "anti-revolutionary" and "anti-Islam" and would be punished in accordance with Islamic laws. In response, the KDPI and Komala called on the Kurdish people to resist the regime.* The peshmerga, who were not equipped with heavy military equipment, withdrew to the rural and mountainous areas, while the Iranian army occupied the main urban areas. After three months of struggle, in which the Kurdish armed forces generally had the upper hand, the Kurds were able to recapture the towns that had been occupied by the government forces. From this point until May 1980, almost all the cities in the two provinces of West Azerbaijan and Kurdistan were under Kurdish control, and negotiations between the Kurdish political forces and the government resumed.

However, the adoption of the new Constitution a few months later, through a referendum held on December 2 and 3, 1979—in which the Kurdish forces did not participate—denied the rights of religious and ethnic minorities in the name of the Islamic *ummah* (community). The Constitution was largely based on the religious doctrine of Ayatollah Khomeini. While the superiority of the Farsi language as a unifying factor in the Iranian nation marked a continuity with the Pahlavi regime,† the concept of *ummah*, unifying Muslims under the *Velayat-e Faqih*,‡ was defended as the most

* Since the revolution, the two Kurdish political tendencies, the KDPI and Komala, had been preparing and training their armed forces. In addition, a number of Iraqi Kurdish armed commanders and even some non-Kurds had been assisting them with training.

† Article 15 of the new Iranian constitution identified Farsi as the country's only official language. Although the Constitution also claims to protect the right to education in minority languages, this right has never been implemented.

‡ *Velayat-e Faqih* (Guardianship of the Islamic Jurist) is a Shia Islamic political theory stating that a qualified Islamic jurist (*faqih*) has authority over political and religious matters in society in the absence of the Imam (Mahdi). It forms the basis of governance in Iran, where the Supreme Leader embodies this concept.

important element of the unity of Iranian society. According to this doctrine, the Islamic *ummah* unifies all Iranian Muslims, regardless of their linguistic and cultural differences, under the governance of a spiritual and secular leader as head of state, the *veli-e faqih* (an Islamic jurist, legal expert, and authority in Islamic law). Article 13 of the Constitution states that the only recognized minorities are non-Muslim religious minorities, such as Zoroastrians, Jews, and Christians.*

Despite the significant shift from the Pahlavi regime's secular nationalism to the Islamic Republic's religious ideology, the emergence of the republic did not radically change the fundamental characteristics of the modern Iranian state. Where ethnic minorities were concerned, the new government shared the attitudes of the Pahlavi regime. As Abbas Vali writes, "The concept of ethnic minority in the Iranian Constitution is strictly cultural; it has no juridico-political identity. . . In the constitution of the Islamic Republic, the identity of political power is uniform and ethnic; Persian ethnicity defines the identity of the sovereign, the conditions of citizenship and hence the boundaries of the state and civil society."[7] The Islamic authorities considered ethnic minorities an obstacle to the development of an Islamic Iranian identity and as a potential challenge to the security of the state. The new regime thus sought to neutralize the issue of ethnicity through the establishment of limited cultural autonomy.

Kurdish political forces, KDPI and Komala, viewed the new constitution as an existential threat to their citizenship and criticized it fiercely. Even Kurdish Islamists joined in boycotting the referendum, highlighting the dual discrimination they experienced as Kurds and as Sunnis.[8] Mutual distrust became embedded, and violent clashes between Kurdish forces and government forces (especially the Revolutionary Guards, known as the Pasdaran)

---

* Ayatollah Khomeini explained in a November 1979 speech his reason for refusing the concept of ethnic minorities: "Sometimes the word *minority* is used to refer to people such as the Kurds, Lurs, Turks, Persians, Baluchis, and such. These people should not be called minorities, because this term assumes that there is a difference between these brothers. In Islam, such a difference has no place at all. There is no difference between Muslims who speak different languages, for instance, the Arabs or the Persians." David McDowall, *A Modern History of the Kurds* (London: I.B. Tauris, 2004), 271.

were increasingly common, with each side accusing the other of instigating tensions and provocations.[9] Kurds expressed their dissatisfaction with government policies through public statements, daily demonstrations, and strikes.* The idea of armed struggle as a "last resort" gained ground from May 1980 onward, and maintained its primacy until the end of the 1980s.

* The Representative Council of the Kurdish People in its eighth statement wrote: "The presence of the Pasdaran [Revolutionary Guards] in Kurdistan had no other result than to cause insecurity and disorder in the region. Their departure from Kurdistan has always been one of the urgent demands of the Kurdish people. But instead of respecting the will of the people, the government, by increasing the number of Pasdaran and insisting on keeping them in Kurdistan, is increasing insecurity in the region." Quoted in the *Etela'at* newspaper, January 4, 1980.

3

The Eruption of Kurdish Women into Organized Political Life

THE SOCIOLOGICAL PROFILES OF THE WOMEN ACTIVISTS

In the immediate aftermath of the victory of the 1979 Revolution, during a period known as the "Spring of Freedom,"* many Iranians became involved in politics. The revolutionary alliance that had united to overthrow the Pahlavi regime began to disintegrate in the first weeks after the revolution, as individuals turned to groups with political positions that aligned with their own. Members of the same family often found themselves divided between several ideologically close or contradictory currents. Thus, while the families of Komala activists Mahin and Sara were associated with Komala, the family of Komala activist Mastoureh was divided across a range of political loyalties, both Kurdish and non-Kurdish. Mastoureh's father was a supporter of the KDPI, while her older brother joined the Iranian People's Fedayeen Guerrilla Organization, while Mastoureh and her second brother, who lost his life soon afterward as a result of his political activism, both chose Komala.

Komala, which positively encouraged women's presence in the movement, offered them significantly more opportunity to participate in politics than women had had during the Kurdistan Republic of 1946. Shahrzad Mojab notes in her study of the republic that its influence on women was confined to the city of Mahabad in West Azerbaijan, and that women's participation was linked to

* In the Kurdish regions this period was interrupted by armed conflict that lasted three months in 1979 and then definitively ended in May 1980, when armed conflict broke out between the government and Kurdish political forces and continued until the end of the 1980s. Political repression worsened in many parts of the country a little later, in mid-1981.

specific conditions, notably family structures and socio-economic status. In practice, only women from a few prominent families were in a position to engage in political activity.[1] Qualitatively and quantitatively, the character and the scope of Kurdish women's political participation between the 1979 Revolution and the end of the 1980s thus cannot be equated with this earlier experience. The socio-economic changes of the 1960s and 1970s, which had enabled some women to gain access to schooling and employment, also opened the door for Kurds to enter political life, particularly through Komala, which attracted many revolutionaries in its core regions.

One of the most striking characteristics of Komala was the young age of its activists, both men and women. Komala was founded and organized predominantly by young people and even teenagers (for the most part unmarried), who continued with political activism in the aftermath of the revolution.* Of the 47 people that I interviewed (both men and women), 13 were under the age of 18 when they joined; 23 were aged between 18 and 25, and 11 were over 25. The age of the activists killed, especially the women, also speaks for itself. We know the birth date of 51 out of 110 female members of the organization who died as a result of their activity: of these, 4 women were less than 18 years old when they died; 25 were aged between 18 and 25; 14 were aged between 25 and 30; and 8 were over 30. Most activists were single: among 47 interviewees, 36 were single when they began their political life in Komala (30 women and 6 men).

The 1979 Revolution was an urban revolution, and at the time of Komala's emergence, the majority of its activists were city dwellers. However, political participation within Komala differed from province to province. While some militants in the provinces of Kermanshah and Ilam were active in the KDPI or Komala,[2] most Kurds in these areas had little interest in the Kurdish cause both because the Shia majority in these provinces was associated with greater sympathy for the Shia government, and there was low level of activity of Kurdish organizations.[3] The Kurdish organizations

* For example, one of the charismatic leaders of Komala, Foad Mostafa Soltani, was only 31 years old when government forces killed him on August 31, 1979.

operated predominantly in the Sunni provinces of West Azerbaijan and Kurdistan, which were themselves not politically or ideologically homogeneous. The KDPI was more active in the northern areas, while Komala was based in the south, where it had significant support in cities such as Sanandaj, Marivan, Saqqez, and Kamyaran. Thus, among 44 Kurdish interviewees, 32 were from areas controlled by Komala, and only 12 from other Kurdish areas that were then under KDPI military control. Additionally, from 1981 onward, as the wave of repression in other parts of Iran intensified, some non-Kurdish activists also joined Komala; thus, of the 110 female Komala members killed in the 1980s, 5 were not Kurdish.*

Another characteristic of Komala members was the diversity of their class backgrounds.† Although the founders of the group were predominantly from families of notables and large landowners in the Kurdish regions, from the outset the new Maoist organization successfully drew in young people from poor families. Thus, while some members, such as Marjan, Monireh, and Nasrin, belonged to prominent families with above-average socio-economic status, others, such as Shilan and Golnar, were from poor urban proletariat families. The diversity of socio-economic background increased further as a result of the organization's withdrawal into the rural areas, which led mainly disadvantaged villagers, as well as non-Kurdish activists from the middle class, to join the membership.

The majority of Komala members did not have education beyond primary and secondary level. Among the 47 people interviewed, five Kurdish men, two non-Kurdish women, and one Kurdish woman had been able to access higher education; 30 left school at the secondary level and five at the primary level, while four were illiterate. Among the Kurdish women who had achieved second-

* These women are Pooran Jam Poor (Tehran), Hajar Faizi (Langerood), Iran Khaksar (Tehran), Arabian Khoshkhu (Mashhad), and Fahimeh Taghadosi (Amol). See Bahman Saidi, *Sé Sal le gel Ebrahim Alizadeh* (Three Years with Ebrahim Alizadeh) (Sulaymaniyah: Ranj, 2009), 80–1.

† The interviewees in this study are divided into three social categories: those from families of large landowners belonging to the upper class; those from families of state officials, merchants, and traders living mainly in urban areas, who belong to the middle class; and those from urban and rural working families or small farmers, belonging to a more disadvantaged class.

ary-level education, eight were still in school when they joined the organization, and nine were teachers.* Among the three women with village origins interviewed, only one had reached primary level education, while the other two could not read or write.

Unlike Kurdish men, who had the liberty to engage in political activity, or some non-Kurdish women who might gain access to politics through education, social class, or urban background, most of the activist women joining Komala, especially the younger ones, whether urban or rural, were engaging in politics for the first time. Few of the interviewees had any previous direct experience of politics. Even Nasrin, whose father had been an important figure in the 1946 Kurdistan Republic, did not enter politics through this family history. In order not to put his children at risk, he had concealed his history from his family and his daughter discovered this family secret by chance, while reading a banned book about the history of that period. While her father refused to allow her to continue with her studies, because she was a girl, her brothers were able to engage in political life at university and it was through them that she was politicized. A similar pattern is found in Fatima's political journey: growing up in a poor family, she became familiar with the world of politics at an early age through the arrest and imprisonment of her brother. Shirin also became politically involved through her brother, as well as through the peshmerga forces of Iraqi Kurdistan who were hosted by her family when they passed through her village. It was thus through interactions within the family or in the village that most Komala activists discovered politics. For some Kurdish men, such as the brothers of Nasrin, Mastoureh, Fatima, and Marjan, and also for some non-Kurdish women such as Sohaila and Mahshid, their post-revolutionary involvement in clandestine organizations was a continuation of their pre-revolutionary political activity. But this was not usually the case for young Kurdish women, the majority of whom joined a political organization for the first time only after the victory of the 1979 Revolution. As Golrokh Ghobadi, one of the revolution-

* During this period, candidates were not required to attend higher education to become a teacher. Instead, they could become teachers after completing a two-year training without the prerequisite of attending secondary school.

aries who joined Komala as soon as it emerged, describes it in her memoir:

> As young women and girls, we had grown up in the dictatorial atmosphere of the Pahlavi regime; a regime characterized by political repression and censorship, a regime that was not open to free association or debate on political and social issues. Our generation knew very little about the experience of previous generations. Everything had to be started from scratch.[4]

FROM EVERYDAY LIFE TO POLITICAL ACTIVISM

As this overview of the social backgrounds and political profiles of Komala's female activists shows, limited access to schooling meant that women who entered political organizations were less educated than men of the same background. However, while they had less experience of political organization and more limited exposure to intellectual networks than men, their entry into the political space of Komala was no less conscious or informed than that of their male counterparts. Their narratives demonstrate how women activists used *everyday life* to anchor their critical analyzes and their politicization.[5] Their political choices, embedded in the domestic space of the family rather than detached from everyday life, arose out of an intention to shift the meanings of organizational politics, understood as a relationship between ideology, program, and action.

According to most of the interviewees (40 out of 47), it was above all the "revolutionary" and "progressive" discourse of Komala that caught the attention of the young, especially women. Unlike other political movements, whether Kurdish or non-Kurdish, Komala was committed both to the Kurdish cause and socio-economic justice. Alongside the KDPI, it was actively engaged in negotiations with the new Iranian government. Its boycott of the referendum called by the Islamic Republic and of the new constitution, and its active resistance to the regime's order of jihad against the Kurds in August 1979, also set it apart in the eyes of young revolutionaries.

In contrast to other Kurdish political forces (KDPI and Islamists), Komala strongly appealed to women. It offered a political discourse aimed at both men and women that insisted on the need for a new social order, one that was more just and egalitarian in terms of socio-economic and gender relations, although it did not specify exactly what forms this might take. To address the "woman question" was among the political goals of the organization as part of its understanding of Marxism, initially as part of its spoken rhetoric, and subsequently in written form. The intensity and urgency of the course of political events allowed members of Komala little time for writing between 1979 and 1983.

It was after the withdrawal of Komala to the rural and mountainous areas in May 1980 that the issue of women came increasingly to the fore. Giving voice to women's aspirations, Komala demanded equal rights for men and women in all spheres of social and political life.[6] In its program for the autonomy of Kurdistan in 1984, the fourth article emphasized "full equality of men and women in all rights and the abolition of gender discrimination." The fifth article similarly demanded "full equality of legal rights for all independent members of the community, without distinction of sex, religion, or political conviction." The organization's attention to women's issues was also reflected in its vision of gender equality within the family. Komala insisted on equal rights for men and women in the event of divorce, equal parental rights over children, the prohibition of polygamy, a minimum age of 18 for marriage, freedom for any person over 18 to start a family independently, and the recognition of civil marriage. Violence against women, forced marriage, the tradition of exchanging women, and dowries were all targets for the critique of existing gender relations.[7] The organization tried to apply these principles internally during the 1980s.

Komala's support for the cause of women was significant in a context where, barely a month after the victory of the 1979 Revolution, the new authorities began to propagate a traditionalist reading of Islamic law targeting women's rights and were already institutionalizing gender inequality in private and public life.*

* Among the changes instituted by the new regime were that a woman was entitled to inherit half as much as a man, and the legal age of sexual maturity was lowered to nine for girls and fourteen for boys, a measure enshrined in the Constitution. Polygamy was legalized by law without the need for the consent of the wife or wives. Men could divorce at any time, without preconditions and without a decision by the family court. Custody of a

Komala's open opposition to these policies was remarkable from the moment of its public emergence. Unlike many opposition groups (including the Marxists, who preferred to remain silent on such matters), the young leaders of Komala such as Foad Mostafa Soltani and Sedigh Kamangar called on Kurdish women to demonstrate against the compulsory hijab on March 8, 1979, in solidarity with the women of Tehran.* Two demonstrations were held in Sanandaj and Marivan, where women chanted: "Neither hijab nor humiliation, down with this dictatorship" (*Na roosari na too sari, marg bar in diktatori*). As Jaleh, a former Komala activist, testifies:

> Although this organization [Komala] was unknown to most of us when it was founded, from the beginning it was very radical and revolutionary, immediately opposing the policies of the Islamic Republic of Iran and advocating equality between women and men. For Komala, the victory of the revolution was only the beginning, not the end.

The presence of Komala peshmerga in rural areas, their involvement in the daily life of the villagers, and their interactions with them attracted the interest of women and girls. Former activist Amineh Kakabaveh recalls her encounters with peshmerga as a young teenager:

> It was the Komala peshmerga who opened our eyes to a new worldview. Above all, equality between the sexes was their principle. They had a lot of respect for women, which was a completely new vision in Iran as well as in Kurdistan. . . . They came to the mosques every Friday to perform plays, to organize meetings

---

child automatically went to the father when the child reached seven years of age. See Parvin Paidar, *Women and the Political Process in Twentieth-Century Iran* (New York: Cambridge University Press, 1995).

* This first attempt on the part of the regime to make the hijab compulsory met with significant female resistance in Tehran on March 8, 1979. Women protested the requirement, calling for the preservation of their rights, including their right to wear whatever they wished, chanting, "We condemn all forms of dictatorship," "Freedom is neither Eastern nor Western, it is universal." See the video about the women's demonstration in Tehran on March 8, 1979, at www.youtube.com/watch?v=NHrTGeGAajc. Accessed November 17, 2017.

> and to talk about our difficulties. They would ask the families if they had any problems. They would talk about women's freedom and secularization. They acted as mediators between the villagers. For example, one time they defended a woman who was beaten by her husband.[8]

For a number of interviewees, especially the women, a further reason for their involvement in the organization was related to their daily life. Former Komala activist Mansoor, himself from a landowning family, points out that while men's wish to escape unemployment or compulsory military service (especially after the outbreak of the Iran–Iraq war) was an added incentive to join Komala, women's involvement represented an escape from patriarchal social and family structures. Marriage, early motherhood, and housework were the only possible destiny for most women; joining Komala offered them access to activities that would never otherwise have been available to them. The entry of women into the organization thus also raises questions about the relationship between constraining social conditions and ideological commitment. Everyday life was the foundation of their critical analyses and their politicization, and all the women interviewees gave prominence in their stories to the connections between ideological choices, social constraints, and daily life.[9] A combination of ideological and social reasons lay behind the commitment of the women of Komala. Miriam, a former Komala activist, explains that she chose to join the organization in part to escape the monotony of her life:

> At that time, the social life of girls like me was limited to home and school at best. We were not as free as our brothers to go about in public. Women's destiny was limited to marriage and motherhood. It was in order to live a different life and to escape this routine and monotonous life that I decided to take part in the revolution, and then to get involved with Komala, which was seen as very revolutionary at that time.

Kakabaveh, as she explains in her memoir, joined Komala not only because of its progressive principles but also to escape the hardships of life as a village woman:

> Life in the village was always the same for the poor. We worked all the time, on the farm or at home, but we could not even meet our basic needs. And also, women's lives were always controlled by socio-cultural norms, so that we had no control over our lives or our bodies. The arrival of Komala in our village gave me the chance of a better future.[10]

Jaleh remembered a friend who had followed other women into the mountains to escape an arranged marriage. In other examples, Komala women, like the Algerian women studied by Danièle Amrane-Minne,[11] made political choices that arose out of personal, emotional, and family motives. While only a few of the women interviewees followed male family members—usually their husbands—nationalist narratives for the most part tend to underestimate women's political engagement. Women's political motivations are largely ignored, and the influence of family and daily village life, rather than being understood as a locus of political consciousness, is seen through the distorting prism of women's emotionality and irrationality. In minimizing the political motivations of the young women who were interested in Komala, the revolutionaries in effect reacted in the same way as the government forces[12] and the religious conservatives. Kurdish women's political engagement was thus subjected to the re-coding of patriarchal norms both by government forces and the organization within which they struggled. In Komala writings, there are only two motives driving women into politics: poverty and the desire to escape sexist customs such as arranged marriage, the exchange of women, and violence. The poem "Be Sar Hat" (Fate), for example, relates the story of a woman from a modest family who, in order to escape a forced marriage to a very old man, leaves her family to join Komala.[13]

By contrast, most of the women interviewees described their choice to be politically active as primarily political, arising out of the revolutionary impulse, even if escaping a routine and monotonous life was also a motivating force. The dominant narrative, which positions Kurdish women's involvement in the struggle as a means of avoiding forced marriage or domestic work, reproduces the division between politics and everyday life, between activist work and reproductive work, between the domestic sphere as the space of private life and the public domain space as the space of politics.[14] When Amineh Kakabaveh highlights the issue of "control over our lives and our bodies," she brings politics into the private sphere: the point was not just to escape from a specific situation but to expose its exploitative characteristics[15] and demand transformation. As Jaleh comments:

> Although it's true that from the outset equality between men and women was not clearly defined—neither for Komala nor us—Komala's insistence on the participation of women as much as men in socio-political life was one of the proofs of the equality that it claimed. That is, women could be free to do everything that men could do in public and political life.

Most of the women interviewees emphasized the difficulty of obtaining information about different political movements; they could acquire even a basic knowledge of the various movements, including Komala, only indirectly. Many women highlighted the influence of family members, such as spouses or brothers, in their initial awareness of Komala. As Laetitia Bucaille shows in relation to the National Liberation Front fighting the Algerian war of independence and the African National Congress waging anti-apartheid struggle, "the political education of women fighters often goes through the family: women are more likely than men to get involved via family or emotional ties, not because they are more emotional by nature, but because they are generally less connected to the public sphere or the networks of militant sociability."[16] The situation was similar for most women in Komala. The young Kurdish women who joined the organization did so as a result of their own assessment of the organization, in the context of their knowledge and experience of male domination within the family. While they might have been dependent on the men around them for political information, they were not passive recipients of this knowledge but evaluated it in light of their own position as oppressed subjects. Shirin learned about Komala from her husband:

> I was also aware of the repression and discrimination we suffered under the previous regime, but because of family restrictions, my only contact with the outside world was my husband. At a time when most women like me were confined to the household, and only allowed to go out when accompanied by a man, it was natural that we only knew about politics through the men of the house. In spite of all this, during that time when everything became political, as soon as my husband came home, I would ask him about everything that was going on.

Susan, another former Komala activist, adds:

> Not only I, but also many of my friends were influenced in our choice of political organization by the men in our family and circles. We knew what was going on only through them, as they knew about the political situation. The world of the men in the family (fathers and brothers, spouses, etc.) was much larger than ours because of their work, their activities, and the freedom they had outside the house, and even in other cities outside the Kurdish regions.

Within the family, the sons gained a degree of prestige through their access to external sources of knowledge; they could enroll as university students, work outside the home, or carry out their mandatory military service in other parts of Iran. Although men from disadvantaged families were generally unable to go to university, they nonetheless had more opportunities than women to learn about the world of politics. Jalil Muin Afshar, a former Komala activist, writes in his memoir that he was compelled to leave school at a very early age to work and support his family, but his shop became a meeting place for activists which led him to an interest in politics and ultimately toward Komala.[17]

Among the men of the household, the young men in particular were influential on the political orientations of the rest of the family, especially their younger sisters. Discussions between the men, enabled brothers to be mediators of political information for their sisters. As the Iranian social demographer Marie Ladier-Fouladi points out, the younger generations of the 1960s and 1970s, better educated than their fathers, were able to challenge their political views and authority on ideological positions.[18] In the course of such debates among male family members, girls generally chose to side with their brothers, who were seen to have a better understanding of revolutionary thinking. While Mastoureh's father had been an important figure in the Republic of Kurdistan, fighting for the Kurdish cause alongside the KDPI, her brothers were significantly influenced by Marxist thought, which they had encountered at university. Between these political orientations, Mastoureh felt closer to her brothers than to her father. Her political choices were shaped by observation of the behavior of her family members, which for her reflected the principles and values of their respective organizations. One of her memories illustrates this point:

> I wanted to take part in a political event which was very important at the time. To do so I had to leave the house for several days and travel to another city with a mixed group of people. My father (pro-DPKI) and my elder brother (a member of the Iranian People's Fedayeen Organization) immediately opposed my decision on the grounds that I was physically weak and the mission was difficult. But my other brother (a member of Komala) supported my decision, and sorted out everything I needed for these few days. So, for me, Komala was more committed to gender equality than other political groups.

As such, at a time when Komala was not yet well known, men's behavior had a practical impact on the dissemination of its ideas, bringing them into the domestic space. For some women, the daily behavior of politicized male family members was an important factor in their political development: identifying gaps between rhetoric and action within the family sphere could contribute to women's choice of political line.

The good reputation and social popularity of Komala figures such as Foad Mostafa Soltani* and Sedigh Kamangar† were enough to attract some women to Komala. Their prominence meant that those who were the only members of their family interested in politics, or who had no one to introduce them to the various issues, had a focal point. Shadi, a former Komala activist, says about this: "Nobody in my family was involved in politics, so I wasn't familiar with the political issues in our city. In this situation, the first thing that attracted me to Komala was the positive reputation of some of the organization's figures, like Kak Foad." Zara similarly explains:

> I wasn't educated, and I didn't know about communist principles. I didn't know about communism theoretically, except through my experience of the actions of people who considered themselves communists. Before the revolution, when we were living in misery and poverty, there was a doctor and several teachers who were known in the region, and who looked out for us. They helped us without asking for anything in return. Without any knowledge of communism, it was above all the way they lived and behaved that led me to be interested in their ideology, and eventually to their political organization, Komala.

* Foad Mostafa Soltani (1948–79) was one of the founders of Komala. He embodied the principles and practice of Komala, earning respect such that he became the most prominent figure in the organization. In Iranian Kurdistan, his name is synonymous with the popular revolution. He and his four brothers were killed by government forces a few months after the revolution. "Kak" means "Brother" in Kurdish. Many Kurds call him "Kak Foad" as a mark of respect.

† Sedigh Kamangar (1946–89), a lawyer known as Kak Sedigh, was one of the leaders of Komala. He was assassinated in Iraqi Kurdistan by an Iranian government agent in 1989.

4
The Obstacles to Women's Political Participation

The "Spring of Freedom" that followed the 1979 Revolution, from February 1979 to May 1980, saw a power vacuum that offered Kurds—along with Iranians across the country—the opportunity to engage in socio-political life. As political organizations and groups of all sizes emerged across the political spectrum, the public space, previously dominated by the government, became the stage where these organizations, their members, and their supporters met. Streets and gathering places in the Kurdish cities were full of stalls displaying newly printed books that had been banned under the Shah. Revolutionary music echoed through the streets, and dozens of newspapers from the various political groups were passed around. Young Kurds, like other Iranians, took part in debates and freely exchanged political ideas. As they met one another at social and political events, the line between private and public life became blurred. For men, this occupation of public and political spaces was normal, while for women, usually confined to their role as wives and mothers for the most part, it represented a great change.

As they made their political demands, Kurdish women had to overcome other obstacles, breaking cultural, social, and religious taboos in order to constitute themselves as political subjects. Where before they had been entitled to enter urban public space only for daily needs—shopping, going to school or to work—now suddenly, thanks to the revolution and the events associated with it, women burst into that space. They joined in demonstrations, strikes, debates, speeches; they went out from their homes in large numbers, taking over places previously strictly forbidden to women, such as the mosque, which was usually the only place with audio equipment and a large space for public speeches. Monireh, who like all her family was a supporter of Komala from the outset, comments: “Even though my father was the Friday imam in our city, I had never been able to enter the mosque where he officiated before the revolution.”

The large-scale presence of young women activists resulted both from the call by political organizations for women’s participation, and also from the strategies women adopted to circumvent the expectations of family and society. The urban women interviewees all emphasize in their narratives that their participation in a political movement increased their confidence and their ability to overcome obstacles. As Shilan explains:

> As soon as I started to see myself as a Komala supporter, involved in different political activities, I felt for the first time that I was somebody. I was 17 years old then. Before that I had never been responsible for anything, but suddenly I found myself responsible for other people, and there was someone else who was responsible for me. Life became different; it was really satisfying for me. I really enjoyed it when I went on demonstrations. That feeling of joy is maybe what sticks with me now; at that time, I felt like I was doing something. I didn’t have to stay at home and wait for someone to walk through the door. That was really what it was like before I became politically active.

Nonetheless, this does not mean that women experienced public and political life in this period in the same way as men. While most of the interviewees agree that their participation was enormously empowering for them, traditional ways of thinking often remained intact, even among most Marxist Komala activists. A few months of revolutionary movement could change the country’s monarchical system, but there was no profound transformation of social norms. Family and social restrictions remained in place. While activist men were able to focus entirely on politics, women had to repeatedly defy family and social barriers to access the public arena. Addressing these problems took up a good deal of women’s thought and energy. They were entering a field that was reserved exclusively for men and had to fight every step of the way, a phenomenon described by Madeleine Gagnon as "the war within the war."* Women experienced family structures, social constraints, and even the internal rules of Komala organization as obstacles. Against the will of family, society, and often their male comrades, the women of Komala, like other Iranian revolutionaries, had to adopt a range of strategies.

FAMILY OBSTACLES

One of the major obstacles, encountered by most women during this period, was the family. Some men had to confront their families too, but to far a lesser extent. Parents, especially those who remembered the many years of political repression of the Pahlavi regime, were anxious, fearing irreversible consequences for their children.

For a few women, such as Marjan, Sara, and Mahin, their interest in Komala was in line with their family's political sympathies. They faced far fewer restrictions from their families, and were even encouraged to commit themselves to the organization and its aims. Sara's entire family, including her parents, had been Komala sympathizers since the party's emergence, and their home became one of Komala's political bases in Baneh. Similarly, Pershing recalls:

> I was the eldest in my family, as well as the only girl. When I was just 16 years old, I easily got involved in the political life of the time. My family was always behind me, especially my father. He was not restrictive, like in most Kurdish families. It was easy for me to leave the house and join in whatever political event was going on. Whenever I had a problem or a question, the first person I consulted was my father.

However, the testimonies of the interviewees show that most families, regardless of their differences, were not in favor of their

* The Canadian writer, poet and novelist Madeleine Gagnon articulates the idea of "the war within war" as, traveling through several countries at war (Macedonia, Kosovo, Pakistan, Israel–Palestine), she explored women's approach to conflict. See Madeleine Gagnon, *Anna, Jeanne, Samia* (Paris: Fayard, 2001).

children's involvement in politics, especially not their daughters. They understood politics to be a man's business and saw women's participation as contrary to prevailing norms. Families feared above all that unmarried girls might lose their virginity or be raped in prison. Women's political participation was often identified with the risk of rape, dishonoring not only the women themselves but also their families; such a risk carried a high social cost. Farzaneh describes her father's reaction when she was reading the story of Algerian activist Djamila Bopacha,* who had been raped in prison because of her activism. Her father, seeing the book in his daughter's hands, could not hide his fear that she might, one day, suffer the same fate. As Susan, another Komala supporter, states:

> The families' concerns were more focused on us than on our brothers. They were above all terrified of the bad things that could happen to us. Men involved in politics might be killed or imprisoned, and the family reputation would benefit from having a member who was a martyr or political prisoner; but for us, it was the question of honor [*namûs*] that became a nightmare for our families, especially our parents.

Jaleh likewise recalls:

> From the beginning, my family, especially my father, prevented me from participating in politics. He constantly reminded me that politics was not for women, and emphasized the particular dangers it might lead to. He had no problem with my brothers, but it was different for us. For my father, women's participation in politics definitely involved the risk of being raped.

Some women interviewees, however, confirm that family restrictions were less severe after the revolution than they had

---

* Djamila Boupacha, born on February 9, 1938, in Bologhine, was an Algerian National Liberation Front activist arrested in 1960 for an attempted assassination attempt in Algiers. Her confessions, obtained by rape and torture, gave rise to a sentence that was transformed by Gisèle Halimi and Simone de Beauvoir into a media trial of the French army's methods in Algeria. Sentenced to death on June 28, 1961, she was granted amnesty under the Evian agreements and released on April 21, 1962.

been before. There were girls who had not been allowed to attend school by their families but were now able to get involved in political life. Women teachers could take advantage of their freedom of movement in public, as well as their financial independence, to support their activism in the public domain. Female high school students also took advantage of their freedom of movement to take part in political events. By contrast, housewives like Shirin, who had responsibility for family and children, faced more restrictions on their movements.

Domestic restrictions were also reinforced by families' hostility to the Maoist tendency in Komala. Marxists were widely regarded as "unbelievers," "infidels," and "miscreants."* That many of the pioneers of Marxism had held critical views of the family also damaged the reputation of Iranian Marxists in general and of Komala in particular; they were perceived as lacking ethical and moral principles, not least in relation to sexuality. Reputedly unbelievers, and therefore immoral, they were regarded as a threat to the social order. Women who contributed their time and labor anywhere other than within the bosom of the legitimately married family risked being called prostitutes, a slur which, as Gail Pheterson theorizes, can be mobilized to target all women who step outside their assigned positions.[1]

Komala activists, above all women and their families, thus had to constantly deal with rumors of immorality. Such insults, designed to punish transgressive behavior, served as a concrete means of social control to limit women's movements outside the home. Women activists were thus frequently represented as "monstrous bodies," abnormal and immoral, because they challenged the dichotomy of gender roles and the boundary between family and politics.[2] Hence some families saw Komala as "deviant" and "degenerate" and refused to let their daughters join in political life within the organization. According to Serveh's account:

* Ayatollah Khomeini said in a speech about the Marxist Kurds: "We are not fighting against the Kurds, but against the communists, those who want to erase Islam from Kurdistan. They issue negative publications against us. They use internal and external means against Islam. Kurds are Muslims and they belong to Islam, Muslims do not fight. It is the Kurdish political parties that want to deceive the Kurds and keep the Muslims away from Islam." Quoted in *Kayhan*, August 22, 1979.

> My father was a nationalist and a supporter of the KDPI. There were endless rumors circulating about the left, especially Komala. Although my father agreed to my political activities, he was completely opposed to Komala. Right up to the last moment, he wanted me to join the KDPI. I had to overcome many obstacles, but the family was the biggest of them.

Komala itself, however, in assessing the commitment of its activists, did not recognize such barriers. For example, one of the conditions for joining the organization was "that they are willing to accept a life of labor, and have already set out on that path."[3] An activist seeking to become part of the movement had to be known in his or her neighborhood, city, or village and had to work alongside the poor in the factories and fields. Some key members, who had gone through higher education before the revolution, worked in factories or rural areas, with the aim of developing a full and textured understanding of the plight of the workers and poorer classes. For example, Mohammad Hussein Karimi, a key figure in Komala whose death day was chosen by the organization for the official proclamation of its existence, had been engaged in construction work among villagers. To undertake this type of work, however, was impossible for most women. The definition of exploited work as limited to wage labor and agricultural work made unsalaried domestic and reproductive work invisible.[4] With the exception of some female teachers in rural areas, most women, faced with the restrictions imposed by family, could not move in social settings other than their own. Nasrin reports: "I really wanted to go and join in the work for the benefit of the poor, especially in the rural areas, but my father did not let me take part in that kind of revolutionary work at all."

Some non-Kurdish women in large cities, like Solmaz, were able to leave home in order to pursue their political activities, but most Kurdish women lived in small towns where everyone knew everyone else, and found it almost impossible to escape from the family home. They had to find ways of evading supervision, or else have open discussions with family members to try to convince them of the rightness of their decision. Zara explains that her family did not want her to identify herself as a Komala activist:

> My uncle, a religious figure in the village, was totally opposed to my political choice and accused Komala of being an anti-religious organization with no moral commitment. But I always argued against him by reminding him of Komala activists who had helped the villagers before the revolution (some teachers and a doctor), who were considered very respectable and reliable. I tried to persuade my uncle and others who thought as he did by asking them how they could be suspicious of an organization that had such supporters and sympathizers.

While some Kurdish women managed to gain the approval of their families, others pursued their involvement in political life despite family opposition. Neither beatings nor insults could stem their determination, and the strategies used by girls and women to sustain their militancy in this period were diverse. Mehri explains that the strength of her convictions enabled her to continue her political activities, even though she was repeatedly beaten by her father. These women tried to lead a political life while simultaneously complying with the disciplinary order imposed by their families. Nasrin explains that she decided to marry an activist in order to get around the family obstacles:

> My father was opposed to my political activities. But in spite of his fruitless attempts to discourage me, he agreed that I marry a Komala activist. The marriage was a way of relieving my father's anxieties. From his point of view, my marriage would not only neutralize the rumors about my morality that were directed at me as a Marxist woman; also, if there were any political problems, my husband would be the one to blame.

Another strategy was to try and balance domestic and political lives. Farzaneh says: "The main thing was, I had to deal with all the domestic chores; once I'd done them, I could go out and do what I wanted politically." Others managed to keep their political activities hidden. Shadi, for example, continued her activities in Komala in secret (the only person in her family to be politically involved) even after her father withdrew her from school. Shilan and her sisters did the same, planning their political lives around the activities of their male family members: they went out when their father and brothers were not there and came home before them.

Most women activists were single, but those who were mothers found it even more difficult to be politically active, because they had to reconcile activism with their family responsibilities, in what Jules Falquet calls the "work-family" duality.[5] While Roonak's husband pursued his political activities in another city far from the family, as the mother of a young daughter she could not do so herself. Instead she had to satisfy her parents-in-law (who accused her of politicizing their son) by doing the housework, while she sought to take part in socio-political activities whenever possible. To discourage this, her parents-in-law refused to look after her daughter while she was out, so she often took her along, which in turn incurred the disapproval of several of her comrades.

In such an environment, the women interviewees did not experience family life as a space in which they could freely develop their militant creativity. While the women faced varying levels of restriction, most of them had to struggle to varying degrees to convince their families that they should be able to participate in public and political life. These limitations were unquestionably central to their political formation, contributing to a collective awareness of patriarchal structures and their articulation with the struggle for Kurdish liberation. Indeed, women's political struggle was inseparable from their daily struggle within the domestic sphere. The specific position of women at the intersection of several social hierarchies allowed for the politicization of the domestic sphere and the transformation of relations within it. Like their brothers, who used their pro-Komala political engagement to interrogate the authority of fathers and age-related hierarchies in the family structure, female Komala activists brought the struggle into the family to challenge gender inequalities. They thus contributed, along with their brothers, to the dissemination of the values and program of the Komala organization both within the family and in the wider population.

SOCIAL OBSTACLES

The restrictions imposed by families, dovetailed with social mores that also constrained women's entry into and participation in the political world. The unprecedented presence of women alongside men in the public domain was regarded as shocking by a general public unaccustomed to such scenes. Nasrin recalls:

> It is true that thanks to the revolution, many things had changed—the political system of the country, the emergence of a number of different groups, the increase in the presence of women in the public space. But the views of the majority of the population, especially in small towns where everyone knew one another, had not changed. So as young people, especially women, we had to be careful about our activities.

While political participation among men was viewed as a normal part of their social role, among women it was problematic. Farzaneh explains: "Some people saw the extensive presence of women as a potential threat not just to society, but also to their own family culture. They were afraid that if it continued, their own daughters would one day get involved."

This panic was amplified when it came to activists identified with Komala, an organization that in the public imagination was atheist and therefore without sexual morality. Women in particular were jeered at and their political beliefs discounted; they were accused of having joined in order to find a husband—in a context where social norms dictated that a woman should be passive in matters of marriage—and their families faced abuse. Marjan shares her memory of this period:

> Although the revolutionary atmosphere significantly lessened the obstacles, reactionary attacks on communists, and especially women, carried on. Communists were constantly faced with insults and criticism about their morality. They said that we had no restraint in our sexual relationships, and that we slept with everyone.

It was largely rumors like these that led Serveh's father to forbid his daughter from getting involved in Komala. Although he was not at all opposed to her being politically active, he wanted her to support the DPKI, which was not seen to violate the moral values of society.

Women's political activities might also be obstructed by family friends and acquaintances, especially if they were involved in politics secretly without their family's permission. Shilan and her sisters, who unlike their brother became politically active, were forced to hide their activities not only from their brother, but also from their brother's friends and those who knew their family. Subjected to gossip and sexist insults, they were also sometimes banned from entering the mosque on the grounds that they were communists. Sayran remembers a sign at the entrance of one of the mosques in her city, where she had gone to listen to a speech, which announced, "Entrance is forbidden to communists." This meant in practice that entrance was forbidden to women: while it would be difficult to distinguish men's ideological affiliations on the basis of their appearance, women attending such events could be assumed to be Marxists, and specifically Komala supporters.

The social constraints on women activists might be greater or lesser, depending on factors such as age, marital status, and location. Fatima, who was only 16 years old at the time, did not regard social restrictions as a significant barrier for girls her age, although she recognized their existence; for teenage girls like her, the major obstacle was the family. Most of them were students, organizing collectively from within the school, which perhaps reduced the deterrent effect of social restrictions on their political activities. Single women of marriageable age, by contrast, were more vulnerable to constraints and rumors in the public domain.

The region in which the Komala activists lived might also be significant. Although after the revolution, the two Kurdish political forces (KDPI and Komala) united in defense of the Kurdish cause, this alliance did not eliminate the longstanding tensions and rivalries between them, which eventually resulted in armed conflict from 1985 to 1988. In the cities primarily under Komala's control, such as Marivan, Sanandaj, Kamyaran, and Saqqez, rumors about the morality of women activists could be more or less neutralized by the influential presence of charismatic leaders, while in the areas dominated by the KDPI,* Komala sympathizers had to endure insults against their morality of a kind much less familiar to those living in Komala-held areas. Nasrin, who lived in a KDPI town, explains:

> Everyone thought that we spent our time sleeping with each other, even with our family members. This tells you something about how we were regarded in that society! They thought we were constantly in bed with our classmates. It was a rare thing for me not to hear sexual insults as I walked by.

Golnar, from a town largely occupied by the KDPI, gives a similar perspective:

> Although my entire family was Komala-oriented and had no problem with my political activities, the more traditional residents of Mahabad, most of whom belonged to the KDPI, were very ready to put pressure on us. The KDPI spread a lot of propaganda against our organization, especially against women. They particularly emphasized our so-called sexual immorality. However, those who knew the Komala supporters knew that this was in no way the truth.

CONFRONTING ORGANIZATIONAL OBSTACLES

For a time, Komala succeeded in becoming a significant political force in the Kurdish regions. However, as a new organization, it lacked experience, and although it saw itself as a revolutionary group committed to the service of the oppressed, it struggled to break with dominant social norms. Its young leaders, members,

* The northern parts of the Kurdish regions, including cities in West Azerbaijan and Kurdistan province such as Mahabad, Sardasht, Piranshahr, Bukan, Baneh, and Oshnavieh, were predominantly under the control of the KDPI. In contrast, parts of the southern Kurdish regions, particularly cities in Kurdistan Province like Marivan, Sanandaj, Kamyaran, and Saqqez, were largely under the influence of Komala. Certain cities, such as Paveh in Kermanshah province, experienced shared control between the two Kurdish political factions.

and sympathizers remained for the most part embedded in their society, reproducing the same conventions and applying them to women activists. Facing family and social constraints as well as scandalous rumors, Komala reacted in ways that while not hard to understand, certainly reproduced dominant norms and constituted an obstacle to women's involvement in the organization.

At the moment of triumph of the 1979 Revolution, men and women stood side by side in collective actions, but this social mixing dwindled with the waning revolutionary atmosphere. As the demonstrations, public debates, and exhibitions that had brought men and women together were increasingly replaced by small meetings in the organization's headquarters, and as occasions of militant sociability took place on an ad hoc basis, gender mixing gradually lessened. As Golrokh Ghobadi writes,

> When our activities were made public, and the headquarters of the various political groups and organizations gained official status, the number of women involved steadily decreased, and they attended fewer meetings. This was a situation we understood; we knew that neither families nor wider socio-cultural norms were liberated enough. It was more acceptable for young women to join in rallies and open gatherings than in private meetings in closed spaces.[6]

Such semiprivate meeting places, neither entirely public nor entirely private, constituted important spaces for militant socialization, political training, and the development of common interests and political orientations. The female activists of Komala were thus excluded from the "backstage"[7] of militant activity, an exclusion that reproduced the unequal gender relations in revolutionary work. Some men aimed as far as possible to avoid mixed gatherings in these intermediate spaces that escaped the collective gaze of the larger gatherings. Women's political activity was legitimized by the collective framework, which functioned as a gaze, offering both a guarantee and surveillance of their morality. Women had to neutralize the danger of gossip and immorality by keeping a distance from their male comrades, but the effect of this was to remove them from the intermediate spaces of the organization, from the backstage, and from the spaces of militant sociability in which hierarchies took shape. The exclusion of women from these semiprivate intermediate spaces resulted in their absence from positions of authority and kept decision-making power in the hands of men. Ghobadi writes:

> Traditional society, restrictions on gender relations, and reactionary forces all pushed women to be cautious and to keep their distance from the political forces of the far left. At times some intellectuals, rather than fighting against these conservative tendencies, went along with them, and refused to allow women's presence in rallies and meetings. A few brave women fought courageously against these reactionary responses, but overall, women had little desire to stand for [party] positions occupied by men.[8]

Nonetheless, young women who had just found a political voice were reluctant to give it up too easily. Some of them—Komala activists, independents (Kurds and non-Kurds), and members of other Marxist political organizations—set up their own women's democratic institutions in various Kurdish cities. Although these institutions were short-lived, their emergence testifies to a serious response to the organizational obstacles in mainstream political groups, buttressed by family and social pressures.* The strategy of making these groups women-only guaranteed access to the spaces of sociability and training necessary for women's political existence, as well as defending women's legitimate place in the public political arena of Marxist organizations. At the same time, it countered the gossip about sexual immorality that weighed so heavily on them. Sayran, who along with her comrades had attempted to oppose the restrictions they experienced in mainstream politics, set up a group for the women of her city, as she describes: "These organizations were created by women for women. Their creation was an innovation arising out of our own experiences and difficulties. If socio-cultural norms did not allow us to take part in mixed

* These women-only organizations are discussed further in Chapter 5.

meetings, we would establish our presence by founding our own groups, as something our male comrades could not ignore."

In opposition to the previous regime's homogenizing policy of imposing European dress, most Kurdish activists, regardless of gender and ideology, appeared in public wearing traditional clothing. Komala activists were no exception. Much as the chador had become a symbol of resistance for some Iranian women during the revolution, traditional dress was used by Kurds to assert their political and cultural rights. Naser Mohadjer, an Iranian writer and researcher, points out that following the overthrow of the regime, "if in some Persian regions of Iran, as a symbol of the revolution, the pseudo-modern norms of the Shah's era were replaced by religious norms, in Kurdistan it was the cultural symbols of the subjugated and repressed Kurds that were restored."[9] According to Ghobadi, although the style of Iranian Marxists had been fashionable among Kurdish revolutionaries during the revolution,* when "teachers, employees, young students, young boys and girls joined in the demonstrations in jeans and sneakers,"[10] subsequently traditional dress became the distinctive mark of the Kurdish revolutionaries. Marjan recounts: "We decided to wear Kurdish clothes, which had previously been forbidden in public places like schools and offices. In a way, they represented the illiteracy and poverty of the villagers. Even to go to school, we would wear Kurdish clothes."

As Iranian Marxists had done before the revolution, members and supporters of Komala rejected the values of consumerism and luxury that had characterized the previous regime. Activists were generally expected to dress like the common people, and a true revolutionary would also avoid luxury consumer goods, such as cosmetics. Many Komala activists spontaneously adopted the clothing and habits of the oppressed and disadvantaged people they lived among. But as always, the appearance of young women was more closely policed than that of their male counterparts. Dif-

---

* As Parvin Paidar describes Iranian Marxists before the revolution: "The Marxist-Leninist woman, dressed in the same way as her male comrade, wore her hair short, did not wear makeup, and avoided wearing high heels. She was encouraged to be tough and to suppress her emotions. The Marxist-Leninist remedy for the treatment of women as sex objects was the 'masculinization' of women." Parvin Paidar, *Women and the Political Process in Twentieth-Century Iran* (New York: Cambridge University Press, 1995), 171.

ferences in Kurdish men's clothing were negligible; male militants wore clothes that were more or less the same, in plain colors, fabric, and shape. Traditional Kurdish women's dress, by contrast, was much more varied in color and pattern and also in price. The revolutionary discourse of the time pushed women activists toward the simplest and cheapest clothes—gray in color, plain and austere—in order to distinguish themselves from the "extravagant" habits of the "Westernized" elite and middle-class women. In so doing, the young activists were attempting to achieve the ideal of femininity advocated by Iranian Marxist organizations, including Komala. Susan recalls:

> Unlike men's clothes, our [traditional] clothes were very bright and colorful. However, during this period when even appearance was seen as a symbol of revolutionary identity, we tried to avoid colorful clothes, which were supposedly attractive and not revolutionary. We increasingly wore cheaper and less colorful clothes, in gray, dark blue, and so on. All the women activists of Komala were aiming to get closer to this ideal. We tried to wear the simplest and cheapest clothes. We tried to be less attractive so as to be more revolutionary.

In promoting this version of femininity as the only legitimate one within a revolutionary framework, Komala effectively endorsed a model of behavior and appearance among activist women in the public domain that ran directly counter to the discourses of individual freedom and autonomy simultaneously disseminated by the organization. The norm of revolutionary femininity was represented by a "desexualized" female figure, whose adoption of masculine attributes affirmed the greater value of the male; men also faced socio-cultural restrictions on their behavior, but the revolutionary was a resolutely masculine figure. This style was nonetheless welcomed, especially by women, not only because it conformed to the political goals of the organization but because dressing simply and going without makeup radically distanced Kurdish women from the model of femininity of the Pahlavi regime, which had been considered corrupt and degenerate. This distancing could to some extent neutralize the rumors that targeted revolutionary women. As Miriam explains: "This kind of appearance could not completely prevent the spread of rumors against us. But it was not totally ineffective either. Because of our appearance, some people did not believe the rumors that were going around about us."

However, some women activists were unwilling to conform to the style of dress and the codes of femininity that were expected in their political milieu; still others tried to find a compromise between their individual desires and revolutionary standards. Pershing used to spoil or even tear her already simple and inexpensive clothes in order to look more like a poor woman and to get as close as possible to the revolutionary lifestyle, while Mahin, who considered herself just as revolutionary, attempted to make space for her personal desires: "For myself, I felt that copying the lifestyle of oppressed people at all costs was too much for us teenage girls and young women. I would wear Kurdish clothes, but I tried as far as possible to choose them in my favorite colors."

In a context where the political struggle was considered the ultimate priority, not only was appearance monitored but behavior as well, and the use of alcohol or drugs, as well as any kind of extramarital sex, was prohibited. Even the most personal decisions, such as marriage, might be subject to criticism if they were perceived as nonrevolutionary. The debates at the first Komala congress in 1978—which took place in secret before the party made itself public after the revolution—illustrate how marriage was seen to risk alienating people from activism. Young revolutionary leaders frequently referenced concerns that militants who married would become politically "passive": "What might lead certain comrades to 'deviate' from the political fight was their excessive attachment to the family, the root of all problems and the origin of fears and conservatism."[11] Monireh nevertheless explained her decision to marry for love as an individual choice:

> I remember that time very well. As soon as we [my husband and I] decided to get married, we encountered incomprehension from everyone around us. Everyone was astonished, and they didn't hold back from open criticism. "What? They want to get married? Then they can't consider themselves real rev-

olutionaries any longer." Everyone was incredulous, because at that time we weren't supposed to think about anything except politics. Personal life was dominated by political issues.

Importantly, the Komala leadership appears not to have been fully committed to addressing the violence and sexism of some of its activists. While the reality of political life was very different from the rumors about sexual behavior within the organization, not all activists behaved according to their principles, especially when it came to women. Three of the interviewees recall incidents of women who were harassed or even raped by their comrades, but neither the rank-and-file nor the organization's leaders were willing to take these problems seriously. There were several reasons for their silence. Because sexism was regarded as relatively insignificant in comparison with revolutionary political activity, some leaders were reluctant to combat or even to discuss it. Moreover, if activists, especially women, were to admit the reality of the problem and attempt to discuss it at any level, their testimonies were liable to confirm the fears of families and society at large about the risks of female participation in the political sphere. These reasons alone cannot, however, explain the widespread silence on the subject, which can essentially be attributed to the indifference of most activists; violence against women was considered "normal" and "natural." Susan relates:

> I worked with several other girls in our town, all of us under the age of 18, in a group under the guidance of a comrade. But the demands of our leader, who took advantage of his status, sometimes spilled over into our political activities. It was said that he had raped some young activists, but we tried not to make it public because we were afraid of the reaction of our families and others.

At the time Susan explained the silence of her comrades as lack of awareness, but ultimately realized that she was wrong:

> It was in prison that I realized that the other comrades [the men] were aware of it, but didn't want to get involved. One of

my interrogators, who had heard everything from one of the detained comrades, was always insulting me, talking about a rape by my group leader. I felt so let down by this. That's why after my release I abandoned political life in Komala forever. The organization never condemned our rapist leader.

5
The Socio-Political Activities of Female Militants

The brief period of the transition of power following the 1979 Revolution was marked by the emergence of several political organizations. All aimed to mobilize their members to have a voice in the construction of the country's new political system, in the light of their various understandings of the situation and the ideals they promoted. As activists in these organizations, women played an important role during the transition of power, connecting the general interest as defined by their organization with the specific issues of their own condition in society. For Kurdish activists, this period—which began in the aftermath of the victory of the revolution—lasted until 1981, at which point most Komala activists joined the armed struggle as peshmergas. Although Komala, in line with the sexual division of revolutionary labor, had been willing to accept young women only as activists in the urban areas, their role intensified and developed throughout this period as conditions changed.

THE EMERGENCE OF WOMEN'S DEMOCRATIC ORGANIZATIONS

As a new political organization, lacking experience and as yet little known to the public, Komala in its early days collaborated with various Iranian Marxist political organizations to establish groups such as the Society for the Defense of Freedom and Revolution and the Emancipatory Society of Workers to organize their political work. These groups did not generally survive for more than five months, as they were suppressed during the first attack by the government forces that began on August 19, 1979. However, during this period, they were the main centers of decision-making and organizing important events, and they succeeded in drawing significant numbers of younger people into political activity.

Women who had been active participants in the revolution were compelled to distance themselves from these groups, which with the decline of the revolutionary atmosphere became increasingly the preserve of men. This prompted some women, particularly teachers, to set up their own democratic organizations in order to prevent women from being forced back into the home. Women's groups were set up in cities with a significant number of women teachers or experienced activists, including the Women's Council in Sanandaj, the Women's Union in Marivan, the Saqqez Women's Activist Association, the Women's Association in Oshnavieh, and the Women's Council in Naghadeh. There was a close link between Marxist groups, particularly Komala, and these women's organizations.

Kurdish women's political participation was not limited to such organizations, which in any case did not have a base in every town in the Kurdish regions. Not all women chose to join these women's groups; in particular teenage girls, who were less affected by family and social obstacles, cautiously continued their political activities alongside men and in mixed groups. Shilan, who was a member of a very active student council, emphasized that seven out of twelve of the group's members were girls, and they were encouraged to take part in demonstrations, strikes, and special events.

These democratic women's organizations proved crucial for women's political engagement. Members of the Women's Union in Marivan and the Women's Association in Oshnaviyeh were Komala activists, while the Saqqez Women's Activist Association was composed both of Komala activists and non-Kurdish women belonging to other Marxist political organizations. The Sanandaj Women's Council was set up by a group of politically active women working cooperatively, most of whom had no definite political orientation. Galawij Rostami, an activist in the Women's Association in Oshnaviyeh, recalls: "We had a number of high school girls accompanied by active pro-Komala teachers from middle- and lower-class backgrounds who decided to set up our association. . . . It had no manifesto or program. Each day we held a meeting and decided what to do."[1] In contrast to the restrictions that a large majority of women activists faced, single-sex organizations offered an entirely new experience, as Golrokh Ghobadi elucidates: "These groups enabled us to get around family, social, and organizational barriers, creating spaces for camaraderie based on affinity of interests, along with political initiatives so that women could defend their legitimacy in the public domain."[2] Founded in response to women's marginalization from semiprivate meeting places, which had become a main space for doing politics, these groups also gave women a tactical way of circumventing rumors of sexual immorality. Mastoureh, a member of the Saqqez Women's Activist Association, recounts:

> After we had founded these organizations, we never went to the men's meetings. We did not attend their events; we organized our own, separately, under the supervision of the political organizations. We sometimes went to the homes of our male comrades to hold a meeting, but I don't remember any form of mixing.

The only manifesto known to survive from these democratic groups is that of the Saqqez Women's Activist Association. This document declares:

> The February [1979] uprising, although it succeeded in bringing some victories, did not succeed in achieving the final victory of uprooting all the imperialist forces from the socio-economic and cultural life of Iran. Therefore, in order to neutralize all the conspiracies of the reactionaries and to continue our struggles until the liberation of all the laboring classes and the abolition of the exploitation of individuals has been achieved, the activist women of Saqqez present their organization under the name of the Saqqez Women Activists' Association.[3]

The manifesto lists the conditions necessary for the accession of new members:

> 1. The association is not linked to any party or organization from a foreign country. 2. The member accepts the association's objec-

tives and makes efforts to advance its projects. 3. Community members must not be under 16 years of age. 4. Their socio-political qualifications must be confirmed by the Saqqez Women Activists' Association.[4]

Although these organizations were composed entirely of women, and decisions were taken by and for women, they initially focused on the general aims of Marxist-oriented political currents and did not develop policies relating specifically to women's interests. On the contrary, their members used the organizations as a way to participate in the politics of already existing organizations, particularly Komala which invited them to speak at debates and gatherings. As Sayran, a member of the Sanandaj Women's Council, points out, women from these organizations brought their own slogans, confirming both their solidarity with the proletarian class and their commitment to the project of Kurdish autonomy. Participating directly in socio-political activism, they took every opportunity to contribute to debates.

According to Marjan, a member of the Women's Union of Marivan, no important political decision was taken without the presence of this organization; two or three members of the Women's Union were present in every local Komala meeting in Marivan.

Activists in these groups focused their efforts on two main aims. They worked to support underprivileged women living on the city margins and in the villages, who because of the discriminatory system of the Pahlavi regime had little access to social services. As far as possible, they attempted to provide healthcare, basic education, sewing and knitting classes, and in some cases, financial assistance. They also attempted to mobilize the most disadvantaged to demand their daily needs. Thus, for example, women in a very poor neighborhood of Sanandaj were mobilized to campaign for access to drinking water, while the women carpet weavers of Saqqez were encouraged to go on strike to demand better wages, hours, and working conditions. Former activists look back positively on the efforts they made at that time. Farzaneh, a member of the Marivan Women's Union, explains:

> Unlike some Iranian Marxist organizations, which were more intellectual and had less contact with ordinary people, we tried to be as close to them as we could in order to understand their daily lives and help them as much as possible. So, we did not hesitate to support poor and people in need in rural and urban areas.

Through such mutual aid projects, the activists in these groups also aimed to raise awareness among impoverished women of political issues both national and regional, including the Kurdish cause and socio-economic discrimination. They sought to expand the circle of political awareness into the most disadvantaged members of society, especially women, who were confined to the home and often illiterate. In contrast to those who saw poor women as devoid of political will, women's democratic organizations aimed to politicize the networks of everyday life.[5] Thanks to this grassroots work, activists could count on the support of these women during political events, as well as their participation in street demonstrations when needed. Ghobadi, who was a member of the Sanandaj Women's Council at the time, writes:

> In every place where women were not present, we would go and find them, usually near their houses or inside their homes. We would get talking with them and give them the political news of the city. Usually they didn't know about it, and they listened to us attentively. Sometimes they would welcome us warmly into their homes and listen for hours; but sometimes they were reluctant to accept us, because they didn't see any connection between our ideas and the reality of their lives.[6]

While members of these organizations started out by focusing on the general programs and goals of the Marxist groups, the working-class women were seeking solutions to their everyday problems, including domestic violence, polygamy, and forced marriages. It was thus working-class women, in their exchanges with the activists, who pushed activists to become aware of and to advocate for specifically women's issues. Farzaneh, a member of the Marivan Women's Union, explains:

> Underprivileged and village women talked to us about their everyday difficulties, like problems with marriage, divorce, and so on. We realized we had to add these issues to our political programs, and we tried, as far as possible, to help them solve their problems, for instance by initiating a court case, and so on.

In a similar vein, Sayran, a member of the Sanandaj Women's Council, relates: "Sometimes, with issues like female genital mutilation, we didn't know much about it at all. It was practiced in some regions and villages and we, as activists, did not have enough knowledge to tell them about it." Ghobadi confirms women's growing awareness of these issues but clarifies:

> Our goal in creating our own organizations was not to focus on women's specific problems. We just thought that it would be easier for women to participate in politics in single-sex institutions. But we realized that women had their own specific demands, other than political demands, that were mainly concerned with different kinds of gender-based discrimination.[7]

Women's democratic organizations, although initially intended as a route to political participation, thus became spaces for a specific politicization and for the articulation of common interests. They made it possible for women activists to build independent links to women from working-class areas, deprived neighborhoods, and villages. These organizations allowed members to distance themselves from the revolutionary consciousness as defined by the men of the organization, or what the English feminist and historian Sheila Rowbotham describes as "the paralysis of consciousness in a male-defined revolutionary movement."[8] Moreover, these institutions had no desire to limit themselves to events in the Kurdish regions. Although the activists had rarely visited other regions of Iran, they expressed their wish, as leftist revolutionary forces, to serve oppressed people throughout the country. For example, when the new government's military attacked the popular forces in a region of northeastern Iran on March 28, 1979, three members of the Sanandaj Women's Council volunteered to help the wounded there. They were killed in a car accident with six other comrades before reaching their destination, however.[9]

Marivan: Women at the Center of Protest

The establishment of the Islamic Republic of Iran was met with resistance and protest. The new regime deployed a range of strategies to silence opposition and monopolize power, particularly through its security organizations, among them the Islamic Revolutionary Guards (Pasdaran), neighborhood committees, and revolutionary courts.[10] These played a decisive role in the violent suppression of opposition forces (leftist, liberal, and even other Islamists), claiming that they were anti-revolutionary, internal agents of world imperialism or of the Americans. The Revolutionary Guards struggled to control the Kurdish regions in particular. The new government and the Kurdish political forces accused one another of creating tension. It was in this context that on July 22, 1979, the population of Marivan, at the instigation of the town council as well as other democratic institutions including the Marivan Women's Union, decided to leave the city in protest for an indefinite period, settling near Kani Miran, a village located 15 km from the city of Marivan. "If you insist on occupying the city militarily so as to massacre us," the Women's Union declared, "we will evacuate."[11] Known as "the historic displacement of Marivan," this protest is embedded in Kurdish collective memory.

During the protest, which lasted for two weeks, about 75 percent of the population left the city. "We will stay until the armies retreat," they proclaimed, along with other revolutionary slogans: "The people: neither war nor surrender"; "State media is lying"; "The real revolution is here, it must be defended or it will be stolen"; "The struggle against domestic imperialism continues."[12]

Large numbers of young Marxists from other Kurdish towns, among them Sanandaj, Baneh, and Saqqez, marched to Marivan to support the protest, demonstrating that the people of Marivan were not alone. Activists from the women's democratic institutions also joined the protest as participants and organizers, despite family, social, and organizational obstacles. Many young women from various Kurdish cities, for the first time, took part in an action outside their hometown and for a number of days. Women were involved in organizing the march and the camp and in setting up committees to deal with health and logistics.

Marjan, a member of the Union of Women of Marivan, explains: "We didn't know how long we wanted to stay in the camp. But what was clear was that even if it was only a for very short time, the action needed to be organized quickly. We planned things well. We set up committees, and we distributed materials and food to the protesters. We had already been working with disadvantaged women and village women, but now most of the population of our city could see that we were capable of organizing things."

While the involvement of women activists in logistics can be seen as a continuation of their usual social roles, they also took up arms to protect the camp, as Marjan elucidates: "In addition, some of the women carried weapons to provide security for the camp. This camp was our battlefield, the stage where we showed the truth of our struggle. In Kani Miran, we were responsible for the night watch." During the displacement, women redoubled their efforts, recognizing that they were under the scrutiny of almost the whole population: Marjan recounts, "We told ourselves that we had to do absolutely the best we could, so that people couldn't say, 'Look at these women, look at these revolutionaries who can't even protect the people of a small town.' So, we tried to sort out everything."

The women activists challenged state policy at every opportunity, justifying their actions to the government officials who came frequently to the camp to try to negotiate. For example, a Komala activist argued with one of the state representatives: "So it looks like the state media won't stop telling lies. They lie to give the army an excuse to attack us. Have you read the report on Marivan? This report claims that enemies of Iran are arming us to fight against the state. But this is not true! We have suffered so many injustices, we've had to cut back our expenses and borrow money to buy weapons; they are our weapons and we will not give them to anyone."[13]

The unprecedented mobilization ended on August 4, 1979, when government officials promised to meet the demands of the demonstrators. However, not only did the central government fail to keep its promises, but two weeks later, on August 19, 1979, its forces attacked the Kurdish regions. During the offensive, which lasted almost three months, the women's democratic institutions were suppressed and the role of the women activists of Komala consequently entered a new phase.

One of the women's democratic organizations' most important actions was the organizing role of the Marivan Women's Union in the massive protest lasting two weeks by the population of Marivan, a border town near Iraq, located in the province of Kurdistan.

WOMEN'S AUXILIARY ROLE DURING THE FIRST ARMED CONFLICT

During the months after the revolution, the new political system's undemocratic measures aiming to consolidate the Khomeinist grasp on power led to increasing discontent among other political forces throughout Iran, including the Kurdish regions. Government forces attacked newspaper headquarters and the meetings of political organizations, intending to silence them. Kurdish political forces were also attacked by order of Ayatollah Khomeini, under the jihad decree of August 19, 1979, only six months after the revolution; the Kurds responded by retreating to rural and mountainous areas in order to resist the offensive. Komala, unlike the KDPI, continued urging women to participate in politics, but in its call it still adhered to the sexual division of revolutionary labor: only men were allowed to regroup in the rural and mountainous areas as peshmergas. The only two women who left the city for the rural areas, Sayran and Monireh, were unable to gain access to arms. Meanwhile Jaleh, unlike her brothers who had joined the peshmerga forces, remained in the city because, as Elizabeth Ferris points out, warfare is culturally defined as a man's activity, a realm of "masculinity."[14]

The exclusion of women from the armed struggle did not mean women were inactive: on the contrary, their role in political activities behind the front lines, in urban areas, intensified and developed. While government forces captured and executed a number of Kurdish militants, women were not as yet under threat. They remained in the city to take care of political affairs, alongside those male comrades who had not gone to the mountains. The role of these auxiliary forces was crucial at this point, because they could move between the city and the struggle's armed front more easily than men since as far as the government was concerned political militants could only be men meaning that women were less likely to be arrested or subject to restrictions.

The outbreak of the armed struggle in the Kurdish regions put an end to the women's democratic organizations. The young women who remained in the urban areas organized temporary committees in the various cities of the Kurdish regions. Women organizers and participants were involved in all the political activities of this period. For example, it was a woman from the steering committee in Sanandaj who set up all the committees in that city and who was responsible for linking with those in other cities.[15]

Like the rest of the community, women were involved in two types of political activity. First, they contributed indirectly to the armed struggle by collecting funds, medicines, and clothes and by transmitting messages and necessary materials to the combat zones. Second, they organized daily demonstrations, with the aim of supporting Kurdish political and cultural demands, condemning the government forces' military attack, and demanding the release of the many political prisoners.* At demonstrations organized by women in Marivan and school students in Kamyaran and Saqqez, participants chanted, "Political prisoners must be freed, the Pasdaran must be dismissed."[16] Shilan, a member of the Sanandaj student council, recalls:

> We organized lots of protests. As a member of the student council, I distributed announcements, newspapers, and Komala publications, as well as calls for demonstrations in support of the peshmerga forces and to free political prisoners. At night, on the door of every house and on the walls, we posted declarations and called on people to join the demonstrations.

After three months of armed struggle, on November 17, 1979, the Kurdish political forces and the central government agreed to a ceasefire to negotiate an agreement. The central forces withdrew

* To general shock, in the three months of fighting that followed the August 19, 1979 order for jihad against the Kurds, at least 58 Kurdish political men were executed, whereas previously it had been only senior officials of the previous regime who were eliminated by the new government.

and Komala and the KDPI returned to the cities. Komala's central role in the armed resistance increased its popularity, and in its socio-political activities it increasingly operated separately from non-Kurdish Marxist political forces.

THE ESTABLISHMENT OF THE KOMALA WOMEN'S COMMITTEES

Following the announcement of the ceasefire, the Kurdish organizations' key objective was to ensure the return of Kurdish forces to the cities, and between November 1979 and May 1980 they successfully reestablished their headquarters in several cities. While Komala had collaborated with non-Kurdish Marxist forces in a number of democratic organizations, after the armed conflict it decided to pursue its activities in its own name, operating through various committees in a more centralized way. Women also focused on organizing themselves in the committees that were being set up from the autumn of 1979. While during the three months of armed conflict, the roles assigned to women were predominantly supplementing and supporting the armed forces, in line with the sexual division of labor, the return of the peshmergas to the city and the women's committees allowed them to regain their places as organizational political activists, even if the leadership function continued to be reserved for men.

These committees differed from the democratic women's institutions in two important ways. First, instead of being involved with various Kurdish and non-Kurdish leftist organizations, the women's committees were now exclusively under the leadership of Komala. One or two members of Komala were present at every meeting, and the committees were required to send a monthly report of activities to Komala's central committee. Second, while women's democratic organizations had been limited to only a few towns and cities, women's committees were created in all cities where Komala had a presence. When the first women's committee under the control of Komala was established in Sanandaj, for instance, its mission was to connect up with Komala activists in other Kurdish cities and to create a chain of women's committees. Fatima, from Baneh, a small Kurdish city, recalls:

> In our city, no democratic organizations had been set up, because of the lack of female teachers and more experienced women, but after the Sanandaj Women's Committee made contact, a committee finally came into being in our city. Although I was still a student and a member of the student committee, I became an activist.

As had been the case with the women's democratic organizations, the remit of the committees included political, social, and cultural activities. Activists focused on giving material assistance to the disadvantaged, in both urban areas and villages, providing health services and training to build new social foundations and to organize other women— teachers, housewives, high school girls, or women from working-class neighborhoods—according to the framework defined by Komala.

Women activists were also involved in general affairs, especially in the Kurdish cities in West Azerbaijan and Kurdistan which were controlled by Kurdish political forces. In Sanandaj, for example, 55 local councils were established to run the city. Young people from different localities, among them Komala activists, aimed to gain control across neighboring localities. In addition to maintaining these areas and providing security, when the Kurdish regions were reeling from the economic effects of armed conflict, the councils managed the distribution of food, fuel, and medicine in both prosperous and impoverished neighborhoods. Through these committees, the first female activists were trained in the handling of weapons, as well as in first aid. As Ghobadi describes it: "Following the establishment of these women's committees, we were able to participate in armed training like our male comrades. During these courses we learned how to use weapons. One of the armed commanders of Komala was responsible for our training."[17]

The committees also organized socio-cultural activities, such as photography exhibitions and film screenings; established drug rehabilitation centers; and prepared meals for the peshmerga forces in the cities and for the groups active in the neighborhoods. Thus, in Sanandaj, Shahla recollects:

> After the return of the peshmergas, the towns came under the control of the Kurdish forces. In addition to our organizational tasks, we, like the rest of the community, were actively involved in the administration. We, young people, provided security and distributed the necessary fuel and food in our neighborhood. Some of the women working in the centers were also trained in the use of weapons.

Komala activists were a presence at every anti-government event or protest, including the 24-day strike in Sanandaj in May 1980 against the presence of government forces in the Kurdish areas. Married women activists who had children joined the strike during the day, while some single women and teenagers chose to stay overnight.[18] As well as those taking part in the strike, other women tried to spread awareness of what was happening; they went campaigning in the city and surrounding villages to encourage women to take part, or at any rate to explain the purpose of their action. Women's committees in other Kurdish cities supported the strike by sending material and medical assistance. The committee of Oshnavieh organized a big demonstration and sent food to the strikers of Sanandaj,[19] and as Marjan recalls, Marivan women's committee dispatched two activists to give a speech of support to the strike.

Peaceful opposition to government forces, however, was futile. The final Kurdish protest in May 1980 against a military unit attempting to pass through the town of Sanandaj gave the government its pretext; this led to the outbreak of the second armed conflict, which lasted until the end of the 1980s. Shahla, a member of the student council of Sanandaj, remembers this last demonstration:

> I was at school and the principal told me that I had a phone call. It was one of my classmates from Komala who informed me that an armed convoy full of equipment was passing through the city and that it had to be stopped. He asked me to get the students to stop the column, so my classmates and I met up at the designated meeting point. Most of the townspeople joined us soon after, and we succeeded in our mission.

Less than six months after the previous fighting had come to an end, the government, which had decided to "cleanse Kurdistan of counter-revolutionaries,"* launched a second offensive. This time Komala chose to resist from the towns of Sanandaj, Saqqez, Marivan, and Baneh, but one after another, these towns fell quickly into the hands of government forces; for example, the resistance of the people of Sanandaj during this period has become known as the "24-day resistance." The Kurds paid a heavy price, enduring war, terror, bombing, serious injury, and death.

Despite the presence of women at all levels, the sexual division of revolutionary labor did not appear to change. The prestigious role of the armed peshmergas remained the preserve of men. However, most of the women actively participated in the resistance, as Roonak describes:

> The armed conflict in the city of Baneh continued for a few weeks, and during this time it was badly shelled by government forces. Even though we had no weapons to defend ourselves, we women did not hesitate to participate in the struggle. Having a young child didn't stop me from working for the popular resistance day and night. In addition to treating the wounded and moving ammunition and weapons at night, we had to prepare food for the peshmergas. For days, while I had my daughter on my back and we had nowhere to go to be safe from the bombing, I distributed food packages wherever the peshmergas were.

* For example, in a speech by Ayatollah Khomeini on May 16, 1980, to a group of military commanders, he emphasized the "necessity of cleansing Kurdistan of counter-revolutionaries." In part of this speech, he stated: "I hope that, with God's will and the efforts of the army and the Revolutionary Guards, Kurdistan will soon be cleansed and restored... I warn you, the brave soldiers, the Revolutionary Guards, the Revolutionary Council, and the Commander-in-Chief, that the insurgents must be removed from Kurdistan. They have corrupted Kurdistan and have horrifically harassed and oppressed the people of Kurdistan. They looted the people and killed everyone. These individuals must no longer be given any respite. The region must be thoroughly cleansed so that their hands are cut off and their hopes destroyed." Sahifeh-ye Imam (An Anthology of Imam Khomeinis Speeches, Messages, Interviews, Decrees, Religious Permissions, and Letters), Volume 12, (Tehran: The Institute for Compilation and Publication of Imam Khomeini's Works, 2008), 294.

WOMEN'S UNDERGROUND ACTIVITIES IN THE TOWNS

The government's second offensive and the outbreak of the armed struggle immediately put an end to any hopes among the Kurdish political forces for negotiation with the central government. The KDPI and Komala found themselves once again engaged separately in resistance in the rural and mountainous regions. During the earlier fighting, there was low chance of women activists being arrested, but this time some of them were captured and executed. Most women therefore chose to take refuge in the rural areas to become peshmergas as well, even though they were not accepted on the same basis as the men. As a former Komala activist explained, "Many men like me took up arms and joined Komala in 1980, after the Iranian army invaded the city of Sanandaj in that famous 24-day battle,"[20] but this was not an option for female activists. While men, simply because they were male, could join the ranks of the organization, women were not accepted in the armed struggle—notwithstanding Komala's commitment to equality.

In this situation, Komala's women activists had only two options. If they were unable to return to the city for security reasons, they were sent to villages, both to spread awareness and to learn about the daily life of village women—a type of mission highly valued at the time. Otherwise the Komala leadership encouraged women in danger to stay in urban areas or to travel to other cities, Kurdish or not, where they were not identifiable, so as to develop the organization's clandestine activities. Unlike men, women had little alternative, since they were still denied participation in the armed struggle.

With Kurdish political forces abruptly forced to retreat to rural areas, underground activities could to some extent compensate for logistical weaknesses in the Kurdish regions and in the rest of the country. In this respect, the role of women was crucial during this period. Some women initially refused to go underground, but given the spectacular defeat of the organization and the rout of its young and inexperienced leaders, many women activists ultimately consented. As Ghobadi explains, "In a joint meeting with the women, they [the men] asked us to do everything we could to stay in the cities, managing the organization and engaging in underground activities. This was an unexpected approach for us, as we had hoped to join in armed training courses and then organize ourselves in our respective units. But there was a visible reluctance to have us present in this area."[21] In the event, this period did not last long, and from 1981 onward, most of the women activists were forced to leave the urban areas.

In this new phase of their activism, most of the Komala women established themselves outside their hometowns in order to be less identifiable, alone or in underground groups; some were also sent outside the Kurdish regions. Those who were least at risk stayed in their own towns. Thus while Sayran went to Mahabad in West Azerbaijan, Shilan and her sisters remained in their homes, taking more precautions than ever, while others such as Farzaneh took refuge in Tehran. Like their male comrades, some women (students, teachers, or civil servants) gave up their studies or jobs in order to work full-time for the organization. Others, such as Azita, continued their work as teachers to mobilize students in schools and high schools.

Activists were required to live in a "team house" with their male comrades as if they were a family, posing as siblings or as husbands and wives, so as to avoid moral stigma or recognition. Team houses, an entirely new experience for Kurds, became popular as women found themselves living with their male comrades in cities where no one knew them. Already in existence before the revolution among non-Kurdish Iranian militants in the 1970s, this practice spread throughout the country, where according to the new Islamic laws, any type of mixing in public space outside the family could be punished. As Yassaman Saadatmand writes,

> For women in general, it would have been strange to live alone; they had to either live with their family or get married. The security aspect was also important within the organization: single people were more readily suspected than married couples. Moreover, it was dangerous for the two sexes to be seen together in public. People could be stopped while walking with someone of the opposite sex in the street, and if they could not show that they were related or married, they could be imprisoned. It was a risk that political activists could not take.[22]

The main activities for the women of these groups, despite the danger, were printing and distributing Komala's magazines and newspapers, both in the Kurdish and in other regions; meeting the immediate needs of Komala members by delivering money, medicine, and clothes; passing messages between the organization and its underground groups; driving militants to safer areas of Kurdistan (the free areas); and supporting the peshmerga forces to take part in occasional armed operations in the city. As Golnar describes her activities during this period:

> I did whatever I could for Komala: collecting money, sending letters, hosting peshmergas in my house when they were going to launch an armed operation in town. However, my most important job was to deliver documents, like letters, newspapers, and money. I was a sort of post office. I went back and forth between towns and villages, as well as to different Kurdish regions and sometimes even to Tehran. I did everything in my power. With everything strictly monitored by the government, we were the most reliable means of communication. For example, I remember very clearly the time I went to a border region in West Azerbaijan in the early morning to deliver a package. But in spite of my tiredness, as soon as I got home, I was asked to deliver another letter, this time to Tehran.

The increasing strictness about wearing the hijab also meant that women could more easily pass unnoticed than men. Jaleh recounts:

> One of the things that was most helpful to us in carrying out our various organizational tasks was wearing the hijab and the chador. After the withdrawal of Kurdish political elements and the regime's takeover of the city, the hijab was increasingly common, and I, who had not previously worn it, started to do so in order not to be easily identified by the regime. So, I wore the hijab against my personal preferences, but being veiled was very important to the success of my activities.

After the outbreak of the Iran–Iraq war on September 22, 1980,* the Iraqi government was keen to strengthen forces opposed to the Iranian regime. It provided logistical and financial support to Komala, especially in the years 1984–5. Notwithstanding the financial aid from Iraq, public donations—although insufficient—remained important to Komala, as they had been previously. Activists also tried whenever possible to support the organization through their personal finances, or through their families if they could afford it. For example, Nasrin, whose family was financially comfortable, did not hesitate to ask them for financial contributions. Roya supported Komala as a teacher; she and other teachers regularly distributed Komala newspapers and writings among high school students and devoted a significant part of their monthly salary to the service of the organization. Some political tasks could also provide activists with financial support. Farzaneh, for example, worked nearly seven hours a day in a factory in Tehran. This allowed them at once to earn a living, to strengthen their ties with workers, and better understand the difficulties of their daily lives in a context where the space for activism was increasingly restricted. This type of political activity had previously been impossible for most Kurdish women because of family and social restrictions.

In the team houses of non-Kurdish activists of Marxist tendency in the 1970s, any kind of intimate relationship was forbidden, and violation of this rule could even mean the assassination of the alleged "guilty" persons.[23] An activist from the Iranian People's Fedayeen Guerrilla Organization recalled a romantic relationship between a man and a woman within the organization that had resulted in the man's assassination in 1978. According to another activist, in the team houses they "were very careful about romantic relationships. Our relationships had to be very disciplined. Relationships between men and women were considered taboo. We censored ourselves heavily. We even controlled our smiles."[24] However, this

---

* The Iran–Iraq war (1980–88) arose out of multiple hostilities linked to border disputes between the two countries, and out of apprehensions about the consequences of the Iranian Revolution of 1979 that brought the Islamic Republic to power. This war did not lead to any territorial changes. See Karsh Efraim, *The Iran–Iraq War 1980–1988* (London: Osprey, 2002).

was not the case among Komala activists and other leftist political organizations after the victory of the revolution, who accepted emotions and relationships between men and women in the team houses. While Sayran refused her comrade's marriage proposal because she did not reciprocate his feelings, Farzaneh married one of the comrades with whom she was living in Tehran. Their married life did not last long, however; they were arrested by government forces a few months later, and Farzaneh was sentenced to seven years in prison while her husband was executed nine months after their arrest.

These underground groups played an important role, but it was not only militants who engaged in such activities. The support of family members of militants was fundamental for clandestine operations, which were continuously under the surveillance of government forces. Golnar relates:

> Elderly mothers with peshmerga sons also had an important role in the underground activities of that time. One of the mothers, who had already lost her two sons in the fighting, was always trying to collect funds and send messages and letters. The mothers whose sons were peshmergas did a lot for the organization under the pretext of visiting them.

Young Kurdish women, who were actively present in political life, were confronted by the sexual division of militant labor within Komala. They took advantage of every opportunity to constitute themselves as political subjects with a recognized and legitimate place. Within a year, however, as the wave of repression and arrests continued to grow, these underground groups were gradually identified, and women, like their male comrades, were compelled to leave the urban areas.

6
Becoming a Peshmerga Under State Repression

After almost a year of armed struggle against government forces, Komala finally accepted women into its ranks as officially identified peshmerga in March 1981. This decision, revolutionary in its time, was essentially pragmatic, a response to the immediate situation rather than an ideological position based on a discourse of gender equality. In other words, it was material and historical motives that led to the acceptance of women into Komala as peshmerga.

BECOMING A PESHMERGA TO SAVE ONE'S LIFE

Repression intensified in the Kurdish regions in May 1980, spreading out to affect the whole country. Under the pretext of protecting national sovereignty and independence, the government took advantage of the Iran–Iraq war, which started a few months later, to crush and severely punish any dissenting voices seen as likely to weaken the Islamic Republic of Iran. Large numbers of activists were captured, imprisoned, and executed. Many went into exile. At the same time, women—despite their massive participation in the revolution—not only lost their rights in public and private space under Sharia law, but also suffered severe repression if they were activists in political organizations that were now considered anti-revolutionary. This wave of political repression in the 1980s radically changed the lives of activists. In contrast to the first wave of repression in the Kurdish regions from August to November 1979, which was primarily aimed at men, the second wave also targeted women, regardless of their age, marital status, or degree of political involvement.

The initial attack in May 1980 was swiftly followed by a wave of arrests of Kurdish activists who were considered anti-revolutionary. Almost all the activists who had been engaged in political and public activity in small towns were identifiable. Their revolutionary appearance, especially the women's plain and dark Kurdish dress, made them easy to identify and arrest. The collaboration with government forces of some local groups, known as *jash* (traitors) by the Kurdish movements and as "Muslim peshmerga" by the government, was another important factor in the rapid and widespread arrests of male and female militants. According to Golrokh Ghobadi: "Almost all the members and supporters of Komala had gone about their political activities visibly, without taking precautions. They were known to almost everyone, both friends and enemies. Two years after the revolution, everyone knew each other. Everyone was involved in the process of promoting the revolution, and revolutionary work seemed extremely difficult to do clandestinely."[1] Susan corroborates this: "We were so confident about the revolution and the power of the people that we didn't believe the new regime would be able to occupy Kurdistan for a second time so quickly and easily. So, we weren't really taking precautions in our activities."

One of the first Kurdish women to be executed was Mastoureh Shahsavari, a 17-year-old student from Saqqez who was put to death on May 24, 1980, in Sanandaj prison.[2] The execution of teenage girls was not unusual. Fereshteh Golanbarian (a member of the People's Fedayeen Organization of Iran), Farideh Golnasab, and Khanom Khormali were also sentenced to death and executed. Shahin Bavafa, a nurse who was not a member of any party, was executed in Sanandaj on June 14, 1980, for treating the wounded during the attack by government forces.* Before her death, she spoke to the French weekly *L'Express* about the situation in the city.

* According to a report published by the Kurdistan Human Rights Network on March 9, 2023, at least 96 Kurdish women have been executed on political charges since the establishment of the Islamic Republic in 1979 up to 2023. Of these, 93 were executed during the 1980s alone. The last Kurdish female political prisoner to be executed was Shirin Alam Holi, who was hanged in Tehran's Evin Prison on May 9, 2010, without prior notice given to her lawyer or family. The report states that no cases of Kurdish women's executions were recorded during the Pahlavi regime. The report can be found here: https://kurdistanhumanrights.org/fa/?p=20503. Two female Kurdish political activists, Werisheh Moradi and Pakhshan Azizi, are currently at risk of execution. On January 8, 2025, the death sentence of Pakshan Azizi, was confirmed by the judiciary of the Islamic Republic of Iran.

In an article published a few days later, *L'Express* gave the date of her death as June 17, 1980, and stated that "she insisted to Christian Hoche [the journalist] that her name should appear, so that no doubt would remain about her testimony. Christian Hoche warned her of possible reprisals, though he confirmed that her testimony would carry more weight if the source were not anonymous." But she responded, "I am not afraid of death. When you return to France, shout out loud about what you have seen. And I beg you, ask your government to intervene so that this butchery stops."[3] *L'Express* reported that this nurse was arrested and tried by an Islamic court on the grounds of "sabotage in her work and publication in a foreign newspaper of a counter-revolutionary insurrectionary call." The article concluded: "But who would dare to say that the Ayatollah was a reactionary regarding the status of women? In front of the firing squad, the only remaining effective production unit in Iran, the genders for him are equal."[4] In addition to Shahin Bavafa, two nurses and sisters, Nasrin and Shahla Ka'abi, were executed not long afterward, on August 30, 1980.[5]

Thus, barely two years after the revolution enabled these activists to enter the political scene, the heirs of that very revolution killed them. If during previous repressions the role of Kurdish women had been to mourn the men killed for their political activity, this time women were themselves among the first victims. From the 1980s

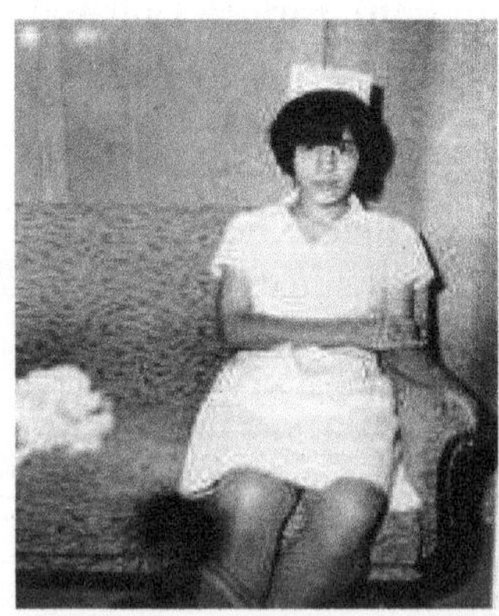

Figure 6.1 Shahin Bavafa, a nurse, executed June 14, 1980.

Figure 6.2 Nasrin and Shahla Ka'abi, nurses and sisters, executed August 30, 1980.[6]

on, the division between martyred men and grieving women was destabilized. For the first time among Kurds in Iran, women joined the rank of martyrs or *shaheeds*, those who sacrifice their lives in the service of the organization. Women were being executed for their clandestine activities even while they were denied the opportunity to be full peshmergas in the armed struggle. Although there is no precise estimate of the number of Kurdish women executed, it can be confirmed that among the 110 Komala women killed during the 1980s, 41 died in prison.

Faced with the imprisonment of their comrades, most female activists from Komala chose to embed themselves fully within Komala. Saving one's life by dedicating it to the cause seemed logical in a context where hundreds of activists were being arrested and sentenced to death. Paradoxically, women took refuge in the ranks of Komala in order to save their lives. For as Lætitia Bucaille theorizes in another context, "when life becomes precarious and death is likely, joining the struggle is a rational decision not only for increasing numbers of men, but also for those women who did not initially choose to be involved. Their presence in the struggle, in response to the irruption of violence into the home, reinforces the porosity between public and private spheres."[7] Although there is no exact record of the number of women executed by the government, estimates demonstrate heavy repression during the 1980s. Between June 20, 1981, and June 20, 1984, at least 3,895 people were executed in Iran, including 580 women.[8] Nor were executions confined to the first half of the 1980s; a few days after the end of the Iran–Iraq war, in August 1988, the regime unleashed a second wave of executions of Iranian prisoners of Islamist and Marxist tendencies. The evidence suggests that more than 5,000 prisoners were hanged in secret within two months in a number of prisons across Iran. Among those executed were over 300 women who had been sentenced to a few years in prison.[9]

Sanctions also targeted the families of activists: relatives might be arrested in the place of absent militants or their property confiscated.[10] The family of Mahin, for example, bore significant human and financial costs: "Within the space of a few months, a female cousin of mine was arrested and executed. One of my Komala peshmerga brothers was killed during an operation; my sister was captured, and all of our family property was confiscated by the government. We were forced to leave the city and join the Komala in the rural areas."

The threat to life was thus an important motive for militants to leave the cities and join the ranks of Komala. The women also had a specific gendered motive for abandoning the towns and cities: preserving their honor by avoiding the threat of rape in prison. Although any prisoner, regardless of sex, could be at risk of sexual violence, the question of honor, closely linked to women's sexuality, meant that rape became a specific marker of anxiety for activist women during this period.

BECOMING A PESHMERGA TO SAVE ONE'S HONOR (*NAMÛS*)

The fear of rape and of the consequent loss of honor led families who had previously been unhappy about their daughters' political activities to encourage them to leave home and join Komala, which now seemed more positive about women's participation. The Iranian authorities denied rape, claiming that these were rumors spread by enemies of the revolution and that rape was prohibited by Islam.* There were nevertheless widespread accounts of women activists being systematically raped in prisons. The subject of rape, especially that of unmarried women, was a general topic of conversation. Several interviewees mentioned a rumor, widely circulated among Kurdish families at the time, that after executing female prisoners, government forces would bring flowers and sweets or sugar cones to their families and tell them that their daughter was married to a Revolutionary Guard the day before she was executed.

---

* Ayatollah Montazeri said: "During the 1980s, when the subject of the execution of [Islamist and Marxist] prisoners was topical, I protested by saying that women, even if they were a minority, were also executed. Arguing that [unmarried] girls should not be executed according to Islam, the imam [Ayatollah Khomeini] said 'so don't execute them.' But afterwards, it was claimed everywhere that I had said that [unmarried] girls should not be executed, but that they should be married before they are killed." Hossain Ali Montezeri, *Khterate Ayatollah Montezeri* (Memoir of the Ayatollah Montezeri), Etehadiye Nasherane Irani Dar Uruopa (Baran, Khavaran, Nima), 1379 (2000): 344–5.

The fate of unmarried women, as Amir Hassanpour points out, was linked to their virginity. Women's honor was maintained through chastity, and this in turn represented the honor of the men of their family and indeed of the wider community A woman who was raped thus suffered not only the violence of the act itself but also the shame that she had "dishonored" her family.[11] As Christine Guionnet and Erik Neveu point out in another context, "doing politics has gender-differentiated costs."[12] The stories that identified rape as part of the experience of female political prisoners inflamed collective panic and fueled social control over female activists.

Although most researchers have so far remained silent on this subject, my interviews with four female Komala activists who were imprisoned—as well as the results of the only study conducted so far, by two Iranian researchers, Shadi Sadr and Shadi Amin—confirm that notwithstanding the Iranian government's denial, sexual abuse and assaults aimed at humiliating female political prisoners were committed. Sadr and Amin report that while "only four of the women we interviewed . . . told us of being raped themselves, most of them reported at least one incident of rape amongst their cell mates, and some reported multiple incidents."[13] They go on to explain:

> The testimonies of female political prisoners all agree that the rape of female political prisoners in the 1980s did not extend to the majority of the female prison population. They also all confirm that rape occurred in Iranian prisons in the 1980s. However, they give varying accounts of the reasons and the aims as well as of the categories of prisoners who were raped. Some witnesses suggested that the likelihood of rape increased when female prisoners had resisted all other types of torture. In these cases, rape was used as a method to break their resistance. Rape was still more likely if the prisoner was beautiful, or if she had boldly defended her position during interrogation and refused to provide any information—behavior considered audacious and brazen—or if she or her family was for some reason the target of particular hatred and desire for vengeance in the interrogator.[14]

The fear of rape unquestionably plagued the minds of women activists, and it was one of the chief reasons that hundreds of young women throughout the period left their cities to join Komala in the countryside. In a society where the concept of *namûs* or honor determined the fate of women, regardless of their marital status, some women prisoners who were raped, chose to kill themselves to escape dishonor and the shame associated with rape. Azar Al'é Kana'an, a Kurdish member of an Iranian Marxist political organization, imprisoned between 1981 and 1986, recounts her suicide attempts after being raped:

> After the rape, I attempted suicide twice in prison. The first time, I cut my wrist. I saw it bleeding. It got infected and that was all; they sent me back to my cell. The second time I attempted suicide with sleeping pills, the same pills they gave us. I left mine at the cell door, in exchange for a few from another prisoner, and I picked some up in the corridor. One way or another, I was seriously determined to kill myself.[15]

Roya recounts the story of Shawbo Sa'id Zahedi, a Komala political prisoner, who set herself on fire in prison after being sentenced to death by the Marivan court. There were two versions of the death of this activist: that she killed herself after being raped or did so to avoid rape. Other women killed themselves after their release from prison. Susan, who was incarcerated for six years, relates: "A friend of mine from Oshnavieh was raped in prison. It broke her mentally, and after her release she died by suicide. The intensity of the pressure was too strong for her."

In addition to the severe physical and psychological effects of rape as torture on prisoners, regardless of gender, these suicidal acts suggest that if women could not protect their honor, they would be considered guilty not only by others but also themselves. In this society, women's honor was not a personal value but a collective one. The women prisoners were considered guilty because they had chosen politics; they had stepped out of line, going against the sexual division of labor, and thus they had been unable to protect their honor in prison.

The fear of rape was shared by all women prisoners regardless of the level of their activism. Shadi, sentenced to five years in prison, recalls: "Under the whip, instead of thinking about my immediate suffering, I was thinking about my virginity. Every time, I checked myself to see whether I had bled or not. Although I was lucky not to be raped, the fear of rape was a permanent stress and nightmare during my five years in prison." This fear increased when the prisoner was alone with her torturer. Soraya, who was sentenced to two years in prison, said: "Every moment, I was afraid of being raped. I thought, 'This is it, this is the moment.'" Mojgan, sentenced to one year in prison, was also threatened with rape many times during her imprisonment: "Despite the fact that I was not raped, prison guards often threatened me with it so as to break my resistance."

To humiliate the women prisoners, prison authorities reduced them to the status of sexual objects in the service of men. They might be forced to undergo or threatened with so-called "virginity tests." Susan was frequently threatened with the virginity test allegedly to confirm whether she had had sexual relations with other activists. Women prisoners were constantly accused of having been sexually loose and were regarded as nothing more than sex slaves to their comrades. Soraya, another Komala prisoner, recalls:

> They considered me a slut, a prostitute who slept with any man. This kind of insult was not easy to bear, especially for me, having grown up in a traditional society. It scared me. They asked me repeatedly if I had slept with my male comrades or not. And I was ashamed to the bottom of my heart to hear their words.

Some prisoners were forced to marry prison officials in order to be released. Shilan's twin sister, for example, was forced to marry her torturer to secure her release. This decision cost her dearly; her family rejected her for years.

In general, unlike men, women on their release from prison were neither welcomed nor seen as heroines. Some were even asked to prove that they had not been raped. The reaction to a woman's imprisonment could be reduced to a simple question: *Has she been raped, yes or no?* Her answer to this question eclipsed everything else, to focus solely on her virginity or sexuality. Even those who answered no to the fateful question remained suspect. Despite this, among the four prisoners interviewed who were raped in prison, three rejoined Komala on their release, while one, Susan, abandoned political life even though she was fortunate enough not to be harassed with such questions by her family and the people around her. A Kurdish detainee quoted in Sadr and Amin's study recalled that two of her comrades who had passed out under torture feared they might have been raped. This fear persisted for years after their release, up until their marriages. In the case of one of them, the whole family waited outside the bridal chamber for hours on the wedding night to check the bloodstained cloth following sexual relations that demonstrated that the bride had been a virgin and thus to confirm that no rape had been committed in prison.[16] Such pressures reveal how significantly the cost of political engagement was gendered. According to Susan: "The torture women endured was ten times worse than that of men. It was an endless nightmare of fear of rape and terror of disgracing our families and the people around us."

Kurdish women who left the cities thus did so in order to save their lives and honor, joining the ranks of Komala in the rural or mountainous areas, traveling alone, with one or two family members (husband, brother, or sister) or as a family. Narmin's parents, who had opposed her 14-year-old sister's activities, ended up driving her to a Komala base in a village near Sanandaj; she had been identified by the government forces, and they feared she would be arrested and raped. Some activists from other organizations also decided to join Komala. For example, Pershing, a Kurdish member of the Iranian People's Fedayeen Guerrilla Organization, explains:

> I was the only girl in the family, and I was 16 years old when the wave of arrests and torture and executions of militants began. My family, especially my father, could not bear to imagine me being arrested and raped. That is why, despite his personal wishes, he encouraged me to leave the city. My own political organization was divided, so I joined Komala, the only Marxist political organization to engage in armed struggle.

For those who had to join Komala alone, departure was more difficult. Young women, who normally never left their families on their own, were reluctant to step into the unknown, but they had little choice. As Asrin emphasizes, "Setting off for an unknown fate is not an easy decision for activists, regardless of gender," and it was still harder for girls from religious or conservative families. While many women had tried to maintain the separation of the sexes in their activism, joining Komala far from the cities meant it was no longer possible to keep away from male peshmerga. Such a prospect was too much for women like Shadi. Her father had not even allowed her to go to school, so she had participated in the movement without telling him. She thus could not find the courage to leave her family to become a peshmerga and in the end chose to stay at home, whatever might happen. She said:

> I was sure I would be arrested and jailed, but I grew up in a very conservative family. I couldn't leave the town without my family. I couldn't even imagine such a thing, because I was very shy; I couldn't even look my male comrades in the eye. How could I separate myself from my family? So I simply preferred to stay and be arrested rather than to go away in the company of unknown men.

Her choice cost her dearly, leading to her imprisonment for five years.

WOMEN ACTIVISTS IN RURAL AREAS: PRECARITY AND UNCERTAINTY

The intensity of the repression gradually led opposition activists, non-Kurds as well as Kurds, to take refuge in the ranks of the DPKI and Komala. Fearing for their safety, activists from other Iranian organizations were compelled to leave the cities in increasing numbers. Most of the Marxists, especially women, joined the ranks of Komala, which took a more positive view of women's political participation. However, while men who joined the organization could readily be integrated into its armed and unarmed activities, this was not the case for women. Despite the daily increase in the numbers of women joining, Komala failed to assign them a specific role. Ghobadi described this period as "the beginning of uncertainty."[17] The women who had previously worked alongside their male comrades in the urban areas suddenly found themselves idle. The young leaders of Komala, who had not anticipated the intensity of the repression, were unexpectedly dispersed to different Kurdish regions. Lacking the logistical equipment that would have enabled them to resist, they also had no plan for the women. Susan explains:

> Neither Komala nor any other political organization at the time imagined that government forces would easily be able to force them to withdraw from urban areas. They had not planned for such a situation, either for themselves or for the women. But one thing was obvious: the peshmerga forces were composed only of men, and no women could play this role.

On leaving the cities, single women were required to group themselves into teams, while those who were married moved into separate houses with their families. With no official mission, they were nonetheless expected to continue with their activities. The organization of activities in rural areas during this period was based on the sexual division of labor: men were peshmergas or warriors, while women provided support and food, as in most war contexts.[18] At the same time as women supported the peshmergas by preparing meals and doing housework, they were directed to help the villagers in their daily agricultural or domestic work, such as cleaning, childcare, cooking, animal care, field work, and harvesting. These activities had two purposes, in line with their activism in the urban areas: understanding the hardship of the lives of masses, and raising awareness among the population of the socio-political situation in Iran, especially for Kurds.

However, according to the women interviewees, it had been much easier for them to raise awareness in the city; in the countryside, the struggle with daily tasks prevented them from effectively transmitting political awareness to village women. The young women were worn out by the demands of the daily labors that consumed their time and energy. Roonak testifies:

> Being accepted as official members of Komala was not easy. As we could not go back to the city, we worked as hard as we could to be admitted as official members, which we saw as a great honor. So, we aimed to redouble our efforts at every level, especially by helping the villagers. I put my daughter on my back, and I was busy with these activities from morning to night.

Although the work was challenging, most of the women regarded such activities as necessary to prove that they were true revolutionary activists. Many of them welcomed village work. Susan, who lived for a short time in a small village before her arrest, emphasizes its importance:

> In order to prove to ourselves that we were true revolutionaries, we worked and lived alongside the village women. These activities were consistent with our revolutionary ideals and goals. We, the women and men of Komala, were mostly educated and urban, but we believed completely in what we were doing. It was through this work also that the villagers became closer to us.

Women assigned to full-time village work increasingly developed an explicit critique of the sexual division of political and domestic labor. Even if performing the village tasks was considered proof of revolutionary commitment, the women activists of Komala, newly arrived in rural areas, and having previously participated with their comrades in all socio-political events in urban spaces, were not prepared to be confined to such activities. Not only the women themselves but also the families who had supported their daughters' political commitments expressed dissatisfaction. Marjan describes this period as the "worst" of her life as an activist; she also faced criticism from her mother:

> My mother didn't like to see me focus only on the day-to-day affairs of the villagers, especially the women. She thought I and the other women deserved much better than that. According to her, if we had to spend our days doing domestic chores and taking care of other people's children, then what was the point of getting involved in politics? We might as well get married and

> start our own families; after all, it would be more rewarding not to be in politics and to take care of our own children than to be in politics and take care of other people's children. My mother kept saying, "If you want to get involved in politics, then take up arms and become real peshmergas. You are just as good as the men."

In this situation, women activists ended up feeling isolated and distant from the real politics of the time. As Ghobadi describes it: "We were in total ignorance. We had no access to books or publications, not even to the radio. We were easily sidelined and, in some cases, humiliated by comrades in the organization. For many of us, the struggle was gradually reduced to a monotonous, tedious life. When we protested, we were called 'whiners.'"[19] Women began to protest their position, taking every opportunity to make themselves heard and to demand changes. Notable here is Marjan's epic journey: with the aim of expressing her frustration at being confined to menial tasks, she set off on foot from a village near Marivan and walked for 20 days to the city of Bukan, where the central committee of Komala was based. Dissatisfied women hoped that such actions would lead to concrete change.

At the second congress in March 1981, the organization consented to discuss the situation of women within the movement. However, in the event the discussion was deferred by the leaders, who took the view that other subjects should be given priority—including the reform of Iranian society, the right to self-determination of the Kurds, the challenge to populist ideologies, and support for the most deprived classes. Once again, the issue of women was relegated to the margins. It was regarded as a "non-subject" and did not capture the attention of the organization, despite the presence of two women at the congress. Ghobadi, who was one of them, stated: "I did my best to raise the demands and expectations of women activists, but 'they' [the leaders] did not listen to us. They looked down on us and despised us. None of the demands concerning women, whether about the taking up of arms or about the taking of decisions, was met."[20]

Despite the continuing strength of this ideological reluctance to fully accept women as political subjects, in 1981 the Komala leadership was compelled to accept women into its ranks as official members with the title of peshmerga. This was for two reasons: the increase in the number of women taking refuge in rural areas, and the dissatisfaction of female activists with the situation in which they found themselves. While the exact date of women's official entry into Komala as full members is unclear, it is generally placed a few months after the second congress in March 1981. Komala thus became the first Kurdish organization to accept women into its ranks as peshmerga, even if it was a development resulting chiefly from the immediate pressures of the moment. Without denying the political conviction that drove many women to engage in armed struggle, most women who joined Komala in this period seem to have done so primarily as a response to the constraints of their desperate situation, and as a strategic attempt to escape the tragic outcome of their political commitment—namely, being killed or raped.

While the massive presence of Kurdish women in political life in the post-revolutionary period was certainly a distinctive and unprecedented development, this participation in no way led to their representation in all areas. Only two women had left the city for rural areas during the initial attack by the government forces; most were not yet ready to take up arms. Although women expressed a desire to enter this field, in practice most families and indeed the women activists themselves were reluctant to take part in what was considered a male monopoly; Komala leaders were generally no exception in this regard. The admission of women into the organization was the result neither of a principle of gender equality nor of independent demands by a majority of women. Rather, it was the consequence of the massive influx of women activists into the rural areas seeking to escape rape and the stigma of dishonor.

PART III

Patriarchy in the Lives of the Komala Peshmerga, 1981–91

From March 1981, both women and men, whatever their field of activity (armed or not), could be considered official party members or peshmergas. In consequence, a degree of mixing between the sexes would henceforth structure social relations within the organization. Alongside the Kurdish urban women who had been active since the movement's emergence, hundreds of new members were joining Komala in the 1980s; these included non-Kurds as well as villagers from poor and uneducated families, sometimes with no political background.

THE POLITICAL CONTEXT: THE KURDISH REGIONS IN THE 1980s

Confronted by attacking government forces, the two main Kurdish political forces (KDPI and Komala) organized their membership, forces, and armed operations independently, without consulting each other, and indeed were in open conflict for over three years. The term "peshmerga," first used during the Kurdistan Republic in 1946 to designate people participating in the armed struggle, took on another dimension during this period. Bloody confrontations pushed the Kurdish political forces into the mountains and the rural areas known as "free zones" where they became better trained, more experienced, and better equipped.[1] The exact number of peshmergas in Komala is unknown, but various estimates put the total at 3,500 to 4,000, including nearly 500 women. In the 1980s, it was the villagers who constituted the popular base of the Kurdish forces, even if not always willingly; the presence of fighters in the villages provoked a strong reaction from government forces, who saw the locals as collaborating with the "rebel" or "counter-revolutionary" forces.*

Several factors contributed to the defeat of the Kurds. The Iran–Iraq war, rather than weakening Iran as a whole, as the Iraqi government had hoped, weakened the Kurdish regions far more. While the war gave Kurds access to some financial and military

* Kurdish political forces were not the only ones present in rural areas. The villagers, often poor, hosted various members of Kurdish and non-Kurdish groups that had taken refuge in these areas.

resources from Baghdad, its destructive effects hit their region especially badly.* In the province of Kermanshah alone, according to the Iranian government's official statistics, nearly 22,000 civilians and soldiers were injured and 9,800 killed.[2] The Iranian state authorities effectively mobilized nationalist principles and the idea of national integrity,[3] taking advantage of the war to present the battle against internal and external enemies—the Kurds and the Iraqis—as a single front, thereby justifying increasing repression.† The Kurdish political forces, finding themselves increasingly isolated, allied with other Iranian opposition groups. Although the KDPI's efforts at such alliances were largely unsuccessful, Komala succeeded in forming a union with some non-Kurdish Marxist group Iranians to form the Communist Party of Iran (CPI) in 1983, in an agreement that lasted until 1991.‡

Conflict between the KDPI and Komala, which lasted from February 1985 to April 1988, also accelerated the defeat of the Kurdish political forces. Neither the continuous clashes of the Kurds with the government forces nor the war between Iran and Iraq could neutralize this conflict,§ which was driven primarily by a struggle for hegemony in the Kurdish regions.[4] Reliable data on

---

* This aid never pushed the Kurdish political forces to directly collaborate with the Iraqi forces. See David Romano, *The Kurdish Nationalist Movement: Opportunity, Mobilization and Identity* (Cambridge: Cambridge University Press, 2006), 237–8.

† The government's repression was not limited to Kurdistan. The war gave the government an important opportunity to suppress dissent throughout the country. Farhad Khosrokhavar describes this period of repression as "the promotion of blind violence." Farhad Khosrokhavar, *L'utopie sacrifiée* (The Sacrificed Utopia) (Paris: Presses de la fondation nationale des sciences politiques, 1993), 87.

‡ The number of non-Kurdish members of Komala, who joined especially after the beginning of the wave of repression from 1981 onward, is not recorded anywhere. According to the estimates of some interviewees, they made up only 3 or 4 percent of the peshmerga. The number of non-Kurdish women is much lower than that of non-Kurdish men.

§ Internal conflicts among the Kurds have a long history and are sometimes described as Kurdish fratricide. These conflicts are deeply rooted in ideological and geopolitical divisions, often exacerbated by external manipulation. They have weakened the Kurdish movement in its quest for self-determination and struggle against oppressive states (such as Turkey, Iran, Iraq, and Syria). The reasons for the armed conflicts between the KDPI and Komala during the 1980s are numerous, including the decline of the revolutionary atmosphere, attempts to assert dominance in Kurdistan, and mutual ideological accusations. See David McDowall, *A Modern History of the Kurds* (London: I.B. Tauris, 2004), 275; Michael Gunter, *The Kurds: A Divided Nation in Search of a State* (Dallas: Markus Wiener, 2018); Abbas Vali, *Kurds and the State in Iran: The Making of Kurdish Identity* (London: I.B. Tauris, 2011).

the number of casualties on each side is hard to find, but a former KDPI peshmerga estimates the number of deaths at "376 on the KDPI side and 348 in the ranks of the Komala."[5] Twenty women are also mentioned among the Komala casualties.

In this context, the Iranian government's success in defeating its Kurdish opponents was not surprising. Little by little it recaptured almost all the Kurdish regions, thanks not only to superior military equipment but also to those local forces that chose to fight alongside the Iranian army against the peshmergas, their intimate knowledge of local geography opening the way for government forces. Between 1980 and 1984, towns, villages, and roads alternated between government and peshmerga control, while in the free zones, the KDPI and Komala built their bases, with schools, radio stations, and hospitals. However, from 1984 onward, as the government offensives intensified, the Kurds gradually lost the free zones, and the border areas that had previously been held by the peshmerga came under government control.

From 1984, as Iran began to prevail in the war against Iraq, the Kurdish regions were steadily retaken, forcing the Kurds to withdraw into Iraq, where their troops were stationed in camps that were less well equipped or provisioned. With support from the Iraqi government, they were able to launch raids into Iran, but were no longer in a position to represent a serious threat to the Iranian government, especially after the announcement of the 1988 ceasefire between Iran and Iraq.[6] During this period, although again there are no exact figures for the number of casualties, the Kurds in general and the political forces in particular paid a heavy price. David McDowall estimates 27,500 dead between 1979 and early 1984, including 2,500 fighters. The general secretary of the KDPI revised this figure upward in 1990, reckoning 45,000 fatalities, of whom 5,000 were combatants.[7] An unpublished Komala list indicates that 1,545 of its peshmergas were killed during this period,[8] and in addition to those killed in combat, several activists were executed in prison.

By the 1990s, most of Komala's peshmergas were leaving the movement to go into exile. The reasons for this growing trend were multiple, encompassing the defeat of the organization both militarily and politically, lack of security in the camps, and the intensifying internal tensions within the party, including the first split in 1991. Komala members had already taken refuge in Iraqi Kurdistan to escape government forces; now most of them, losing hope in the possibility of continuing the struggle, went into exile again, seeking political asylum in Western countries such as Germany, Sweden, Norway, and England.

7

Peshmerga Women and the Problems of Integration

The early organizational structure of Komala reproduced the patriarchal division of labor: men in combat in rural and mountainous areas, women as auxiliary forces in urban areas. This was challenged in 1981 when Komala accepted female peshmergas into its ranks. Women peshmergas—particularly those in the armed wing—faced many difficulties because, at an ideological level, the organization's leaders were themselves cautious about the issue of gender mixing, while in practical terms the reproduction of conventional gender relations in the interactions of daily life further complicated the position of women.

THE OFFICIAL STATUS OF WOMEN IN KOMALA: UNARMED PESHMERGAS

From March 1981 onward, young women, whatever their marital status or level of education, could join the ranks of Komala, by choice or by "necessity." However, the organization accepted them only hesitantly, and the level of their integration was limited. Although women were involved in all other areas of activity, bearing arms was still the prerogative of men; no woman was permitted to do so until 11 November 1982.* Whereas men were provided with arms as a matter of course, women who joined between March 1981 and

* Neither the exact date of women's admission as peshmergas nor the date of their admission into the armed branch is mentioned anywhere. Nor do any of the interviewees know these dates. The exact date of the arming of women is mentioned only in a book by one of Komala's former peshmerga women. Malakeh Mostafa Soltani, *Sébari Qalabard La Sar Almane u Talasowar (The Shadow of the Qalabard on Almane and Talasowar)* (Sweden: 49books, 2023) 257.

November 1982 became peshmergas but were left without weapons, even for self-defense. As auxiliary forces, they supported their male comrades in tasks such as publishing newspapers and propaganda pamphlets, running the radio station, teaching, organizing logistics and supplies, catering, and caring for the wounded—work identified by Manuel Cervera-Marzal as "shadow tasks."[1] Nonetheless, the women interviewees agreed that becoming a peshmerga was a great victory. Even without weapons, this status allowed them to move beyond their roles as wives and mothers. While the work performed by men can be seen as a continuation of their social roles, for women, joining a political organization constituted an important break with family guardianship and the roles socially assigned to them. Recognized henceforth as peshmergas, rather than as sympathizers without official title, they were able to make use of their still unequal circumstances to claim autonomous political existence. Miriam recounts: "Initially, I was assigned to work in a publishing house for several hours a day. I didn't mind, what was important was to be useful to the organization." Shirin, who was the mother of one child, started out by working as a cook—one of the most difficult jobs, especially at a time when Komala was suffering from supply shortages: "I worked with the minimum of ingredients. The peshmergas were relieved when they saw me, because they knew that I could prepare something to eat no matter what. They trusted me. My only slogan was 'You can't fight if you can't feed yourself first.'"

Among the characteristic features of the gendered division of labor is that women may take on a wide variety of tasks in a single day, and as the French historian Christine Bard points out, women's responsibilities in wartime are particularly diverse.[2] Such labor is always assigned a lesser value than unvarying work[3] and is a modality specific to women. In a situation of armed conflict, the men in Komala were also required to participate in services such as cooking and cleaning to some extent, but women's responsibilities were more various than men's. After their daily work, they would organize meetings for village women and offer classes to illiterate peshmergas or to children with no access to schools. Many women carried out these multiple activities while pregnant or as mothers of one or more children. They did a bit of everything: looking after organizational tasks such as holding meetings, cooking, cleaning, and in particular joining the health brigades.[4] Roonak described her usual daily tasks:

> I already had one child at the time, and when I became pregnant with my second, I chose to continue my political activities with Komala. I divided my time between visiting the clinic where I treated the sick, and collecting and distributing educational books for the village children. I also never missed an opportunity to gather the village women together to discuss politics.

In breaking away from the family unit to commit themselves to a political organization, the peshmerga women challenged the traditional sexual division of labor. Nonetheless, the differentiation of access to weapons reproduced a gendered division of functions. In the early 1980s, there was an acute need for fighters, and women felt they had been "relegated" to the rear base, assigned to the least visible or valued tasks. They were eager to join the most prestigious branch of the organization, namely the armed wing. Like their male comrades, almost all of them saw armed struggle as the best way to defend themselves and to avenge the attacks of the Iranian regime. Narmin explains: "We were losing friends and relatives all the time, either under torture in prison or during military operations. Although every field of action had its own value, it seemed to me that the sphere of armed struggle was the only way we could be avenged on the regime that had forced us into this situation."

Nonetheless, Komala continued to resist accepting women into the armed wing. Three reasons may be identified. The first is founded in the idea of nature. As Nicole-Claude Mathieu explains: the supposed physical and mental weakness of women is seen to make them unsuitable to work in such a strongly "sexed" field.[5] Komala peshmerga women were not free of this stereotype, and indeed were regarded as weak, fragile, gentle, and sentimental. Shaho, a former armed commander of Komala, recalls: "Certainly, women were present in all areas of unarmed activity, but we still thought that fighting was far too violent for them, and they could not be involved in it. We were convinced that making war, that is to say killing and being wounded, was not a woman's business."

Reduced to being merely the negative counterpart of men, who were identified with attributes of courage and bravery, women had no autonomous identity or existence. Yet as French sociologist Sonia Dayan-Herzbrun points out, "This weakness which defines women does not prevent them from being constantly perceived as eminently dangerous. . . . Women arouse passion and desire through their fragility; if they were to occupy public offices there would be a risk that citizens, unable to resist their seductiveness, might lose their reason, leading to unmanageable disorder."[6]

Some Komala men, notwithstanding their claim to be "revolutionaries," were unable to move beyond the essentialist clichés that considered women as "the source of evil," seducing men by "trickery" and distracting them from their goals. Most peshmergas were young, single men under the age of 30; this in itself was seen as a threat to discipline. According to Amir, a former Komala peshmerga: "Many feared that the peshmerga men and women, living alongside each other, especially at night in the mountains, would be distracted from their political goals and turn to sensual pleasures instead. Putting men and women side by side was like putting a match to gunpowder."

A second reason relates to the mystical value of the armed combatant and his weapon. A peshmerga was seen as a "real man" and as such was assigned an indisputable moral value. He was regarded as a hero, ready to sacrifice his life; this semi-sacred mission was the most visible and prestigious task of the struggle. Some men were unwilling to share this prestige with "weak" and "fragile" women. There were those among both senior and ordinary peshmergas who feared that women's inclusion in the armed struggle would undermine and discredit the organization. Even worse, they believed that the presence of women might undermine the achievement of political goals and prove counterproductive. Sayran echoes the testimonies of other women who bore arms when she recalls: "If a woman took up arms, the men would immediately lay down their own to protest against this insult."

The third reason for the organization's reluctance to include women in the armed wing was its continued vulnerability to rumors about "morality," associated with being leftist or communist. While the organization had come to accept women's participation in unarmed activities, gender mixing had remained under their control, as well as that of the villagers. The entry of women into the armed wing would limit this control as armed peshmergas generally operated in mobile units, and it was feared that anything might happen between the members of a mixed group.

Mixing genders was thus seen as a potential threat to the popularity of the organization, as it would fuel rumors of immorality, especially in rural areas. Komala was dependent on the support of the local population for protection and access to food, as well as other logistical assistance, and the organization feared losing this support. As Ebrahim Alizadeh, one of Komala's former central committee members, explains, "The situation we found ourselves in led us to believe that traditional Kurdish society would never accept female peshmergas. We had internalized this view, and we concluded that our society would never accept them."[7] Women were therefore relegated to the rear base to take on the less visible tasks: organizing supply chains, cooking, caring for the wounded, and performing mourning rites for loved ones killed in action.

However, as the number of women grew, so too did their demands to join the armed wing. When they could not be incorporated any further into the unarmed branches, the support of prominent men in the organization such as Mansoor Hekmat* ultimately resulted in their integration into the armed branch in November 1982.[†] Shaho recalls:

> There was a debate among the young leaders of our organization. Half of them were against and the other half were in favor of the idea of accepting women on the battlefield. This second group emphasized the undeniable contribution of women

---

* Mansoor Hekmat (1951–2002) was an Iranian Marxist theorist who became the main theoretician of the CPI from 1983. After the first split in the organization, he founded the Worker-Communist Party of Iran in 1991.

† In addition to Komala, the People's Mojahedin Organization of Iran, with many male and female members, also began an armed struggle against government forces in 1986. After creating the National Liberation Army of Iran, it launched an armed operation called Eternal Illumination (*Foruq-i Javidan*) against government forces in 1988. According to the PMOI in 1998, 1,300 fighters were killed in this operation, see www.bbc.com/persian/iran/2016/09/160912_l44_albania_iraq_mujahedin. Accessed January 20, 2025.

during and after the revolution, and argued very forcefully that women should be allowed onto the battlefield.

THE CREATION OF BATTALIONS OF WOMEN PESHMERGAS

In November 1982, Komala set up an experimental single-sex armed group of women fighters, composed of ten Kurdish women educated to at least secondary level, so that they could read and speak in public. These women were given a mission that was political rather than military: they would go to villages in the free zones and speak publicly to villagers, while remaining under the supervision of male peshmergas. They were required to be familiar with the political contexts of Iran and Kurdistan, to be capable of explaining their points accessibly, and to answer questions, argue, and persuade in public debates. This first group, named Golriz in memory of an activist killed in a car accident shortly after the revolution, consisted of students and teachers aged between 18 and 25, both married and single.* According to one of these women, Komala had three objectives: "To explore the reactions of the villagers to the presence of these armed peshmergas, to get the internal opposition to accept the fact that women as well as men could bear arms, and to open the way for other women fighters, especially rural women."

Although the group's objectives were more political than military, the women received a month of high-level arms training from a senior Komala officer so as to be able to defend themselves in the event of an attack. However, being part of a selected group and receiving arms training was not seen as sufficient for women to qualify as full-fledged fighters: they were required to go through an additional rite of passage in order to receive the peshmerga's

* Long before the revolution, Golriz Ghobadi (1951–79) was one of the first women activists to operate clandestinely with the group that later became Komala. She tragically lost her life along with eight other comrades in a car accident just two months after the revolution on March 29, 1979, while she was part of a team of volunteers providing medical care in the northeastern Iranian town of Torkaman-e-Sahra, which had been attacked by government forces. She was the sister of activist Golrokh Ghobadi who was also a Komala activist and wrote a memoir.

Figure 7.1 The Golriz battalion—first group of armed Komala women, all of whom are alive and living in exile in Europe. *Back row, left to right:* Fouzieh Nosratpour (armed leader), Shirin Khakbaz, Mehri Godazgar, Nahid Bahmani (political leader), Nadereh Panah. *Front row, left to right:* Shahnaz Naderi, Parvin Darayi, Shahin Pishyari, Fouzieh Nosratpour, Badri Tawhidi.[8]

most sacred weapon, the gun. A ceremony was organized in a small village, Hajikand, to which the most important members of the political bureau and the highest-ranking officers, along with ordinary peshmergas and the local villagers, were invited—more than 100 guests in total.

Here political leaders delivered speeches about the importance of women's role in the revolution and the armed struggle, the main purpose of which was to contain any challenge to the new policy. A cadre of the Patriotic Union of Kurdistan in Iraq (PUK) delivered a vibrant plea for gender equality, although his own party accepted women only as activists.[9] Archival videos and photos of the ceremony show audience members holding up signs reading "Without women, no struggle is possible."[10] At the end of the proceedings, the battalion sang a song "Women in Struggle," composed by a member of the movement, celebrating the entry of women into the armed struggle: "The hour of the uprising has come; rise for the revolution, women of all countries. / Women, join the struggle alongside your male comrades."[11] Finally, the women were officially given their weapons.

Figure 7.2 The ceremony of handing over weapons to the peshmerga women[12]

The movement sent these women to villages in the Kurdish regions to propagate and spread Komala's revolutionary socialist ideas. They were, therefore, generally assigned political tasks, rather than being sent into military confrontation against government forces alongside the men. Their job was to meet with local people in villages and mosques, where they opened their speeches with their song "Women in Struggle." Their presence in mosques was highly significant in Kurdish and rural societies, as it broke the fundamental taboo against women's visibility in public and religious space. Group singing was also seen as a radical act that might offend the villagers. The speeches and debates of the Golriz battalion among the villagers are described in a report, *Political Activities and Propaganda of the Armed Women of Komala,* published on January 21, 1983, by the National Committee in Exile. Themes discussed included the socio-economic inequalities plaguing rural people, and women in particular; the brutal policies of the Islamic Republic of Iran; and global capitalist domination. These discussions and debates were intended to convince the rural population, that Komala was fighting on their behalf and that they should offer their support.

While the movement had previously been composed primarily of middle-class urban Kurds (and some non-Kurds), by this point many women from the countryside had joined the organization. Indeed, from this period on, the majority of women joining the movement came from the villages. A Komala 1986 report stated that 25 percent of new volunteers were women, 90 percent of whom came from the rural proletariat.[13]

Following the Golriz battalion's first mission, two village women joined the group. One of the women in this group—here given the pseudonym Shilan—recalls:

> From the beginning, we focused our efforts on the village women and did everything we could to establish bonds with them. At first, they were afraid to enter the mosque. It was difficult, but we managed to get them to come. This wasn't our only success, either; in the first week, two women from the village decided to join us, and of course we welcomed them with open arms.

According to the women's testimonies, most villagers responded positively to the women peshmergas. Three peshmerga members of the armed group remember as particularly respectful those villagers who not only welcomed them and provided shelter but also assisted with their political activities, provided information about government forces, and passed on necessary equipment, including weapons. Conversely, some women who later joined the armed wing describe how they were, at times, perceived as prostitutes or as women of "bad character." As Komala was a refuge for village women— fleeing intolerable family pressure and violence, escaping lives of labor in the fields, or hoping for a break from the drudgery of everyday life—some families in rural areas met the presence of Komala, and especially of Komala women, with hostility.

Three women from this single-sex group describe a feeling of having to justify their new roles to their male peers, especially by energetically engaging in debates and propaganda among rural people. Despite their efforts, some men continued to refuse to accept their presence and would humiliate and mock them in public. In the experience of these women fighters, the main obstacle to their integration into the organization was not the villagers as much as Komala members, whether ordinary soldiers or senior officers. Most of the Komala leaders who had opposed allowing women into the armed forces justified their position with reference to the supposed conservatism of the villagers, which enabled them to avoid any engagement with sexism within the organization. The experiences of the armed peshmerga women show that notwithstanding the arguments of these Komala leaders, it was Komala members themselves who verbally and mentally abused women. One of the women from the Golriz battalion—here given the pseudonym Fatima—recounts:

> In the early days, some of the more conservative members did not admit their opposition to the peshmerga women. They claimed that it was the villagers who were opposed to us and would not want us to take part in the armed struggle. It was very difficult for us to convince our comrades of the legitimacy of our presence when there were some peshmerga who did not even have any political convictions. They had only joined Komala to "pass the time," to escape unemployment and poverty in their region. Sometimes they even refused to give us access to the camp so that we could rest.

After this experimental women's battalion finished its first mission, its members wrote a letter to the central committee in which they expressly asked the leaders to accept their presence alongside men in mixed combat units. Their demand was accepted at the end of December 1982. All women who had the personal desire and the physical and mental capacity could now choose to join the armed branch alongside men in mixed units, like their counterparts in Latin America, Algeria, and Sierra Leone. As Golrokh Ghobadi writes: "It was thus that women broke another patriarchal tradition in Kurdistan."[14] Alizadeh, one of Komala's former central committee members who had initially argued against including women in the armed wing on the basis of the villagers' likely reaction, recalls: "We quickly realized that our fears were unfounded. Kurdish civilians not only understood women's participation in the armed struggle; more than that, they supported it. This is why men and women could then fight together in mixed units."[15]

Despite the delays in permitting women to join, Komala subsequently used their participation as evidence of its own progressive attitudes—a move that obscured women's struggles within the organization. Thus, Alizadeh states: "Of course, women are also present in other Kurdish movements, but Komala differs fundamentally for two reasons. Firstly, we have extensively involved women in all the Kurdish regions both in our political activities and in the armed struggle. Second, women's political and armed activities were inseparably linked to the defense of gender equality. This assertion of equality between men and women had the backing of all of our peshmerga."[16]

The pioneering presence of the ten newly armed women opened the path for others to take up arms. Roonak, who had taken part in a range of unarmed activities, recalls: "Once the first group of women had taken up arms, it was possible for all women to do so. This did not mean we abandoned our other activities. For my part, I carried on with the tasks I had before alongside my armed missions, such as surveying the terrain."

Meanwhile part of the education and training of all new peshmergas was devoted to "women's issues and full equal rights," and the official discourse of the organization encouraged women to join by promising them equality.[17] A 1986 Komala publication summarizes its official position:

> The liberation of the working class is not achievable without the liberation of women. It is futile to talk about democracy and solidarity with the working masses without fighting for the liberation of women. The Komala Party will work for greater equality between men and women, aiming to transform mentalities on the essential question of patriarchy, which undermines society. For this reason, Komala encourages women activists to take up arms and join the ranks of the peshmerga. The

> oppressed women of Kurdistan will find in Komala the opportunity to claim their freedom, as well as answers to any theoretical questions they might have within the ideological framework of the party.[18]

With the entry of women into the armed branch, Komala became the first Kurdish political organization (in Iran, Iraq, Syria, and Turkey) that was prepared to arm women as fighters, although it continued to differentially identify armed combat as a duty for men and a right for women. With the exception of Margaret George Shello (1941–69), who joined the ranks of male fighters in Iraqi Kurdistan, women in the Kurdish collective imagination had previously played a narrow role, always mourning, suffering, or sacrificing their sons for the Kurdish cause. By taking up arms they were able to overturn this essentialist image, and it was the peshmerga women of Komala who were the agents of this change.

WOMEN WITH GUNS: BETWEEN DENIAL AND ADMISSION

While the number of women in the armed wing gradually increased, their participation in combat remained relatively low; out of the ten women fighters in the first group, only two decided to remain in armed struggle. There are no precise statistics on the number of women and men in the armed branch. One list records 110 women killed during the 1980s, of whom only 48 were killed on the battlefield (28 fighting government forces and 20 fighting Kurdish rivals in the KDPI),[19] while more than 1,500 men are estimated to have died during this period, primarily in the course of armed struggle.* Women thus appeared on the battlefields in much smaller numbers than men.

A major factor discouraging both women and men was the harshness of the war: fighters faced the probability of a violent death, the failure of military actions, problems with supply chains, and war against both government forces and the KDPI. This intra-Kurdish

* An unpublished list of Komala casualties sent to me by a former member included the names of nearly 1,500 men killed.

conflict had a particularly demoralizing effect and led to peshmergas leaving the ranks of both forces. The Iran–Iraq war further complicated the situation. Among those who had been unable to flee and had run out of ammunition, many surrendered to the Iranian army or died of exhaustion, hunger, disease, or injury. The losses were very high. The end of the 1980s was a period of great change for Komala, with a drastic and continuing reduction in its troops. According to a former peshmerga, "In the spring of 1987, Komala had no more than 40 or 50 people in its ranks, whereas a few years earlier it had been at the head of a mini army."[20]

The difficulty and danger of the terrain contributed to the low morale of women. Mahin remembers:

> We were often forced to walk for hours on end, suffering from hunger, thirst, and lack of sleep. Sometimes we had to fight several times in one day, either against the government forces or against the KDPI. Most of us found these situations intolerable, regardless of gender. This eventually led many fighters to surrender to the regime forces.

The testimonies suggest that women were often reluctant to fight or chose not to continue. Although for the most part they regarded the armed conflict as legitimate resistance, these women rejected violence and refused to cause bloodshed. Shirin and Nashmin are notable examples. While Nashmin refers simply to her fear of fighting and violence, Shirin invokes her pacifism—she could not reconcile the reality of war with her humanist convictions. This pacifism was linked to an understanding of social reproduction and life in general that was ideologically distanced from the armed struggle, one that remained deeply rooted even when the clashes between Komala and its many opponents were at a critical stage. Although Shirin had dreamt of becoming a peshmerga from a very early age, she realized that the role of a fighter did not suit her. In fact, she hated it:

> Although I considered Komala's participation in the armed struggle against the Islamic Republic to be legitimate, I did not like the idea of using weapons myself. In my view, supporting

Komala's goals was not limited to taking up arms. I would have preferred to contribute to their cause without having to carry a weapon.

Women also refer to paternalistic, contemptuous, humiliating, and sometimes insulting treatment by some of the men. This sexist behavior was more evident in the early days of women's admission to the armed branch, before gradually lessening. Serveh remembers the numerous difficulties she suffered, in particular at the hands of one commander who refused to accept her into his unit because he could not conceive of a woman in any role other than that of wife and mother. A recurring problem, cited by many women peshmergas following their arrival in the battlefield, was the gendered distribution of weapons. Several of them—including Sayran, Serveh, and Mahine—relate that women were given the heaviest weapons, such as the G-3, while the men were armed with light weapons, particularly the Kalashnikov.*

Not all men were willing to accept that their behavior toward women reflected a sexist outlook; some claimed that the inequality in weapon allocations was caused by the general shortage of equipment and women's lack of experience in handling arms. Nevertheless, a former peshmerga in his memoir explains men's attitudes toward their female comrades as the result of women's inexperience, but also sees that they are evidence of male opposition to change: "Men carried Kalashnikovs, and women, though they were less experienced, carried heavier weapons which were called G-3s. If a woman ever picked up a Kalashnikov, the men would immediately protest."[21] Even in the mid-1980s, when the supply situation of the organization improved and there were enough Kalashnikovs to equip women as well, sexual discrimination continued to determine access to the peshmergas' preferred

* The G-3 rifle is renowned for its great reliability, but it is heavy and cumbersome, over a meter long, and weighing more than 5 kg when loaded with powerful ammunition. Kalashnikovs, automatic rifles that were developed by the German army in 1942 during the Second World War, are generally considered to be the first modern assault rifle. These weapons rarely jam and are resistant to water, sand, and dampness—hence their popularity with guerrillas and members of revolutionary armed groups fighting in deserts, forests, and other hostile terrains.

weapon.[22] Another female fighter, Zara, explains: "Although the shortage of Kalashnikovs was no longer an issue, some people still thought that since women were not involved in major operations anyway, there was no reason to let them carry Kalashnikovs."

Women describe how the men undervalued them and had little confidence in their abilities. Zara testifies: "Some men considered the mere fact of marching alongside women as an affront to their manhood." At times men would offer false excuses, claiming that women tired too quickly or that it was not "appropriate" for a woman to do a certain thing, so as to exclude them from the most important operations. And even when women had the "right" to participate, they were rarely on the front lines. Serveh recalls: "Some of the commanders were very reluctant to send us to the front lines or to include us in ambush operations. In all my years in the armed branch, I only took part in two major actions. They only gave us support roles, with the men on the front lines."

Some armed commanders cited the fear of rape as a reason for keeping women away from the front lines. In addition to rape in prison by government forces, KDPI forces were rumored to rape captured Komala women. However, this principle of systematic exclusion from major operations applied only to operations that were planned in advance. When groups found themselves trapped or ambushed by the Iranian army or KDPI forces, both men and women took part in operations. It was probably in situations such as these that 20 women died in battle against the KDPI.

The transformation of women into peshmergas in the armed struggle was not a consequence of the egalitarian discourse propagated by the organization. Rather, it was linked to the reality of women's daily interactions with men during combat, in which they proved their courage and competence. There was ultimately no way to compel these determined women to give up. As long as Komala was able to continue its operations, women not only remained in the field, weapons in hand, but also succeeded in winning respect and recognition for their determination. These women readily acknowledge that their presence at the front did not change the final outcome of the war: defeat at the hands of the Iranian army and a forced retreat to Iraqi Kurdistan. Nonetheless, their efforts were not in vain. They succeeded in demonstrating that women had a legitimate place in the armed struggle and that they were capable of waging war on the same level as men. As Jaleh explains:

> Despite the challenges, women showed great courage. Men began to respect us when they saw that we were capable of sacrifice, that we could provide additional support or even save a man's life. They finally recognized that women put their hearts into their work and were not afraid to go into battle, even in situations where the most battle-hardened of men might retreat. They gradually began to see us as equals.

Shaho similarly recalls: "Resistance to the presence of women gradually decreased, and although they faced constant pressure, the women managed to show what they were capable of. They became accepted and appreciated as full-fledged peshmergas in the armed struggle, as well as in the villages in contact with the people."

The public visibility that resulted from women's involvement in armed struggle also had an impact on the development of Kurdish literature. Literature and poetry at the time, domains dominated by men, celebrated the "ideal" women who joined the organization's ranks driven by the spirit of revolution and the desire to bring the working class to power. Their struggle to liberate themselves was seen as also showing the path to liberation for all women. "The Peshmerga Young Woman," a poem translated into Kurdish by J. Rebwar in 1989, praised Peshmerga women as far superior to princesses, nobles, or the wealthy and elegant women of the bourgeoisie.[23] In Komala publications, the women represented as particularly worthy of respect were those who joined the fight for the unity of the workers of the world, with the aim of emancipating themselves along with others.*

Kurdish poems paying tribute to women killed in battle reiterate this new version of femininity. If women's physical beauty had previously been the sole source of inspiration for poets, their presence in the armed branch provided new ones. Poets portrayed

* The play *Yaxi le Sitem* (Revolt Against Oppression) depicts a group of women workers in a weaving mill. After enduring years of exploitation in the factory, hard work for low wages, constant bullying within the family, and forced marriages, they suddenly decide to leave this life of misery and join the ranks of the peshmerga. *Peshang*, no. 2 (1986): 29–41.

the women fighters of Komala in a laudatory light, extolling their courage and strength of character. A poem by Ahmad Bazgar testifies to this change:

> Before you appeared, women of the trenches,
> I had eyes only for the beauty of your necklaces
> My poems described only the perfume of cloves on your skin
> and the powder on your faces
> Then suddenly you appeared
> You women of the trenches, like sparks of fire
> Since that day, the women of my poems appear with guns on
> their shoulders.[24]

In order to better grasp how certain women became involved in armed struggle regardless of formidable challenges, let us now consider the narrative of Zara, an illiterate village woman who took up arms. A mother of young small children, she defied gender stereotypes by entrusting their care to various families so that she could fight. Throughout her journey, from the moment she joined Komala until her departure from Iraqi Kurdistan for Sweden, she showed steadfast commitment. Zara's life story is unique, while also reflecting the broader conditions that led women to become politicized and join Komala.

Portrait of Zara, Peshmerga of the Armed Wing

Zara was born in 1957 into a modest village family. She married at the age of 13 without ever having attended school and had five children. When one of her sisters died in childbirth, everyone said it was God's will, but the doctor told her that on the contrary, it was a social injustice. In this way, she came to learn about Marxist ideas from the village doctor. This political awareness was reinforced shortly before the 1979 Revolution, when Marxist activists came to try to help the poorest villagers and to share their way of life.

When Komala emerged a few days after the victory of the revolution, Zara and her husband were drawn to this new Kurdish organization of Maoist tendency. With the encouragement of her comrades, she ran for the municipal elections in her village and won most of the votes. After the outbreak of the armed struggle in May 1980, as militants retreated from urban to rural and mountainous areas, Zara learned more about Komala. She officially joined in 1982, when women were joining the movement as peshmergas to participate in the armed struggle. Zara was one of the first to do so. To enable this, she split her five children, aged one to eight, among three households in safety away from the battlefield.

Her courage and determination were well known by her comrades and her region. She recalls the difficulties the fighting entailed:

> Engaging in the armed struggle at that time was not so easy. In addition to facing the government forces, which were more numerous and better equipped than us, we also had to face the armed forces of the KDPI. On a number of occasions, in the course of a single day, we had to take part in two or three operations. When we had spent several days preparing to attack a center of government forces, an operation that could take more than four or five hours, it might happen that on our return, regardless of the results of our mission and the condition we were in (tiredness, hunger, thirst, lack of equipment), we would also face the armed forces of the KDPI. These fights could be more dangerous than the first ones, because they happened suddenly, without us having had time to prepare for them, and they sometimes lasted several hours.

The rest periods, as she describes them, were not pleasant either. Most of the time, far from Komala bases, peshmergas were forced to rely on villagers as their first and last popular base. In addition to the poverty of most villagers, their political orientation (pro Komala, pro-KDPI, or pro-government) could change the situation: "We usually went to the villagers' houses in the late evening, when there was almost nothing to eat, but it was better than nothing. And even worse, if the families were against Komala, they might give us a hard time."

According to Zara, the role of the peshmerga was not limited to armed struggle. She explains, "We also carried out Komala's propaganda, distributing its publications and magazines, and when necessary, helping villagers with business affairs, such as litigation. Peshmergas, especially women, played an important role in cases of domestic violence, forced marriage, and similar issues."

In the early 1990s, when Komala was both militarily and politically defeated, Zara's husband was killed by government forces. She managed to get all her children back and went into exile in Sweden in 1994. Since then she has worked as a caregiver. She is no longer a member of any of the branches of the now-divided organization.

8

Bodily Discipline and the Peshmerga

Following the admission of women and the formation of mixed units, peshmergas of both sexes lived in close and constant contact. They shared the same places of relaxation in the homes of villagers and mosques, and at Komala headquarters, located in rural areas or in camps in Iraqi Kurdistan, and they would encounter each other at the canteen, during work, and at meetings. In order not to offend the sensibilities of the villagers, Komala sought to reduce the visibility and the potential problems associated with this mixing of the sexes, particularly in a time of war, when discipline was a priority more than ever. The organization thus developed a set of regulations "to discipline the fighters, to make them true professional revolutionaries driven by a single political objective."[1] As Luca Greco points out, "while the body does have a materiality, it is historically, socially and ideologically constructed by a set of regulatory practices that make the body 'docile,' at the service of an ideology of power and a historically situated anatomical model."[2]

Whatever their gender and field of activity (armed or unarmed), Komala peshmergas were required to discipline the body in various ways; for example, the consumption of alcohol was prohibited, as were sexual relations outside marriage. There were no written regulations on how this discipline was to be applied, and because of the geographical dispersal of the organization, the rules were implemented with varying strictness from one commander to another and from one area to another. Those who did not respect this discipline might be verbally reprimanded or, in more serious cases, disarmed for a few days to a week.

Before addressing the thorny issue of the restrictions imposed on the peshmerga, two points should be made. First, this type of prohibition is not unique to Komala. As Eric Hobsbawm notes, for revolutionaries "personal libertinism is a nuisance,"[3] and indeed most militantism can be said to exemplify this point. Every socio-political movement, regardless of its ideology and the socio cultural context in which it is embedded, imposes disciplinary order on its members. Komala was no exception, especially when its field of activity shifted from the urban environment to armed struggle in rural areas, which were seen to be more "conservative."

Second, following the settlement of most of the peshmergas in camps in Iraqi Kurdistan at a distance from rural centers toward the end of the 1980s, the severity of body discipline for women gradually diminished, although it did not disappear by any means. Several interviewees, such as Sayran, Marjan, and Jaleh, assert that the restrictions became more relaxed when they moved to the camp. Marjan says:

> After several years of men and women living together, most peshmergas moved into camps, and no longer living among villagers, the discipline and the daily restrictions were no longer the same as before. Even in the late 1980s, the political and armed defeat of the organization enabled peshmergas to discuss and share ideas together more than ever. In the course of these debates some people were strongly critical of the disciplinary orders, and a few even asserted the need for free sexual relations among the peshmerga.

SUBMISSION TO THE DISCIPLINARY ORDER OF THE BODY

Requiring peshmergas of both sexes to submit to disciplinary regulation was one way to reduce or at least control the risks entailed by mixing. In Komala, as with the Tamil Tigers (Liberation Tigers of Tamil Eelam) in Sri Lanka, prejudices about the "dangerous" sexuality of women and the risks of "pollution" for armed revolutionaries were still very much alive.[4] Leaders and commanders could communicate disciplinary orders verbally, directly or indirectly, to peshmergas at any time, and indeed peshmergas circulated them among themselves, whatever their sex. In a revolutionary context where most Iranian Marxists criticized the values of the capitalist system for encouraging the extravagant habits of the middle and upper classes, a simple lifestyle that avoided consumerism was valorized. For Komala, engaged in armed struggle in rural areas, this kind of discipline seemed all the more necessary. Strictness in behavior, austere clothing, self-discipline, and self-denial were thus encouraged and broadly respected. Similarly, the pursuit of personal interests and rights or individual pleasures, such as drinking alcohol, was rejected as "non-revolutionary" and "non-communist."[5] As a former Komala activist recalls in his memoir, "When I was 17 years old, I was friendly with a peshmerga woman. Although we only talked about politics, our relationship was interpreted by others as irregular, even amoral. As a result, we spent a week being interrogated by our commander."[6]

According to most interviewees, while bodily discipline affected all peshmergas, it weighed more heavily on women. Nonetheless, women were not subjected to discipline equally. On top of the organizational directives, peshmergas also took it upon themselves to monitor the behavior of their comrades, especially that of single women; this was one of the main reasons that many women peshmerga were keen to get married. It was with this context in mind that Hammed Shahidian, an Iranian historian and Marxist activist, writes:

> Before 1981 activists lived either with their own families in individual houses, or in what we called "team houses." Contact with others was very limited and the activists were far from the supervision of others. In Kurdistan or Baluchistan, however, living in organizational bases turned everyone's life into an open book. This communal living, combined with the pressure of "local customs," put a great deal of pressure on women.[7]

Although married women continued to face restrictions, the women interviewees describe the control and surveillance of single women as much more significant. Given their economic, political, and symbolic inferiority within the structure of social relations, their bodies became tools to be controlled by men and directed toward service to others.

Other factors might alter the severity of everyday constraints, such as socio-economic status, family background, or preexisting friendships. Those with a spouse or brother higher up in the organization's hierarchy, or with links to old comrades, might be less severely affected by the disciplinary orders. This was also the case for the non-Kurdish members of the small Union of Communist Fighters (UCF).* Since the main work of these activists, whatever their sex, was focused on theoretical issues through writing and publishing, the few women among them had little contact with the peshmergas and the villagers. They were therefore largely exempt from the orders concerning bodily discipline imposed either by the leadership or other peshmerga. Thus in 1981, when women were required upon admission as peshmergas to wear headscarves regardless of their field of activity (armed or unarmed), the women of the UCF resisted.

Among the interviewees, seven Kurdish women from urban backgrounds and whose families were relatively prominent in the region, recall that regardless of their marital status, they were more intensively subjected to the pressure of disciplinary orders than other women. Within a revolutionary organization that valorized the values of the oppressed and disadvantaged, coming from a privileged family background could be problematic. While village women and women from poor families were applauded, those from the upper social class, especially educated urban women, were liable to be seen as upholding bourgeois or capitalist values despite themselves. Some dealt with this by making themselves more compliant with the disciplinary rules than others in order to present themselves as true revolutionaries. As Roonak narrates:

> In our region, where I became a peshmerga, the situation of village women was better than ours, because in line with the ideology of the organization, there was a great respect for the underprivileged. Privileged women were regarded as bour-

* The Union of Communist Fighters, which co-founded the Communist Party of Iran with Komala in 1983, had fewer than 30 members, and fewer than ten were women.

> geois, and were more closely monitored than the village women. In addition, some of us [city women] came from well-known families in the area, like me, and because of this we were more closely watched than others by those around us. Even our most insignificant daily activities were put under the microscope. Although I always tried to put myself at the service of our organization, I often overheard my comrades talking about my past and bringing up my father and his wealth, casting doubt on my loyalty and political conviction. So I tried to obey all the disciplinary orders of the organization, written and unwritten. I observed them more carefully than others, and I would take compliance even further in order to counter their assumptions about my family and me. At the same time, I didn't want my family to hear anything bad about me. The slightest misstep on my part could lead to criticism.

As many interviewees note (26 out of 46), whereas in civilian life women's daily behavior had been primarily controlled by their male relatives, in this context their male comrades took on the role, as the moral guardians of the organization. If the honor of the male members of the family had depended on the sexuality of its women, it followed that now the honor of the entire organization, from the highest- to the lowest-ranking peshmerga, was at stake. According to Ebrahim Alizadeh: "Although our male peshmergas were familiar with Marxist and socialist doctrines, their machismo had by no means completely disappeared. So it was not uncommon to see peshmergas monitoring their female comrades and trying to dominate them."[8] This promoted self-esteem in men and feelings of inferiority in women, as the Iranian sociologist Haideh Moghissi observes.[9] Disciplinary control was concerned not only with women's sexual life but also with the way they dressed, spoke, walked, and laughed. Far more than men, women were required to respect social norms of being modest, demure, and chaste. In other words, they had to stay within the framework of the prevailing patriarchal norms that defined femininity.

Unlike many Marxist-oriented Iranian political groupings, Komala had supported women's protests against the government's introduction of compulsory veiling, but once it accepted women activists into its ranks, it required them to wear a headscarf similar to that worn by Palestinian women activists in the 1960s and 1970s. In other words, the Komala leadership, which criticized the patriarchal policies of the Islamic Republic of Iran, imposed the headscarf on its female members, with the justification that villagers were conservative. Alizadeh said of the veil: "It was a real problem for us. Would the traditionalist villagers accept the sight of women with guns on their shoulders and bare heads? We thought not, so we took the decision to impose the veil."[10] Even though men also frequently covered their heads with Kurdish hats, the imposition of the veil within the organization demonstrated a gender difference: men were free to choose whether to wear the hat in public, but women generally could not choose to appear unveiled. Women who refused to wear the veil were often harassed and called to order by men. The compulsory wearing of the veil did not last long, however, due to constant criticism from peshmergas within the organization, and especially from the women themselves. As part of this shift in approach, articles criticizing the regime's policy of mandating the hijab were published. One such article published in 1987, states, "Under the guise of fighting against inadequately veiled women and Western culture, the Islamic Republic's regime is in fact attacking the tranquility, lifestyle, leisure and peaceful values of its people, thereby halting their march toward progress and condemning them to eternal poverty and isolation from the world."[11]

Women were also required not to deviate from the prevalent gendered norms of bodily propriety; they were to avoid any movements and gestures that were considered vulgar. Narmin observes: "The men could see that we were working as hard as they were and that, logically, we were getting as tired as they were. However, they couldn't stand it when we stretched out our legs to rest, or lit a cigarette to relax. They didn't hesitate to comment on it."

The pressure exerted by some male comrades—in tandem with socialization that had compelled women since childhood to maintain tight control over their bodily comportment and daily behavior—drove some women to go beyond the organization's disciplinary order in their self-regulation. Under this dual pressure, some women went so far as to ask permission from a male superior before doing anything potentially contentious. Shaho comments: "Some women felt themselves to be under such constant surveillance that they would come to me for advice, whether before lighting a cigarette or starting a relationship. They felt that without confirmation from a leader in the movement, they could not take the risk."

Not only were women under surveillance by men; they also monitored themselves and each other. Smoking, talking, laughing too loudly, socializing with men outside the militant framework, and stretching one's legs could all be considered subversive acts that departed from revolutionary ideals. Miriam recalls:

> We were extremely careful not to appear vulgar or immoral, not to talk or joke too much with our male comrades. We monitored our laughter, our gait, and our movements, like when we bent down to pick up an object on the ground. Although we were always dressed in masculine clothing that was absolutely not attractive, we were careful not to let any part of our bodies show.

In her memoir, Diana Nammi describes the policing on the part of women when she participated in a theoretical training of the organization. She writes: "I grew up in a family where boys and girls were free to talk and laugh with each other, so it was normal to talk with boys in the classroom like this. However, one day the wife of a Central Committee member came to the class and saw me laughing with the men. She went back to the Central Committee and interrupted a meeting to say to Azad [Diana's fiancé] in front of the other members that I was shameless. 'Comrade, you love this woman and she is laughing with those men.'"[12]

Many women developed strategies to minimize body shame and stigma. When they needed to use the toilet, they made great efforts to ensure that men did not notice, for example. The situation was particularly difficult for women fighters because they were such a small minority, when there were only two or three women serving alongside 40 men. Women made detours to relieve themselves at a distance from the gaze of men, and when this was not possible, especially during offensives, they might relieve themselves in their clothing so as not to risk exposing their bodies. For the most part, men were unable or unwilling to recognize the social aspect underlying this privacy taboo. One armed commander, for instance, writes in his memoir, "Women had a much harder time than we did in armed operations. We men had no trouble leaving the line temporarily to relieve ourselves. But the women couldn't do so, because of their bodies."[13]

Moreover, the consequences of transgressing body discipline were not the same for the two sexes. In his memoir, one peshmerga recalled a comrade who had an affair with a village girl. He was neither punished nor even questioned by the organization.[14] While clearly some women did secretly transgress the codes of bodily discipline, especially through sexual relations, if they were discovered, the price of transgression was very high, and they faced both stigma and disciplinary sanctions for "sexual laxity."

We should mention here the case of a peshmerga woman who became pregnant as a result of sex outside marriage. Although she was not put to death, as traditional social mores might have dictated, she was under such pressure from her comrades—both men and women—that she killed herself. After her death, she was given a perfunctory burial with no ceremony, and according to Sohaila, a former Komala peshmerga, only eight women had the courage to attend her funeral. The name of this fighter was never mentioned on the organization's radio as the names of martyrs usually were, but her name, Chiman Zamani, now appears among the list of "martyrs" of the organization, where the cause of death is discreetly described as a "horrible incident."[15] As Monireh recalls: "Back then, most of us considered this woman's suicide as normal, because sex outside marriage was seen as very shocking."

THE MASCULINIZATION OF WOMEN: A CONDITION FOR POLITICIZATION

When women joined Komala as peshmerga, even before they were allowed to bear arms, they were required to adapt to the norms and standards expected of men. In practice, this meant taking on characteristics attributed to men—in other words, masculinizing themselves, both externally and internally. There were three areas in particular that these pressures manifested: physical clothing and appearance, the question of physical strength, and menstruation and pregnancy.

First, the masculinization of women's bodies related to their clothing and appearance. At the arming ceremony of the Golriz batallion, the women had to wear men's clothes, which became the everyday attire of women fighters. When asked why they had dressed like the men, several respond that it had not been imposed on them, and that traditional Kurdish women's outfits were made up of long and sometimes loose dresses in which movement was difficult, while men's clothing was more comfortable and convenient. Solmaz, a former non-Kurdish activist, confirms this point: "We chose to wear the same outfits as the Kurdish men for practical reasons, especially in the mountainous areas." Sayran similarly states: "Doing our work in women's dress was very difficult, if not impossible. So, it was decided that women would wear the same clothes as men."

While this focus on the convenience of wearing men's clothing is generally credible, it has a further dimension that is well captured in Miriam's account:

> Whenever I wore men's clothing, I felt very proud and honored. Being a peshmerga meant denying everything that was considered feminine. The further you moved away from your femininity, the more you were recognized as a revolutionary. Some of us became so absorbed in our role that we almost forgot our femininity. From the outset I understood that if I wanted to take up arms, I had to become a man. I was convinced that being a woman would be a handicap in combat; I believed that only men could fight. I said to myself that if I wanted to take part in the armed struggle, I had to behave like a man, a real man.

Second, women sought to be strong and to appear physically powerful, even beyond their actual capacities, to be courageous, fearless, and daring, and to face danger while concealing fatigue, hunger, and thirst. As Alizadeh comments in his memoir: "Women had to make twice as much effort and show twice as much self-sacrifice to win respect."[16] To prove their strength and courage, they took on the same work as men, and at times even more challenging tasks. Asrine remembers that she and her female comrades continually had to hide their emotions and appear tough:

> If the men carried two bags on their backs, I carried three. I knew they were too heavy for me, but I had to do it so as to get the men, who were always making fun of us, to shut up for a while. No matter how hard it was for me, I made myself take part in the major ambush operations. During our long marches in the mountains, I and my women comrades had a trick to stop the men from noticing our exhaustion. It was perfectly natural to be out of breath in those circumstances, but we had nothing to gain by complaining even once; we would immediately be labeled as weak women. We responded to their scorn by voluntarily putting ourselves in danger to show that we were brave.

Aware that men's and women's physical fatigue would be differently interpreted, women developed strategies to get around this differential treatment. After walking for hours, men's exhaustion was attributed to the steepness of the mountain, the cold, or the weight of the loads; women's exhaustion was attributed to their "feminine" nature and their supposed weakness. Thus, for men, weariness was understood in relation to external factors, whereas for women the cause was assumed to be internal. Peshmerga women from the villages, accustomed to the harsh living conditions of rural areas, found it easier to adapt to armed struggle than urban women, and they were more successful in acquiring the "masculine" skills needed for armed struggle, while women from urban areas generally suffered more. Zara recounts: "Having grown up in the harsh conditions of a small village, physically I was one of the strongest women in the organization. My capability was always admired by both men and women comrades, and my comrades from the town would often wish they were like me, and regretted not being as strong."

Women believed that if they managed to conceal their weaknesses and appear strong, it would not only protect them from the scorn of the men, but that in the long run, it would help all peshmerga women earn legitimacy. As Golrokh Ghobadi writes: "I tried never to grumble about anything or anyone. I had to prove not only that I was able to cope with every challenge, but also that sometimes I could do better than the men. It was a very difficult situation. Any sign of weakness in me might be interpreted as a sign of the weakness of all women."[17]

Third, women generally tried to conceal anything related to the female body, such as menstruation or pregnancy. Pregnancy in this context made visible what was supposed to remain hidden. Sexuality was meant to be confined within the intimate relationship of the married couple; the transformed bodies of pregnant women displayed their sexuality in the public domain, shattering conventional norms of secrecy. Menstruation was also perceived as an "illness," representing the impurity of women, their physical weakness, and their fundamental inferiority. "Compared to us men," writes Mohammad Jafari, a former armed commander of Komala, in his memoir, "women face certain limitations in the armed struggle. This is because of their lower metabolism, their monthly 'illness,' the fact that they can get pregnant, and in general their inferior physical strength."[18] Women therefore did whatever they could to hide the signs of menstruation or of pregnancy to minimize the risks of being discredited or shamed.

As a result, women did not even dare to use the term "sanitary pad", and the supply lists sent to Komala did not cater for menstruation. They sorted out for themselves how to get hold of sanitary protection, usually cloth, which they used discreetly. They were also unable to take time off if they had painful periods. By the mid-1980s, the topic was officially addressed in the organization, but nonetheless some women continued to hide their periods. Nasrin recalls:

> For a very long time, our organization paid no attention to this particular issue. However, eventually the leadership came to acknowledge that women might be indisposed, and they proposed to give us two to three days off per month. Unfortunately, this exposed us to the mockery and contempt of our male comrades. As far as I was concerned, I would do anything I could to carry on with my normal activities even when I was menstruating and in great pain.

Figure 8.1 Golrokh Ghobadi (far right) with her friends and husband[19]

THE RESPONSE OF PESHMERGA TO THE DISCIPLINING OF THE BODY

Women responded in two ways to the unwritten laws that sought to control women's bodies and their sexuality: acceptance or defiance. The first was to accept the bodily discipline imposed directly or indirectly by Komala, be it by high-ranking leaders or ordinary peshmergas. They were not necessarily uncritical on the subject, but they rarely expressed disagreement publicly. Alongside their conviction that all socio-economic problems, especially the status of women, would necessarily be resolved by the establishment of a socialist regime, women gave various other reasons for complying with these disciplinary orders.

Peshmergas were fearful of gossip, given the commonly held stereotypes of Marxists as amoral and sexually promiscuous. The KDPI, Komala's Kurdish political rival, which was also engaging in armed struggle against government forces in rural areas, capitalized on these views to spread derogatory rumors about Komala's forces, particularly its women. A former KDPI peshmerga admitted: "For the KDPI forces, spotting the presence of a bloodstained sanitary napkin was all it took for them to vilify the mixing and supposed immorality of Komala members and nickname their HQ 'the walking brothel.'"[20] The Komala leadership responded by tightening control and insisting that the behavior of its peshmergas, especially women, should be irreproachable. Akbar, a former Komala peshmerga, asserts that fear of the rumors spread by the KDPI, as well as of offending the villagers, lay behind the tightening of restrictions, and that most peshmergas, including women, made no protest. Nor was the abnormal situation of war a time to complain; in the words of one armed Komala commander, "there was nothing to eat but bread and [armed] conflict."[21] Nasrin explains:

> It was war. A brutal and unequal war. Our comrades were sacrificing themselves and dying. Almost every day more people were martyred. Under such circumstances, how could we dare to complain that we were being bullied as women? We took it without complaining—it was the only thing to do.

Finally, women were keen to prove to their male peers that their motives for joining the struggle were indeed political, and that contrary to the stereotypes shared by some of their commanders and comrades, they were not there to find a husband or partner. Fear of being judged by others, in a context in which women's participation was subject to delegitimization, made them even tougher on themselves. Miriam testifies:

> I imposed a very strict discipline on myself, because I was terrified that others would judge me. The idea that people would think I was there for something other than purely political reasons panicked me. I went overboard, so to speak, to prove to everyone that I was a political activist with unwavering convictions and that nothing else was driving me. I had totally put aside my life as a woman who might have feelings or desires.

In contrast to the women who complied or preferred to remain silent regarding the disciplining of the body, a few made no attempt to conceal transgressions of the disciplinary rules by themselves or their comrades, whether flagrant or discreet. Many women disliked the compulsory wearing of headscarves, for example. The few non-Kurdish women close to the central committee had always refused it, and women from across Komala contested the headscarf from the outset. Jaleh protested repeatedly and took every opportunity to challenge the organization's leaders. When they replied that they were only conforming to the expectations of conservative villagers, she recalls that she retorted:

> This is totally false. It is not the villagers who are conservative and expect us to be veiled. It is your opinion, the men of the movement, and yours alone. The villagers have already seen me without a headscarf, before the revolution, and even in a mini-skirt, and they never objected. You are the conservatives. You can call yourselves revolutionaries all you want; you have an archaic mentality.

Similarly, the prohibition of sexual relations outside marriage, according to oral testimonies from within Komala, was not always observed. Shahla states:

> When we spent a few weeks in an armed unit, it wasn't really surprising to see or hear things about people. For example, if a man left the ranks for a few hours, we guessed that he had gone to see his lover somewhere in a nearby village. Some women also had this kind of relationship, even those who were married. However, we tried not to talk about it publicly. We acted as if nothing had happened, especially if they were our friends.

Some women came to feel increasingly comfortable in daily life, as they smoked, relaxed, and chatted with their male comrades. Over the course of weeks spent sharing challenges and taking part in joint operations, men and women got to know each other better and established friendly relationships. Women fighters, upon entering the armed branch, were faced with obstacles and experienced more challenges than other female activists, their presence increasingly putting the idea of bodily discipline into question. In contrast to the gendered stereotype of women's frailty, these women not only proved themselves as fighters, they also normalized behaviors that had been permitted only to men: smoking, lying on the ground, laughing, or even proposing marriage. Shilan recalls:

> Being together for a long time in an armed unit created close and friendly relationships between the fighters, regardless of sex. I was close friends with two of the male comrades in our unit. I did not hide anything from them. I even told them that I had fallen in love with our unit commander, who was well known for his determination and courage. I asked them if they thought I could tell my superior that I loved him. Their answer was no, because declaring love and proposing marriage was basically a male prerogative at the time. But although I had respect for my friends, I had even more respect for my feelings. Against all expectation, the commander welcomed my proposal, and accepted it without hesitation.

Fatima also reports:

> After many hours of marching in the mountains and constant military operations, the women fighters generally couldn't even lie down and rest in the presence of the men, who were much more numerous. However, little by little this changed, because we women couldn't go on like that. We needed to rest like the men; and we smoked, we laughed and we lay down as they did.

Women fighters from the villages played a particularly important role in challenging some of these disciplinary orders according to the interviewees. Their rural upbringing meant that they were used to doing not only their household tasks but also agricultural work alongside men, so they were more at ease around men than were urban women. Furthermore, one of the main reasons rural women joined Komala was that they saw the organization as firmly opposed to any restrictions on women. Thus, when they were confronted with bodily discipline regarding smoking, laughing, or expressing feelings of love, they challenged it, demanding to know why an organization known for its commitment to women's rights would impose such restrictions on them. Finally, the organization's particular respect for rural and working women gave them more room to maneuver. Mahrokh says:

> Before I joined Komala I had heard a lot about the organization's efforts to support women's rights. But as soon as I joined I realized that there were still restrictions, especially for women. I didn't want to put up with those kinds of obstacles any more. For example, one time after several operations, we were very dirty and tired, and we happened to arrive at a lake. The men immediately started to bathe, but the women fighters just watched them. This was really unbearable for me, as I'd always bathed in the river in our village; so although no one was expecting it, I suddenly jumped into the lake and swam. This action created a contradictory atmosphere of reproach and admiration. But it didn't matter to me. Any kind of break with tradition comes with a cost, and I was happy about it. Even though swimming didn't become normal for everyone, we were at any rate more comfortable than before around other restrictions like smoking or laughing.

9
Family Life Within the Organization

Komala permitted its members to establish a family unit and have children within the framework of marriage. In this respect, Komala differed from the Turkey-based Kurdistan Workers' Party (PKK), founded in 1978, that officially banned its members from mixing private and political life.* However like members of most militant organizations (such as those in El Salvador, Peru, Algeria, and Palestine), Komala's peshmergas found that their private and family lives complicated their political lives, and in the aftermath of the 1979 Revolution, most activists frowned on marriage. Komala never formally prohibited marriage but regarded it as likely to distract activists from their revolutionary and political tasks. When women came to be accepted as full members of Komala, this changed the calculus, and marriage between peshmergas became widespread. Single peshmergas of marriageable age considered starting their own families as marriage and parenthood were no longer considered "anti-revolutionary." Even the most revolutionary young leaders of Komala, who had previously been committed to their single status as a mark of their devotion to the cause, began to marry.

THE HALF-REVOLUTIONARY, HALF-TRADITIONAL MARRIAGE

Once women entered the ranks of Komala, meaning that young peshmergas had to live alongside one another in mixed settings,

* The rationale for the four-decade ban was that men had not yet broken free from patriarchal norms and would thus struggle to avoid reproducing a relationship of dominance in their relationships. Additionally, having a special relationship could put other fighters at risk. See Olivier Grojean, "Théorie et construction des rapports de genre dans la guérilla kurde de Turquie" (Theory and Construction of Gender Relations in the Kurdish Guerrillas of Türkiye) *Critique internationale* 3, no. 60 (2013): 21–35.

the organization became an advocate of marriage. Peshmergas might marry comrades they had known earlier in their life as militants, or those they met after going to the mountains. Women peshmergas generally got married, but for men it was more difficult given that among peshmergas, men far outnumbered women. Moreover, families were reluctant to agree to the marriage of a politically uncommitted daughter to a peshmerga who might be killed at any moment. Many Komala men thus remained unmarried until they left Iraqi Kurdistan for exile in the 1990s.

Marriage was important to peshmergas for several reasons. First, it was the only legitimate way to have a sexual life. Within the organization, as in the rest of society, sex outside heterosexual marriage was largely unthinkable. Additionally, "in-house" marriage was an ideal way for Komala to counter rumors of immorality and improve its image. Legitimate unions similarly allowed the families of women peshmergas to deflect the gossip that circulated about their communist daughters suggesting that they were "immoral," "anti-family," and "promiscuous." Golrokh Ghobadi records her mother's reaction upon learning of her marriage: "Thank God they are pure, that is all God wants."[1]

Marriage as authorized by Komala represented both a break with and continuation of marriage as it existed in Kurdish society. The fourth party congress, in January 1984, explicitly approved progressive and egalitarian marriage laws in the organization's program for the self-determination of Kurdistan. While these regulations were not expected to be imposed throughout the whole of society, Komala was committed to putting them into practice as far as possible within the organization and among its peshmerga. According to the statutes, anyone over the age of 18 was free to marry the person of his or her choice and to start a family. Spouses had equal rights in relation to divorce and child custody. Polygamy, which had been commonly practiced in Iranian society, including Kurdish society, was prohibited. The Komala leadership was adamant on this issue.

Not everyone complied with all of Komala's guidelines, particularly with regard to bodily discipline. However, while peshmergas might discreetly practice some disciplinary infractions such as extramarital sex, polygamy was neither accepted nor tolerated.

In one case, Komala forced a polygamous peshmerga to divorce one of his two wives before he was permitted to join. In another, Pershing, who wanted to marry a married commander, faced open criticism from her comrades, and the commander was forced to separate from his first wife. Pershing acknowledges:

> I knew that what I was doing was strictly frowned upon by my comrades and forbidden within Komala, but I had fallen in love, and I had no other choice. In spite of all the criticism, my partner and I were determined. But our decision was made on the condition that he divorce his first wife. After that, we got married, but I was never really free from the disapproval of my comrades.

Another progressive change was the recognition of civil marriage. Initially peshmerga weddings were celebrated religiously—to a greater or lesser degree—in line with social norms. Ghobadi writes of her religiously celebrated wedding: "As we lived among the people, we felt obliged to respect their customs. We did not wish to offend them, especially on something as trivial as marriage."[2] This practice came under internal criticism and religious marriage was soon replaced by civil marriage, based on mutual consent between the woman and the man, with no religious element.

The marriage process itself was also simplified. Kurdish tradition specified a fairly complex and highly codified marriage ritual in which there was a succession of stages: the father's consent, followed by confirming the size of the dowry (the sum that the husband had to pay to his future wife) and the *shirbaha* (the sum that the husband had to pay to his future wife's family in order to "compensate" them for taking their daughter); and finally a religious ceremony or *mare brrin* (the religious contract of marriage). Komala's progressive conception of revolutionary marriage was different: the agreement of the bride and groom was sufficient to officially register the union, amounting to a simple civil marriage. However, in rural areas where Komala was particularly well established, it encouraged wedding parties, albeit modest, and invited the neighboring villagers. The aim was to demonstrate that even without the framework of religion, it was possible to lead a moral life. Komala thus confirmed that marriage was the only way to raise a family or engage in legitimate sexual relations.

A further change was that peshmergas, separated from their families and engaged in armed struggle, took the decision to marry without family permission. This was particularly momentous for women. During civilian life, it would have been inconceivable for a woman to marry without the consent of her parents, especially her father; but once they became fighters in the mountains, peshmerga women generally married men of their own choice. Minimal contact with relatives gave women more freedom to decide for themselves, representing a significant break with social mores. Serveh testifies:

> In those days, of course, no marriage was possible without the agreement of the families. But this was no longer the case for us as peshmerga. Because we were in the armed struggle, far from our families, and our contact with them was very limited, most families didn't know anything about their children's marriages, about the date or the person. This happened with me too: I married my commander, who came from another part of Kurdistan and he was totally unknown to my family.

There was also an increase in interethnic marriages. Although there were fewer of these, they were nevertheless a great novelty, especially for Kurdish women. Two of the ten men interviewees had married non-Kurds before the revolution, indicating that men had more freedom in this area, but for women this was almost unheard of. However, after the repression in the 1980s, the peshmerga ranks were swelled by Marxists from all over Iran, some seeking to save their lives, others joining for ideological reasons. Love affairs sprang up and marriages were celebrated, sometimes without the knowledge of parents. Soraya, for example, married a doctor from northern Iran, of Persian ethnicity.

In practice, however, this new matrimonial regime did not always work as intended. Notwithstanding the centrality of free choice in official rhetoric, members of the central committee or the political or armed leaders of peshmerga groups sometimes intervened in the choice of alliances. They might reserve the right to validate a marriage, and they appear to have attempted to "reserve" the "best" women for the leadership. Marriages had a clear political purpose, and the leadership generally sought particularly politicized women who would help them achieve their aims rather than obstructing them. Sara testifies:

> One of my friends wanted to marry a man who held a high position in the organization's hierarchy. The leadership was against it. They told her that the hierarchical difference was too great and that it constituted an obstacle to the marriage. They also told her that, once she and her lover were married, they might "get in each other's way" in their political life.

Pressures were also exerted by comrades. For example, two peshmergas whose relationship was only friendly were obliged to marry on the insistence of their comrades in order to put an end to the gossip. Additionally, single men competed for women, whose numbers were much smaller. A woman might receive many marriage proposals in a single day; Narmin remembers that one of her comrades received 20 proposals in three days. An armed Komala commander recalls in his memoir:

> At that time, it was difficult for us to express our feelings and talk about love. We were too shy for that kind of thing. Instead, we would talk to girls about Marx and Lenin and Engels and Brezhnev and Ho Chi Minh and Enver Hoxha. The girl in front of us would look at us with round eyes. The poor girl! The little she knew of Marx and Engels was almost immediately forgotten, she was so intimidated by all the marriage proposals she received.[3]

These repeated requests, which at times took the form of harassment, were a source of stress for some women, who spoke of feeling "indirect pressure" and "permanent interference in their private life." The same armed commander continues:

> The men were in competition with each other, because the ratio of men to women was not in our favor. We saw all our male

> comrades as potential love rivals. And the women couldn't stand our repeated marriage proposals. They felt under constant pressure. The boys would ask the girls for a walk, talk about politics, and it would end with a formal proposal. The shortage of women, our sexual frustration, our jealousies, and our narrow-mindedness limited human relationships.[4]

Women had to be careful in how they responded to this large number of marriage proposals, as a rejection might have a brutal response. Some men were angry and violent against women who rejected them, while others turned their frustration on their male peers and became even more jealous. Still others took revenge by spreading derogatory rumors about the woman or women who had rejected them. One woman met a particularly tragic fate: when she refused a proposal of marriage from her cousin, he murdered her in February 1984, near the town of Mahabad. Her name, Banafsheh Sabeti, appeared among the "martyrs" of Komala in the 1980s. The cause of her death was discreetly described as a "horrible incident."[5]

According to the accounts given by peshmerga women, marriage could allow them to escape sexual harassment as well as constant demands by complete strangers. Twenty-one women who were married during this period testified that these pressures subsided somewhat after marriage. One of them, Nasrin, interprets this mindset: "Even though I rarely saw my husband due to our different activities within the organization, the simple fact of carrying his name and having the status of a married woman saved me from a number of pressures." However, according to other interviewees (seven women and two men), even married women did not always escape harassment. Roonak comments: "Some married women continued to receive proposals from male comrades. Not to be their wives of course, but to be their occasional mistresses."

While political commitment could be important criteria for a marriage choice, the woman's beauty was also a determining factor. This criterion was less important for ordinary peshmerga men, however, as they had less choice. Women meanwhile generally compensated for their lower position in the movement by opting for what they considered to be reasonable unions with prominent men. The majority of women preferred "hypergamous" marriages—that is, unions in which they were in a position of inferiority to their spouses in terms of age or organizational seniority.[6] Mansoor, a former Komala peshmerga, reports: "A village woman and her lover joined the Komala ranks so they could get married when their families would not consent. But it didn't take long for the woman to receive several better marriage proposals. She therefore decided to marry someone else, more attractive and high profile than her lover." Fatima also states:

> Most women in civil society would opt for wealthy and powerful men out of preference. Similarly, peshmerga women chose men from the central committee of the movement, or at least an influential commander or political leader. If a woman refused a marriage proposal from a comrade who didn't hold an important position, his first reaction would be "So what's wrong with me? You're just set on marrying a man higher up, aren't you?"

Peshmerga couples lived together in a small village house or shared a tent in the camps.* Some worked in different areas and saw each other only occasionally, especially if one partner was involved in the armed wing, but most couples preferred to work together. After marriage, it was the woman who left her previous area of work to join her husband. Azita, for example, married the commander of an armed unit and subsequently left her work as teacher to fight alongside him.

MOTHERHOOD: DUTY IN THE MIDST OF ARMED CONFLICT

Except those who had become mothers before joining Komala (four interviewees) and those who consciously decided to postpone maternity (three)—most peshmerga women bore at least one child in the 1980s. For some, pregnancy during this period of uncertainty had not been part of their plan. It often resulted from

* Singles lived together in groups of four or five people (or more) of the same sex, in a small room in a village house or a tent in the camps in Iraqi Kurdistan.

the lack of contraception, especially during the early years when sexuality remained a social taboo, a nonpolitical and nonrevolutionary topic that was not talked about. Nasrin recalls: "Politics and revolution occupied all our time. Talking about trivial things like sex education and pregnancy was frowned upon. We would be criticized for our passivity on serious issues and our lack of revolutionary fire."

Some women, however, became pregnant because they wanted to, justifying their desire for motherhood as a personal choice or a shared decision with their husbands. Not knowing when the conflict would end, and recognizing that the road to victory would be a long one, these women decided not to wait to have a child on the grounds that afterward it might be "too late" for them to become mothers; they did not want to be left with regrets at the end of the conflict. Serveh and her husband explained their desire for parenthood as the wish to "leave a trace of their time on earth," not least in case they did not survive the war.

Although women often insisted that their desire to become mothers was personal, they made their choice in a culture that considered motherhood to be natural and instinctive. To not become a mother was still extremely stigmatizing and shameful, and women understood motherhood in an essentialist way as their instinctive and natural task. Their involvement in the armed struggle did not necessarily influence this. Shilan, for instance, comments: "It's so instinctive and natural for us women to want to be mothers. I have never met a single woman who does not have this desire deep inside her. Without motherhood, a woman cannot be complete."

The role of women as mothers was also emphasized within Komala. Although no official texts openly encouraged women to have children, a number of archival sources refer to motherhood as an unavoidable part of the destiny of women workers. These sources also address the moral obligation of communist parties to take care of the children of these mothers. A pamphlet published by Komala in 1983, which identifies the capitalist system as the main obstacle to equality between men and women, also raises the issue of motherhood.[7] The pamphlet asserts that it is in the public interest to support mothers, and once in power, communists must remove all the barriers that prevent women workers from becoming mothers. Nevertheless, it represents motherhood as simply a natural process and offers no discussion of birth control, legalized abortion, or women's right to control their own bodies and their reproductive rights:

> Communists must take responsibility and show unity on this issue [motherhood]. We must not treat it as a private issue. As communists, we must create optimal conditions, particularly with regard to hygiene and material conditions in general, so that women can become mothers in safety. We must abolish the difficulties and oppressions that hamper women in capitalist society.[8]

The injunction to become mothers thus continued to weigh heavily on women even in the midst of the armed conflict, both in liberated areas and the camps, despite the harshness of the living conditions. In order to avoid being stigmatized as barren women, many peshmerga women became mothers, often shortly after marriage.

Some women describe their pregnancy and the first months of motherhood as the worst period of their political lives. They became pregnant during a war that intensified on several fronts, amid a lack of supply lines and provisions, loss of life, the deaths of comrades, husbands, or brothers, regular displacements to the border areas, the withdrawal to Iraqi Kurdistan, and finally resettlement in the camps in Iraqi Kurdistan where they lacked even the bare necessities. These women were often ashamed of their individual desire for children—which had nothing to do with their revolutionary ideals—especially in a situation where at any moment their comrades might fall in battle. Pregnancy disrupted not only their private life but also their participation in political life.

Except for a few privileged women who were close to the most prominent men, the majority of women who became mothers at this time emphasize the hardship of their experience, and the fact that they went through all the stages of childbearing on their own, from the announcement of the pregnancy to the delivery and the care of the newborn. Those who became pregnant by accident faced additional shame and guilt, and sometimes even disgust not only with themselves but also for the child they were carrying. Roonak admits:

> Before I became a peshmerga I was already the mother of a little girl, so I didn't want to have any more children, especially in a period of total war when our fate was not clear. But I got pregnant for the second time by accident. It was one of the worst things that could have happened to me during that time. From the moment I found out I was pregnant, I felt so bad, above all about my friends killed in battle, who were sacrificing themselves for us. I felt guilty. I thought of the fetus in my belly as a bastard. I wished it would never be born.

Moreover, in the context of armed conflict, motherhood represented women's "weakness." Women had sought to become like men by proving their physical strength and endurance, and dressing and behaving like them. Pregnancy, especially in its final months, changed all that. Ghobadi recalls:

> I felt really bad, I had pains all over my body and almost no appetite. I felt totally unable to do anything. For the first time in my life, I felt weak and vulnerable. I needed help. It was a really unpleasant feeling. As a peshmerga, I was supposed to help others, not to be asking for help myself. I was so stressed that it spoiled all my pleasure in carrying a child and later spending time with my baby.[9]

Pregnant women's sense of guilt was fueled when some comrades, from the highest ranks to ordinary peshmerga, made derogatory and even insulting comments. They were told they were "irresponsible" and were blamed for getting pregnant at the worst possible time; some were suspected of using their pregnancy as a Machiavellian plan to escape their political duties. They were accused of being selfish and of not paying attention to what was happening around them. Despite the rhetoric suggesting that motherhood was not the burden of women alone but should be a shared responsibility for communists, the experience of the peshmerga women tells a different story. Mahin remembers:

There was no law against conceiving a child during wartime. However, if we became pregnant, as soon as we announced it, people's views of us changed. Between one day and the next, we turned into a "liability." Some of our male comrades would make fun of us or even insult us. When I got pregnant, I felt extremely guilty and was afraid to tell anyone. I didn't feel I could do it. It was a nightmare, I almost felt as if I were carrying an illegitimate child.

The blame fell on women, not on their husbands, even in the case of planned pregnancies when the decision to conceive was made jointly with their husbands. And it was almost always women who were held responsible for unwanted pregnancies in line with patriarchal notions of gender. According to the sexual division of labor, the business of childrearing, from pregnancy to education, was the responsibility of women. During the pregnancy, it was only women who could no longer carry out the tasks assigned by the organization, especially during the last months. Even a well-known Komala leader, whose wife had become a mother twice during this period, expressed criticism of mothers. Nashmin recounts: "I remember very well one time when one of the well-known figures of the organization, talking about the medical equipment available to women during childbirth in Europe where his wife, taking advantage of her status, had given birth twice,* vigorously criticized peshmerga women who had children, taking it as a sign of passivity."

For the same reasons, they tried as long as possible to conceal their pregnancy, continuing their normal activities until a very advanced stage, when they could no longer bend down or tie their belongings onto their backs without help. When it was no longer possible for a woman to deny a pregnancy, she might claim that it was accidental and contrary to her wishes, so as to alleviate her shame and guilt. While few women admitted to wanting to get pregnant in the middle of a war, most of them carried their pregnancies to term. When Roonak got pregnant, during the first

* It was said that the presence of the families of Komala leaders would prevent them from focusing on the organization's main goals. As a result, a few families were transferred to Europe.

few months she did everything she could to hide her condition, tying her belt even tighter than before. The wife of Aram, a Komala peshmerga, tried to hide her belly by wearing Kurdish women's dress, because it was long and loose.

Childbirth was also particularly risky. Before Komala was forced to withdraw to Iraqi Kurdistan in the mid-1980s some women, such as Mastoureh and Roonak, gave birth in the infirmary located in the free zone. Others, like Azita, were sent to urban hospitals in Kurdistan or an Iranian city like Tehran or Tabriz. Since the women were clandestine Komala militants, they registered under a false identity; discovery would have been extremely dangerous, and fear of identification and arrest was thus added to the stress of childbirth. Some women died in the armed conflict while pregnant or as young mothers. Records mention two women from Komala who were killed in armed conflict against KDPI forces while pregnant: Farah Adman on November 16, 1984, and Monir Modaresi on November 14, 1985.* To escape from government forces, some women were forced to flee, leaving their babies with the villagers immediately after giving birth.

After Komala withdrew to Iraqi Kurdistan, where peshmergas lived in more or less improvised camps, pregnant women were sent, a few days before term, to give birth in hospitals in cities of Iraqi Kurdistan. Most of them continued with their activities during the final stages of pregnancy, sometimes up to the day before their delivery. A few women active in the armed wing requested to be allowed to carry their pregnancy to term in one of the camps, to undertake different activities. Shilan, for example, was assigned to domestic work until she gave birth:

> My favorite area of work was the armed branch, but when I got pregnant, I went to "finish" my pregnancy in one of our camps (on the Iraqi side), because it was dangerous for me at the front, and there was not enough food. It was around this time that we lost most of the free zones. For security reasons we would

* Unlike Farah Adman, Monir Modaresi's name is not mentioned in the list of Komala martyrs. Her name, which came up during my interviews, has been included in the list of Komala activists killed. See Appendix 1.

> go to the villages very late at night to get supplies, and usually there was nothing to eat. Once I had arrived at the camp to carry my pregnancy to term, I continued to carry out tasks such as cooking and cleaning until the last moment before I gave birth.

PESHMERGA MOTHERS AND LOST MOTHERHOOD

In line with the gendered division of labor, it was women who had to manage the dual responsibility of children and politics, whatever their field of activity. They continued as combatants, but care of their children was their sole responsibility. The presence or absence of a father was not relevant as far as childcare was concerned. This division of reproductive labor was produced and reproduced within Komala's political domain, even as new challenges arose from the context of armed struggle. Sometimes, for instance, women had no access to basic necessities (food and hygiene products) or childcare items. Akhtar Kamangar, a peshmerga mother, appealed to a supply officer in a vain attempt to get milk for her baby: "In those days the camps had no facilities for children and the party gave us no help."[10]

Fathers saw themselves as bearing no responsibility for family life, while most women took on responsibility for both activist life and parenting. Young mothers returned to work, either at their old job or a new one, within days of giving birth. For several hours a day, they performed various duties: radio, editing, communication, teaching, and so on. While Jaleh and one of her comrades struggled to cope with this schedule, they both agreed that what was most important to them was their work for the organization and not their life as parents. Sometimes fathers agreed to be more active in caring for their child and helping their wives but these occasional involvements did not make a significant difference to the sexual division of labor which was ultimately structural. Amir acknowledges:

> Sometimes we helped our wives with childcare, but most of the childcare responsibilities were handled by our wives. For most men, these things were totally foreign. The women took care of everything related to the children. We didn't get involved

> with them at all. The women meanwhile continued with their assigned duties. We men didn't pay any attention to them, we didn't try to help them, but the leadership still expected them to spend time on their political activities, as they had done before.

Motherhood could weigh even more heavily on the women who married men with high positions in Komala's hierarchy. Ghobadi, for example, who married a member of the party's central committee, reflected on discrimination against mothers:

> It was assumed that all the work would be done by the women, who carried everything on their shoulders. If Sa'id [her husband] ever helped me a little bit, for example by washing Shaho's [her son's] clothes, everyone would find something to object to. People would come and see me and tell me off for letting Sa'id do this trivial work, as a member of the central party committee who had more important things to do. Ironically, I was also criticized for doing too much for my son and not doing enough organizational work.[11]

In the end, almost all peshmerga couples were compelled to send their children away, to be cared for by their paternal or maternal families. This was the case both for women who already had children when they joined Komala, and for those who became mothers later. All the women interviewees who were mothers in the 1980s reluctantly made this choice, for three main reasons.

The first related to the lack of material support, and the inability of the organization to provide adequate conditions for childrearing, particularly in the first half of the 1980s. The situation was somewhat better in the camps in Iraqi Kurdistan, with aid from international organizations as well as the Iraqi government. But the government, itself engaged in a murderous war against Iran (1980–8), was in no position to provide long-term support to the camps. It was thus very difficult for parents to keep their children with them in the camps, living in tents through the freezing cold of winter and the unbearable heat of summer.

The second reason many couples chose to send their children away was insecurity; the Iranian army was advancing rapidly, and the camps on the borders of Iraqi Kurdistan were subjected to frequent bombing. Finally, the third reason was the hostility that the mothers experienced. Endlessly confronted by insults and scorn, they had to face mockery, criticism, sighs, and raised eyebrows every time they asked for a day off, a little help with their daily chores, or supplies for their children. They were accused of being lazy and using their motherhood to escape organizational tasks. Ghobadi, who was busy from morning to night, writes:

> The men were always scolding me. They were especially hard on me, as my husband was away and I was alone at the time, but my comrades whose husbands were around were subjected to the same attacks. All the women who had young children and had to leave for a few hours a day to take care of their little ones were given a hard time about it. For me, it was always hurtful and humiliating.[12]

Almost all peshmerga couples thus ended up sending their children to safety away from the front. This broke up the family nucleus for the second time, the first being when they had left their families to go to the mountains. Couples who had no one to look after their children entrusted them to volunteer families. According to some interviewees, a few couples, who found no one to take their children in, had to raise them in the camp throughout the years of conflict. All the couples, especially the mothers, spoke of the decision to be separated from their children as the most devastating they ever had to make. In a short letter that distances itself from the ideological propaganda of the organization, Galewej Rostami, a mother, addresses her child:

> My dear little heart, the distance that separates us from each other, a mother and her child, is so great that the day we meet again and I take your sweet body in my arms, the scene will be strange to you and I will be a stranger to you. Maybe your innocent gaze will be unable to accustom itself to your mother's. And with your playmates, who have the same bright eyes as yours, you won't know how to talk about your parents.[13]

Another peshmerga woman, Kamangar, similarly describes in her memoir the pain of separation from her children: "It is impossible for me to describe what I feel. I wish I could put my feelings into words and perhaps ease my heart, but I never can."[14]

If women felt guilty about not fulfilling their political responsibilities when they became pregnant during wartime, they felt further guilt when they had children for not fulfilling their responsibilities as mothers. Adrienne Rich writes that the "institution" of motherhood, which "obliges" mothers to care for, feed, and educate children, makes them feel guilty for failing in their duty.[15] While men who became fathers progressed through political life smoothly, on a linear and continuous path, women felt that they definitively failed to be "good mothers" in line with what society expected from them. The war interrupted the process of motherhood and broke the mother-child bond. Their participation in politics, as they saw it, had affected not only their public but also their private lives.

For mothers who were separated from their children, their sadness and guilt might be alleviated in three ways. The first was that this was a general experience. While women peshmergas experienced separation from their children as terrible, the fact that it was collective and shared by others could offer solace. Miriam remembers:

> A month after my daughter was born, I had to send her to my husband's family. I could never put into words how I felt during that time. I clearly remember one night when it was raining, and my breasts were overflowing with milk. I couldn't stop myself from thinking about my daughter. My breasts were full of milk, but my daughter was far away from me. When I saw the milk flowing, my throat hurt. I couldn't even breathe. But I didn't want my friends in the tent to see me crying. Then I heard a cat who had just given birth mewing with her little kittens, and I felt that only this cat could understand my feelings. I went out in the rain and followed the sound of her mewing, and suddenly I realized that some of my other comrades, who had also sent their children away, were sitting next to her and crying. We had each other for comfort.

Second, some mothers dedicated themselves entirely to their political activities as a way to alleviate their guilt. While the institution of motherhood required women to become mothers as soon as they were married, and Komala did not officially prohibit motherhood, equally it did not recognize the place of mothers in militant work. Peshmerga mothers were thus caught in a contradiction between two roles that were impossible to reconcile. Sara remembers:

> I was overwhelmed with sadness as I couldn't have my son by my side. I felt like I had committed a crime against him. I, the one who brought him into this world, was unable to fulfil the duty of nurturing him. To ease the torment of my conscience, I devoted more hours each day to various activities. All this was meant to convey that if I don't fit the conventional image of a good mother, it's because I have more important, more revolutionary roles aligned with collective objectives.

Finally, some parents were able to see their children while they were on missions in cities or villages. Zara, a mother of five, explains:

> During my missions I was able to see my five children, who were being raised by three families: two of them with my husband's parents, the next two with my husband's sister, and the last one with a family in Sanandaj. I could see them from close-by during my missions, especially those in the villages, but it was not always possible to meet them for security reasons, or because of the presence of government forces. So, while my comrades were resting, I would watch, in hiding and from a distance, my children playing in the street.

Others were able to see their children in the camps, though it was not always pleasant. Sara recalls:

> I wasn't able to see my little girl for three years. However, so that my little girl would recognize her parents, my husband's family would always show her a picture of me and her father,

Figure 9.1 A child visits his parents in a camp.[16]

> saying "This is your mother, this is your father." When I saw my daughter three years later, I thought I would go crazy, I felt like the happiest mother in the world, but it wasn't the same for my daughter. I knew she was my daughter, but she didn't know me and had no feelings for me. Every time she heard the word mother, instead of looking at me, she turned her head to my picture and ignored me completely. I was filled with shame before my daughter, and disgust toward myself.

Others did not have this opportunity because of the great distances and the difficulties of travel. Moreover, the government, which closely monitored the relations between members of scattered families, was always ready to use children as hostages and bargaining chips. Monireh was unable to see one of her twins for nine years—who she had she sent to her husband's family, keeping the other twin with her in the camp—after her in-laws were exiled to another part of Iran on the orders of the government, which sought to sever familial ties.

In a few cases, specifically gendered reasons prevented mothers from seeing their children again. If the father died while the child was staying with his family, the family might refuse to return the child to the mother, because children were regarded as belonging to the paternal family. Keeping a child was considered even more important when the child's father died in combat. Additionally, in divorce cases, the father would often instruct his parents not to let the child see their mother again. While peshmerga women had the same right as men to divorce in theory, the risk of losing their children was great, and they were thus more cautious than men about seeking a divorce. After separating from her first husband, Solmaz was unable to see her daughter for 15 years. In these cases, the children were hostages not of the government but of the father and his family. During this period, with a few exceptions, the majority of couples lived for several years away from their children and were able to reunite with them only in the late 1980s and early 1990s.

MALE DOMINATION IN PRIVATE LIFE

Komala condemned inequality between men and women. In its theoretical discourse, it asserted that the root of domestic violence and all forms of discrimination against women lay in capitalism. This view is articulated in a letter written by a peshmerga called Bayan, who was killed in March 1985 by KDPI forces:

> I come from a poor village family. Throughout my life I have experienced many forms of violence and discrimination within my family, mainly from my father and brothers. My family never let me go to school, simply because I was a girl. I had to take care of the household chores and animals. Before I met the peshmerga, I blamed my family, my father, my brothers. But after spending time with Komala peshmergas in our village, I understood clearly that capitalism was the cause of this discrimination, not my family.[17]

There were men who sought equality within their marriages. Shilan recalls: "Some peshmerga men had great respect for their wives and did everything they could to support them. So other women also trusted these men, and relied on them if they were having difficulties." Zara similarly affirms:

> I was among the first women to join the armed wing, where we were few in number, and my husband, who was a commander, always encouraged me. Our relationship went beyond that of a couple. We were more like friends than spouses. He passed on his experience of the armed struggle to me, and he always encouraged me.

Marxist theory argues that in any society, the dominant ideology is that of the ruling class. In other words, if the lower social classes are superstitious, if they believe in miracles, divine laws, or nationalism, it is derived from the dominant classes. As a 1984 article in the Komala journal put it: "The working masses follow what capitalism seeks to impose on them. It is our duty as communists to explain to them that customs such as exchanging women or dowries are debasing. These customs only serve the interests of the propertied classes."[18] Accordingly, peshmergas would often involve themselves in family disputes and domestic violence in rural areas. Zara explains:

> We didn't have many ways of influencing affairs, but as soon as a woman complained about family problems like domestic violence, polygamy, or forced marriage, we would always intervene in the woman's interests. For example, if the issue was polygamy, we would first try to persuade the husband [against it]. If he was obstinate, we would threaten him.

In one case, Diana Nammi and a group of peshmergas found themselves facing a complex situation. Altun, a village woman who was a victim of early marriage and abuse by her husband, ended up killing him. Most of the villagers, along with some peshmergas, demanded her execution. However, Nammi and a few others opposed this decision. With the intervention of an important figure from Komala via satellite phone, as well as the efforts of Nammi and her comrades to speak to the villagers about violence against women, within two hours the villagers were convinced to forgive the accused woman.[19]

Komala's egalitarian discourse on the family, and the interventions of some peshmergas in support of village women, did not mean that all its men were ready to question male domination in the private and militant domains. The (re)production of inequality in marriage was far from unknown among the peshmerga. Indeed, the practice of women marrying more senior men, reinforced male dominance in couples. Some husbands were violent or would threaten their wives with divorce, separation from their children, or deprivation of their basic rights. Although the role of the paternal family in the private lives of peshmerga women had become marginal, other forms of control replaced it: husbands and military superiors could together exercise great influence over women's lives. Monireh notes: "Although the men posed as energetic defenders of village women against their male relatives, they were generally much more interested in egalitarianism in village families than in their own married lives. As peshmerga, they saw themselves as free (or not) to observe equality between women and men within their own families." Laila remembers one of her comrades who was the victim of her husband's violence:

> Her husband, who was an important leader, raped her regularly. Beatings, marital rape, she was spared nothing. I was the only one she talked to about it. To escape from this situation, she decided to join the armed wing, even though the central committee was opposed to it. They eventually gave way and she went to the front. Later she was killed in a clash with the KDPI forces.

Only in very serious cases was Komala prepared to act. For example, on October 26, 1985, a peshmerga woman and her lover were murdered by her husband.* The husband fled to escape conviction and punishment. The organization could not avoid treating such incidents as cases of domestic violence, rather than as

---

* The name of this woman, Derakhshan Waisi, is not mentioned in the list of Komala "martyrs." Her name, which came up during my interview with a Komala leader on March 16, 2018, in Paris, has been included in the list of Komala women killed. See Appendix 1.

private matters that could be hushed up. But so long as the marks of physical violence were not too visible, the issue would remain unaddressed. According to 16 interviewees, most women preferred to remain silent, believing that this was what was expected of them. Women had joined Komala, one of the most revolutionary movements of the time, to serve the cause of the working class and the underprivileged, including women. Most women who were victims of domestic violence felt that they could no longer present themselves as a force for emancipation, either for themselves or for others. In their view, a peshmerga woman who was beaten or abused in her relationship might be considered a failure, useless, and unable to assert herself. These women, who had succeeded with great difficulty in shattering the image of the "weak woman" by taking up arms, had no wish to return to being considered weak and passive. They thus preferred to keep silent about what they suffered in order to preserve their image as "revolutionaries ready to do anything to help others." Miriam recalls: "Some women did not want to damage their image as 'revolutionaries' and 'peshmerga' in any way. They were there to help the oppressed; they refused to reveal that they were being beaten or kicked by their spouses, for fear of suggesting they needed help."

The other reason for their silence was the lack of appropriate support. To be sure, not all women who were victims of violence remained silent; some were able to speak out about their experiences. But even when women did report domestic violence, the verdict was not always favorable for them. Their case would be judged by a committee of leaders who were usually men, and often the complaint was dismissed. Not surprisingly, the result was that women largely remained silent.

Peshmerga women had the same right as men to ask for a divorce, but when Solmaz took advantage of this in order to leave her husband and remarry, her ex-husband—with whom she had many disagreements—retaliated by preventing her from visiting her daughter, who was living with his parents. To her great shock and greater despair, Solmaz found no sympathetic listeners. No one, not even the influential women, were willing to help her, claiming that it was a "private matter" between two adults. Meanwhile, her ex-husband was taking advantage of his dominant position in the organization to hurt Solmaz in the full knowledge that any case she brought against him had minimal chance of success.

MALE DOMINATION IN POLITICAL LIFE

Male domination and inequality between peshmerga couples were not limited to private life; men could also restrict the political lives of their wives. If a woman acted against organizational discipline, she was often "put in her place" by her husband. Sometimes a peshmerga who did not want to intervene directly in a woman's political life would request her husband's involvement. Jaleh recounts two occasions when her husband curbed her activities. In the first incident:

> It was very hot and I couldn't bear to wear the scarf. My male comrades strongly disapproved, although they were allowed to take off their clothes if they wanted. I told them I had been dying of heat under the scarf. They didn't say anything at the time; they preferred to talk about it with my husband because he had the right to tell me whatever he wanted.

The other interference related to Jaleh's wish to join the armed wing. Her husband, who was at the same time her supervisor and wanted to decide on her area of activity, threatened to leave her if she persisted in this choice. Ultimately, she separated from her husband and joined the armed wing.

It was assumed that more powerful, experienced, older husbands should make decisions for their younger, less experienced wives. Some peshmerga husbands closely monitored their wives' activities. Shilan, who had been a member of Komala's first armed women's battalion long before she married, remembers the obstacles her husband put in her way to keep her away from dangerous operations in the name of safety: "I fell in love with the armed commander of my unit. After we were married, he was afraid that something would happen to me, that I would get hurt or killed, so he refused to let me take part in risky operations. Of course, I always tried to explain that I disagreed with him."

When rumors began to circulate that KDPI members were raping Komala women prisoners, the restrictions imposed on women by their husbands increased.* Shilan says: "Everyone in Komala had heard these rumors of rape by the KDPI forces. When we were fighting their troops, my husband refused to let me go to the front. He would send me to the back. He was terrified that I might be captured."

Male domination in the marital relationship also affected women's decision-making, impeding their freedom of action or sometimes putting a stop to their political life altogether. Certainly, the women held independent opinions, but the marital relationship had a strong influence on their actions. For example, a number of peshmergas who, over time, saw little chance of a positive outcome in their armed struggle against the government forces took the decision to surrender, and several women laid down their arms when their husbands did so. Women often saw their political careers come to an end with the arrest of their husbands; once a woman's husband was captured, she usually saw no point in continuing with her political activities, particularly if she had children from whom she was separated.

Not all women pegged their own fate to that of their husband. When Zara was told that the life of her imprisoned husband depended on her surrendering to government forces, she refused. Her husband was executed shortly afterward, but she never regretted her choice: "I was so afraid for my husband and [five] children and there was not a moment when I was not thinking about them, but I was determined not to surrender."

Facing a choice between continued political engagement and possible reunification with children, Shahla chose family, and she was not the only one. Some women felt validated in their family roles, as wife and mother; without family, husband, or children, continued involvement in politics no longer seemed worthwhile. However, when peshmerga women decided to give priority to

---

* According to the story that circulated, during a conflict between Komala and KDPI forces, some KDPI members insulted, raped, injured, and killed Komala members, especially women. This created an atmosphere of fear in Komala. See Siyamak Shami, *Chekideyi az ancheh bar gordanè 22ye Orumiyeh va man gozasht* (A Summary of What Happened to the 22nd Urmia Battalion and to Me) (Sweden: Chapkhanyeyh Farhange Shamloo), 97.

family over politics, this can be understood not simply as a purely personal choice, but one that reflected the dominant norms of the society in which they had been raised, locating women's primary roles in relation to the home and family.

Like Zara, Golnar, a mother of five children, resisted these pressures. When she came under threat from the Iranian security services, she joined the ranks of Komala alone, and on the advice of her husband and parents, who had always been supportive of her political activities, she became a peshmerga. However, the separation from her five children was not easy. Her in-laws and even her own family urged her husband to take a second wife in her absence, but he refused. For many years after she left, her husband raised the children alone.

While male comrades could consider themselves political subjects in their own right, entitled to move up the Komala hierarchy, women could not claim this right. The figure of the peshmerga woman thus remained to a considerable extent that of the wife and the mother of absent children. She was bound to a man, whose mission was to accomplish great tasks. She could not shed marital ties and exist in her own right, any more than non-activist women could. Despite the best efforts of peshmerga women, the shadow of their husbands largely eclipsed their own efforts and achievements. Some women with husbands high in the hierarchy were able to gain access to benefits or positions within the organization. They might work in the most important areas near the central committees, and they were more likely to be exempted from daily activities such as supervision or cooking, or to be given more time off when they gave birth or menstruated. Galawij relates:

> The circle of power was entirely controlled by men. If a woman managed to rise to prominence, it was usually because of her marital relationship. Marrying a powerful man could easily change the position of a peshmerga woman and enable her to gain status. Unfortunately, there were many competent women who were unable to progress in any way because they didn't have well-placed men behind them. These women were always marginalized.

Women who lacked such a relationship could suffer diminished self-esteem and hopes for advancement. In a context where connections to men took precedence over competence, women who did not have the support of a powerful man generally preferred to focus on their daily tasks without the expectation of ever reaching a more senior position. A woman who gained seniority through her marital relationship was nevertheless in a precarious position as a divorce or separation could change her status irrevocably. One of Mansoor's comrades was a commander of an armed unit, whose wife's position in the hierarchy was completely dependent on him: "When he married an ordinary peshmerga woman, she was given political command of a small group. But as soon as they separated, his wife was dismissed from her position without any explanation."

On the other hand, any change in a man's circumstances could have consequences for his wife, for example if he was discredited. If a married man fell down the organizational ladder, for whatever reason, his wife might lose her own hard-won position. Punishment of a man inevitably led to reprisals directed at a wife whatever her position of responsibility. Azita and Sara were both forced to give up their positions because of their husbands' change in status. Sara remembers:

> At the camp, I was the head of the telecommunications center in a strategic area, a rather important and sensitive position in wartime. I held this position for two years, but following strong criticism of my husband regarding the management of the organization, I was fired. The reason was quite simple. Mistrust of my husband meant mistrust of me.

10
The Disappearance of Peshmerga Women

That women played important roles in Komala, initially as dedicated activists without official title, then as peshmergas between 1981 and 1991, is undeniable. Nonetheless women, whatever their background (Kurdish and non-Kurdish, urban and rural), were significantly less visible within the organization than their male comrades. This could explain why they remain relatively unknown and marginalized in collective memory, even among the Kurds of Iran. Other factors may to some extent account for their invisibility: some of the women's socio-economic deprivation, their limited political knowledge and experience, and the defeat of Komala and its exile to Iraqi Kurdistan and subsequently to other countries. But these external factors do not tell the whole story: the organization itself was part of the process by which women's reproductive labor was absorbed into men's and made invisible.

THE GENDER HIERARCHY OF REVOLUTIONARY WORK

Within Komala, the central factor preventing women from being perceived and seeing themselves as real peshmergas or revolutionaries was the sexual division of labor. Even as women broke new ground within the organization, they were effectively excluded from most leadership positions. Women's entry into Komala undoubtedly enabled them to take up new responsibilities, but they carried out the less visible work, often involving multiple tasks, and always under the supervision of male leaders and commanders, with fewer prospects of internal promotion. Writing about Algerian women during the struggle for independence, Danièle Amrane-Minne comments: "If equality in battle and in the face of death is real, by contrast the taboos around recognition and access to positions of responsibility remain unbreakable."[1] The observation is equally valid for the women of Komala.

Positions within the organization's hierarchy remained the prerogative of men: during the 1980s, Komala's leaders, its central committee members, and the majority of its commanders were men. Few women were able to make their mark. Urban and educated men controlled the theoretical, intellectual, and organizational field, while both educated urban men and poorly educated villagers took up leadership positions in the armed wing. Meanwhile women, regardless of their social rank, level of education, or experience, were largely ignored and sidelined. Even the small minority of non-Kurdish women who had been educated to university level and had gained significant political experience prior to joining Komala were excluded. Not until the fourth congress of the CPI, on February 17, 1989, was a non-Kurdish woman elected a nonpermanent member of its central committee.

Women were not excluded from appointment to high-ranking positions in either the military or the political wing of the party. Nevertheless, when they did hold such positions, their roles were usually temporary, preventing them from becoming enduring and influential figures within the party. While one needed military skills to become an armed commander, for political commanders the main requirement was theoretical knowledge of the organization's ideological discourse. One woman who acted as a political commander was Mahshid, who was appointed to take charge of urban clandestine activities. Similarly, Jaleh and Sohaila were temporarily promoted as political commanders. Sohaila was temporarily appointed political commander of a large peshmerga group even though she was not in the armed wing. A few other women, such as Zara, became armed and political commanders of small groups (less than ten). However, these developments appear not to have been decisive in changing the status of women in the organization.

Even in the rare cases where women were allowed to take command of an armed group, they found it hard to effectively exercise their role because the men under their command constantly questioned their ability and legitimacy. In a world where only men were recognized as leaders, the emergence of a minority of women as commanders of small groups of men was not smooth. One of Azita's friends took on the political command of a small group of peshmerga:

> She was insulted all the time and was constantly criticized by the men who were under her command. For example, she once addressed the men with the words "As your supervisor." This phrase triggered anger and furious criticism from her subordinates, who were outraged that she dared to speak to them as their superior.

Women who were given even minor leadership responsibilities had to constantly prove their skill and determination to the men, meaning they had to make double the effort. Zara, who took command of a small group of men, says: "As women we had no room for error. I tried at all costs never to make mistakes, or at least to minimize them." While some women managed to become fighters in the armed branch, positions that might build self-esteem remained out of reach for most women. Miriam relates: "I worked almost ten hours a day in the Komala publishing house. I trained dozens of people while I was in this position, but the central committee of the establishment consisted of five people, who were always men. Throughout the whole period, no woman was permitted to sit on the board."

Few women dared to complain about the male structure of the organization or to challenge their confinement to subordinate positions. Jaleh attempted repeatedly to get a position as commander, but without success, except once when her commander was absent she was able to take on the political command of a fairly large armed unit for just under a month. While the organization did not prohibit women from any field, it had no promotion policy to support them. More crucially, it condoned individual practices and discourses that blocked women's access to more senior positions. It was assumed that natural gender differences or the supposed shortcomings of women, such as their lack of academic knowledge, confidence, or skills, accounted for the imbalance. As Soraya explains: "At that time, the situation of women very much followed social stereotypes. In line with the dominant ideas of the time, people thought that women were not made for important positions. They were not considered to have the necessary qualities to lead." Roonak similarly comments: "Even though since the early days of women's acceptance into our organization we had made our way into every sphere of activity, we always remained ordinary members and no more."

WOMEN'S LACK OF ACCESS TO THEORETICAL KNOWLEDGE

In the years following the 1979 Revolution, expertise in the theoretical domain was generally limited to individuals and leaders of political organizations who were well known to the public. The militants, however, generally valorized the practical field as the site of revolution. A true revolutionary was one who was "on the ground, in practice," against the regime, no matter their mastery of theory. It was the martyrs, the political prisoners, and those who sacrificed themselves for the cause who commanded the respect of other revolutionaries. An activist with limited political and theoretical knowledge could compensate for this weakness to become a respected revolutionary by engaging in concrete political life. This dismissive attitude toward intellectual activity was very common in political organizations, both before and after the revolution. Hamed Shahidian's work on the Guerrilla Organization of the Iranian People's Fedayeen, for example, clearly demonstrates how little interest the majority of the members had in theoretical issues.[2] The founders of Komala shared this outlook. At its first congress, one of the organization's charismatic leaders criticized the work of a comrade as inadequate, telling him: "You spend your time writing; you put aside political action in favor of endless discussion."[3]

However, in the mid-1980s, following the failure of the war against government forces, the armed struggle—now limited to sporadic operations—diminished in importance, and the peshmerga gradually withdrew to Iraqi Kurdistan. At this point, there was renewed interest in the theoretical domain. Henceforth not only was the armed struggle increasingly marginalized, but in fact came to be seen as a disruptive element, which interfered with the classical Marxist struggle for the benefit of the working class and the establishment of a socialist society.[4] While previously it had been the peshmerga who were most admired, both by the public and within the organization, those who now gained importance within Komala were the most scholarly, those with the strongest grasp of Marxist theory, and the most experienced in the debate of ideas. As Nasrin puts it: "The people who were strongest in the domain of theory were now able to claim the highest positions."

This shift did not benefit women. As Sara observes: "During those years, theoretical knowledge could empower anyone who was an expert in the field; and we women were sorely lacking in it." Most Kurdish women who became activists had little political and theoretical knowledge; their political commitments were shaped by intermediaries, especially their brothers. Their involvement in practical activities in the urban space, and in the armed struggles in rural and mountainous areas, gave them little opportunity to develop their ideas.

Theoretical knowledge was limited to a minority of leaders who mostly belonged to the central committees, along with several political and armed commanders and some peshmergas in the armed wing. Since most peshmergas—whatever their sex, experience, or area of activity—had weak theoretical understanding, and individual efforts alone would have been insufficient to address this gap, the organization took on the responsibility for raising the general level of theoretical knowledge by establishing a series of courses. One of the most significant, the October School, began in March 1984. The topics addressed included the foundations of Marxist theory, the working class, discussions of the programs and the formation of organizations, the methods and strategies of Komala, the armed struggle, and the question of revolutionary sovereignty in Kurdistan. The objectives and importance of this training are summarized in a report that explains: "This course was born out of the need to educate as much as possible the communist cadres who will be responsible for achieving the ambitions of our party. This will equip them intellectually to advance the objectives of the party in Kurdistan."[5] The same report defines the goal of the training as follows:

> Comrades who complete this training will not only improve their theoretical awareness; they will also be outstanding comrades in action tomorrow. More than that, they will be the revolutionary leaders and commanders of the future who will lead the masses toward the achievement of our goals. This training will therefore not only advance the theoretical knowledge of the participants, but also enable them to advance in the field of practice, especially in armed leadership and mass propaganda.[6]

Despite the importance of these theoretical courses in the training of Marxist cadres, few women could access them. (Only four out of 36 women interviewees had attended one.) Numbers were very limited, and the courses were essentially offered to Komala's leaders and commanders, the vast majority of whom were men. The members of the central committees who selected participants also favored men because they considered them more capable of understanding theoretical debates. Monireh, who worked in the administrative department of the October School, recalls: "The general assumption of the central committees of the organization was that the majority of women were not intellectually capable of participating. They believed that the theoretical discussions were beyond women's capacity."

In the 1960s and 1970s, most Kurdish women had been barred by the cultural and socio-economic environment from enrolling in universities, where revolutionary ideas were circulated and debated. In the second half of the 1980s, however, their exclusion from theoretical debates was primarily the result of the sexual division of labor within Komala: men were regarded as the most effective thinkers and propagandists of Marxism. Those chosen by the organization to be trained as future Marxist heroes and leaders, those who were supposed in the near future to become leaders of the people—especially of the working class—were almost all men.

THE MARGINALIZATION OF WOMEN IN COLLECTIVE MEMORY

As Christine Guionnet and Erik Neveu point out, men dominate in the construction of political history as it has traditionally been practiced:

> If we consider textbooks and other works of history, the central characters are men: great men lead countries and engage in diplomacy, other men go to war, resist, work, go on strike, demonstrate, etc. History is thus often a history of male actions in the public space. At most, we now find a few pages specifically devoted to women's struggles or to "exceptional" or influential women.[7]

This marginalization of women in historical inquiries and critical modes of historiography can be explained by what Michelle Perrot describes as the "sexual dissymmetry of the sources."[8] As Laura Fournier-Finocchiaro observes, "for historical and sociological reasons, great men are mostly male,"[9] and the history of Komala is likewise a male story.

Within the organization, "martyrs" and "heroes" were implicitly seen as male, with significant implications for the marginalization of women. The heroes and builders of Komala history are always the great men; the names and faces of the martyrs (*shaheeds*) who have entered the legend of Komala are likewise all men. Two examples demonstrate the importance of these martyrs in the organization's political imagination. Komala chose the anniversary of the death of Mohammad Hussein Karimi—killed during a demonstration in Saqqez on February 15, 1979—to declare its official existence after some years of underground activity. The anniversary of the death of Sa'id Mo'ini, killed by the Iraqi Baathist regime on June 21, 1978, was chosen to mark the annual day of tribute to the martyrs of the organization. Komala also named places, armed operations, and armed units (the Chiuwan unit, the Shahid Arez unit, etc.) after the "great men" of the organization.

Komala's "great men" did not include only martyrs, of course. Its theoretical leader, Mansoor Hekmat, a non-Kurd who was also one of the pillars of the CPI and died of cancer in 2002, had an unchallenged place in the collective memory of the organization's members. Indeed, after the break-up of Komala, the members of one of its divided branches, regarding themselves as Hekmat's disciples, called themselves the Hekmatists. Meanwhile the various branches of the organization that have emerged since the 1990s, each of which claimed to be the true followers of the original, took Komala as the official title of their new organizations. Subsequently, to avoid confusion, these groups came to be identified with the name of their most famous (always male) figure, leading to designations such as Komala of Abdullah Mohtadi, Komala of Omar Ilkhani Zadeh, and so on.

Even as Komala commemorated great men, it did not celebrate comparable heroism and courage among women. In the decade that followed the 1979 Revolution, enemy forces killed 1,545 Komala militants and fighters, including 96 women, but only the names of the male martyrs remain in the "memory" of the organization and of Kurdish society.[10] Although the names of some female fighters are occasionally mentioned and their sacrifice praised, their visibility was temporary, whereas that of the great men was long-lasting. Dozens of women were killed in prison or in combat during the 1980s, but only six of them are acknowledged in *Peshro*, the Komala journal.[11] Fatemeh Hakimi (Shawbo), who was killed by government forces on March 12, 1985, was commemorated by the following account in *Peshro* that year:

> She was born in 1950 to a middle-class family in Sanandaj. The political culture of her family, the 1979 Revolution and the subsequent events . . . pushed her toward politics. It was during this process that she discovered Komala and became an activist in the organization's underground in 1980. She dropped out of school and lived clandestinely for a short time, but threatened with arrest by government forces, she left Sanandaj and joined the Komala peshmerga in 1981. She was a member of the first armed women's groups in the southern regions of Kurdistan in 1982 and proved very courageous in the armed wing. She was among the peshmergas who participated in a celebrated operation in 1983, which lasted for 18 hours. She was repeatedly praised for her courage and determination during this period. This led to her appointment as the political commander of a small armed unit in 1983. She was killed in armed conflict in 1983 with the peshmerga forces of the KDPI while she was the armed commander of her unit.[12]

As this extract shows, women's courage and sacrifice were visible to the leadership and mentioned in Komala publications. However, none of the women martyrs whose courage was praised in the writings became as well known as either their male comrades or the two female pioneers from Iraqi Kurdistan, Laila Qasim and Margaret George Shello. Apart from Golriz Ghobadi, who died in a car accident during a mission in 1979 and whose name was given to the first single-sex group of armed women in Komala, no other women's names were used in symbolic commemoration. The women who died in prison or in combat against either government or KDPI forces were almost all marginalized; their names were never given to committees or to mixed fighting units. This is related to the division between private and public, in which women represent "private life"—in this context, the interior of the organization—and men "public life," the organization's external image, which is associated only with "great men."

THE ORGANIZATION IN CRISIS: EXILE AND DISENGAGEMENT

At the end of the 1980s, the majority of peshmergas went into exile, particularly to Europe, and many also abandoned their political life as members of Komala. This shift helps to explain the invisibility of women; the short period of ten years as peshmergas was not enough to significantly change women's status, as occurred with the PKK fighters over decades in Turkey.* Komala's military defeats by the Iranian regime, the experience of being "trapped" in the camps, and the impossibility of returning to Iran increased the peshmergas' frustration and despair. It was clear to most that the

* The efforts of the PKK's female fighters to challenge the male structure of the organization, such as the creation of single-sex groups in all areas, were significant. However, without the continuation of the organization's struggle over more than 40 years, the change in women's status would not have occurred. Women had been present in the PKK since its inception in 1978, but changes in their status accelerated later, after the beginning of the twenty-first century. See Olivier Grojean, "Théorie et construction des rapports de genre dans la guérilla kurde de Turquie (Theory and Construction of Gender Relations in the Kurdish Guerrillas of Türkiye)," *Critique internationale* 3, no. 60 (2013): 21–35.

organization no longer had any real chance of achieving its goals. Golrokh Ghobadi recalls the intolerable situation of the late 1980s:

> Living in the camps meant a life without political creativity, centered around routine jobs. The peshmergas worked in different departments, like civil servants. We were further away than ever from achieving our political goals. We were a political organization whose dream was to improve people's lives, and we had failed. We were like fish out of water. We were unhappy; we felt that the struggle to achieve our goals had been futile and reckless. Everyone was trying to escape this life and get away.[13]

Meanwhile security conditions in the camps were deteriorating, and the lack of health facilities accelerated the peshmergas' move toward exile. The Iranian air force repeatedly bombed the camps, as recorded in the organization's newspaper: a typical report reads, "The Komala camps were bombed three times by the bombers of the Islamic Republic on April 1 and 2, 1988. This attack resulted in four dead and many wounded." Bombings by the Iraqi regime were also reported, for example, one attack on 15 May, 1988, that killed 23 peshmergas.[14] The lack of security worsened in the 1990s, following Iraq's attack on Kuwait. In this volatile international context, the Iranian regime was increasingly open in targeting the opposition beyond national boundaries. In addition to assassinating Kurdish leaders in Europe,* Iranian security forces took to attacking Kurdish militants, especially from Komala and the KDPI, on Iraqi territory, killing or wounding 207 militants; among them, 13 Komala fighters were assassinated and 15 were injured during this period.[15]

Another important factor leading many into exile was the organization's first split. Destructive internal disputes among the young leaders intensified in the late 1980s. The years of sacrifice, camaraderie, and friendship gave way to hostility between two ideological orientations, resulting in the 1991 split. One group continued as

* For example, Abdul Rahman Ghassemlou, the charismatic leader of the KDPI, was assassinated in Austria on July 13, 1989, and his successor, Sadegh Sharafkandi, was assassinated in Germany on September 17, 1992.

militants within Komala (CPI), while the second founded its own organization the Worker-Communist Party of Iran, on November 30, 1991. The new group, which considered itself more faithful to the aspirations of Marxism, accused its rivals of nationalism, who in turn accused the founders of the new party of marginalizing the Kurdish question. This first split was followed by several more; today there are about eight small organizations that originated from Komala.

Most peshmergas witnessed these debates from a distance, as the powerful men tore each other and the organization apart. This was especially true for the women, who had always been marginalized and distant from the circles of power; they remember these moments as having been filled with great sadness and concern for the future of the organization, as well as their own. The rupture of a political organization that had been such an important part of their individual and collective identities was not easy to accept. Roonak regarded the clashes between Komala's "great men" as a power struggle, commenting: "The more difficult the situation became and the less opportunity we had to fight for our ideas and political aspirations, the more focused we became on small and insignificant issues."

From the perspective of several of the interviewees, the real culprits in this situation were the comrades who were constantly competing, criticizing, and accusing each other of every kind of error. In tearing each other apart, they suggest, these people unwittingly aided the Iranian government. As Fatima laments:

> These rival factions distanced themselves from the people and the realities of Kurdish and Iranian society, and became rootless. As a result, their influence diminished significantly. Instead of working together to find ways to oppose the Iranian state, their endless fights and mutual accusations made them (unintentionally of course) the executive arm of the Iranian regime. This is why I left politics.

Faced with this situation, some chose to surrender to the Iranian government forces. Most of the others, frustrated by the impossibility of continuing the resistance and achieving any gains in Iran, made a different choice: exile, followed by disengagement.

PESHMERGAS ON THE ROAD TO EXILE

In the late 1980s and early 1990s, most peshmergas decided to go into a second exile, leaving Iraq clandestinely and seeking political asylum in other countries, particularly in Europe. While many single people went on to establish families in exile, for parents the first step was to pick up the pieces of their families and reunite with their children, who had been separated from them during the years of conflict. Some parents managed to get their children to the camps in Iraq before their departure, so they could travel together, but the process of retrieving the children was not easy. Zara managed to gather together her five children, dispersed across three families, before she went into exile, but her husband, a famous armed commander in Komala, was murdered by government forces as he was trying to retrieve them.* Other parents were unable to reunite with their children and did not see them again until after they had gone into exile; once settled into the host country, they prioritized getting them out of Iran.

Komala's leadership supported the escape of all members, giving priority to the wounded or sick. They facilitated the journey to exile by providing false passports and cash, "ten dollars to each peshmerga."[16] On their arrival at the destination airport, the exiles would hand over their false passports to a Komala representative so that they could be used by others.[17] Sometimes these sick peshmergas brought one or two other children with them, in addition to their own, to get them out of the camps. Exiles looked after the children of others until their parents joined them. Roonak, for

* According to Zara, her husband was surrounded along with two other peshmergas (his brother and another peshmerga) while he was trying to retrieve two of his children. A peshmerga and family members who had hosted them were killed. Zara's husband and brother-in-law, both injured, were arrested on September 27, 1990. During this period, the government issued a condition: if Zara surrendered, her husband would be released and Zara would be reunited with her family (her husband and children). Zara did not accept and her husband was executed at the Sanandaj prison and his body buried by government forces. The date of death found on the tombstone is July 25, 1992.

example, who was not in good health when she managed to leave Iraq for Germany in 1989 and was hospitalized shortly after her arrival, remained responsible for the care not only of her own two children but also two others she had brought with her.

Most peshmergas arrived in the destination country with false passports, which led to various problems. Zara and her five children were arrested upon their arrival in the Netherlands in 1992 for using false documents and were sent back to Iraq after 12 days in custody in Jordan. On her second attempt, Zara first sent her two oldest children, aged 12 and 13, to Sweden, while she and her other three children went to Turkey because of the lack of security in Iraq. It was not until 1994 that they were reunited in exile in Sweden.

If traveling to Europe with false passports was not possible, especially after Iraq became mired in another conflict following the invasion of Kuwait in August 1990, some peshmergas went to Turkey, where they presented themselves at the office of the UNHCR representative in order to seek asylum in Europe or elsewhere. This process took between six months and a year. Of the interviewees, 31 ultimately settled in Sweden, nine in Germany, four in France, two in the United Kingdom, and one in Norway.

Scattered across host countries, and exhausted by a decade of political upheaval, exiles had to adapt to their situation as political refugees and to living in a new country with no knowledge of its government, language, or culture. Women who had to care for their children needed to find work in order to earn a living. But the path to becoming "good mothers" was a hard one, and for a long time mothers and children struggled to understand each other. Akhtar Kamangar, exiled in Sweden, writes of her relationship with her two daughters: "They could not understand me, and no wonder. That was their right. I couldn't understand them either, and that, unfortunately, was not my right as a mother. What I mean to say is that they deserved better."[18] Unlike children who managed to free themselves from their painful past in the countries where they found refuge, some were never able to overcome their trauma and paid a heavy price. Bayan Shafiyi, born on August 31, 1983, is one such example. According to her mother's account, struggling with her trauma, Bayan chose to completely distance herself from the past and everyone who reminded her of it. To do so, she turned to Swedish social associations, claiming that her family controlled and limited her personal relationships. Despite convincing evidence provided by her mother regarding Bayan's mental health issues, social institutions prevented her from seeing her daughter for eight years. In the end, Bayan passed away in 2016, whilst struggling with her mental health problems and not having received enough medical care.[19]

Some mothers, whose husbands had been killed or did not accompany their wives into exile because of their continued involvement in politics, had to bring up children they hardly knew on their own. Shilan recalls the early years of her exile:

> Unlike my husband, who went back and forth between Germany and Iraqi Kurdistan (while the political groups that emerged out of the party split were weaker and more divided than ever), I chose from the outset to devote myself to my daughter. He thought only about the past. When he got his refugee status, the first thing he did was to go to the market and buy a hundred cigarette lighters for the peshmergas who remained in Iraqi Kurdistan. There was no room in his life for our daughter, or for us as a couple. Politics was everything for him. We just had to put up with this situation. My daughter and I built our future here without my husband's help. For my daughter, I had to be both mother and father.

Most young activists, especially women, had been unable to go to university due to cultural and socio-economic restrictions, as well as the revolution and its aftermath, making earning a living in exile more difficult. Of the 47 interviewees, only six (five women and one man) had been able to access higher education. Twenty-five exiles became nursing assistants, eleven became teachers or public service employees (nine women and two men), three men became cab drivers, three were factory workers (two men and one woman), three people were still involved in the split branches of Komala (two non-Kurdish women and one Kurdish man), and one man worked in the restaurant business. For several of the exiles, the difficulties of their lives during the 1980s were a source of strength to face the obstacles of their new present. Asrin says:

> All those years of struggle in the political arena finally brought results—not necessarily political or social, but rather individual results. Despite the inferior status of almost all peshmerga women, and despite all the clichés of weakness, fragility, and powerlessness, they finally realized that they had real potential. Their abilities had been denied or minimized, but they came to understand that they were capable of accomplishing something.

THE POLITICAL DISENGAGEMENT OF THE PESHMERGAS

Some former peshmergas in exile tended to deal with the successive splits in Komala after 1991 by joining one of the divided branches of the organization—potentially making them political rivals of those who joined another—while an increasing number of activists disengaged entirely. Only 14 of the 47 interviewees (12 out of 37 women, and 2 out of 10 men) were still members of a Komala branch at the time of my research. Among those who remained members, a few women had been appointed to the new central committees. This appears to be consonant with patterns identified by Lucia Bargel in her research on militants of the French Socialist Party[20] and Jules Falquet on the revolutionary movements in El Salvador,[21] whereby the former women militants of Komala became visible only after the organization had split, when positions previously considered prestigious were no longer so important and divided branches lacked sufficient high-ranking members. It was under these circumstances that the appointment of women became more common.

Particularly in the context of splits and acrimony, activism in an organization that had few concrete victories seemed to increasing numbers of members like a waste of time. Once the passion and political fervor had diminished, and bureaucracy and the tasks of daily organization took precedence over the struggle, a number of activists chose to turn away from organized political activity. This was especially the case for women, who had already been largely invisible within the organization. This diverges with the findings of the French historian Annie Krigel on the French Communist Party in which women members remained more loyal to the party than men;[22] this was not the case for women in Komala. However, the disengagement of most Komala activists was not due to a passive approach to political life; nor did it mark it a return to the reproduction of the sexual division of labor after years of conflict, that is to say, a retreat to the private sphere.

Philippe Gottraux suggests that it is important to analyze the moment when political activities are abandoned, as it represents a critical juncture influenced by multiple conflicting factors.[23] The decision to disengage, first apparent in the late 1980s and accelerating later in exile, was not an easy one. The various Komala branches also received news of resignations very badly, especially in the early days, seeing it as a sign of the activists' weakness and infidelity to the revolution and Marxism. Some saw resigning activists as unwitting collaborators of the government, thus Roonak, a member of one Komala branch, regarded the resignations as "a gift to the Islamic Republic of Iran."

Additionally, being an activist had been a central part of these exiles' individual and collective identities. This was particularly so for women in the sense that they had overcome so many obstacles in order to be able to join Komala on the same terms as the men. Their presence in the organization, which had constituted a profound break with their upbringing, was often a source of great pride. Disengagement was thus not an easy decision to make, especially given their deep commitment to the organization. The decision to quit left most with a sense of emptiness, confusion, resignation, and loss of identity. Ghobadi, who resigned two years after her exile in 1990, remembers this period with great sadness: "When I left Komala, I felt like a mother who had lost her child after having sacrificed her whole life for him. It was as if I had lost everything. My soul and the best years of my life were gone without any concrete results or achievements."[24] She continues: "After leaving Komala, I seemed to be wandering around like a lost soul. I felt a huge emptiness inside me."[25] Her comrade Miriam describes similar feelings: "Outside this political movement, I felt that I was insignificant. Life seemed absurd. My individual identity only made sense through Komala. It took me a long time to convince myself that I could lead a life in society without being tied to a political organization."

This disengagement did not mean that women were no longer interested in socio-political life. Nasrin says:

> Even though today I am not officially involved in the life of any political organization, the political world still interests me. I follow closely what is going on, especially in the Kurdish regions. Looking at the women guerrillas in Turkey and Syria, I remember everything I experienced in the 1980s in Iranian Kurdistan.

While some former peshmerga disengaged from Komala, they sought alternative ways to take part in socio-political life, involving themselves in other Kurdish or non-Kurdish political organizations in the countries where they had settled. Susan, who abandoned political life in Komala after her release from prison in the Islamic Republic of Iran and her subsequent exile, continues with political activism as a PKK sympathizer. Diana Nammi established IKWRO (Iranian & Kurdish Women's Rights Organization) in 2002 in UK which provides advice and support to Middle Eastern, North African and Afghan women and girls living in the UK, who have experienced, or are at risk of all forms of honor-based abuse, including; forced marriage, child marriage and FGM or domestic abuse. Mandana and Amineh Kakabaveh are active in Swedish political parties. Mandana, who has been in exile in Sweden since 1978 has been involved with the far-left party Ung Vänster for two decades, while Amineh Kakabaveh served as a member of the Swedish parliament for several years, first representing the Left Party and later as an independent.

Two main perspectives emerge among the women interviewees about their political involvement in Komala. They all paid a heavy price for their political involvement: family, societal and organizational pressures; prison and torture; the loss of friends and relatives; the terrifying character of the armed struggle; the lack of access to the most basic sustenance or health services; the estrangement from their children and break-up of families; and finally exile. Nonetheless, three decades later, some agree that the period of their active involvement in Komala was the best time of their lives, despite those costs. When asked if they would choose the same path again, they answer in the affirmative, validating their youthful choice. They remember with nostalgia the values of those militant years: self-sacrifice, the primacy of collective over individual life, and the experience of working within an organization that for its time was progressive in its fight for the defense of oppressed peoples, equality between men and women, and socio-economic justice. Soraya captures this shared nostalgia:

> When we get together with our former comrades, we only talk about this period—our difficulties, our collective memories, our missing comrades, and so on. We only talk about those moments, not about our lives before or after that time. We are forever drowned in our memories.

Others, however, without denying the positive aspects of their involvement in politics, emphasize the very "high" and "different" price that women had to pay. These women suggest that their participation in Komala, with its masculine structures of power, had cost them dearly: they had been forced to sacrifice their family lives. A few go so far as to say that if it were possible to go back in time, they would not choose politics as a way of contributing to public life. Shahla reflects:

> There is no doubt that this commitment changed my vision and approach to the world. I became more self-aware as a woman and a Kurd. But my family life was sacrificed; I lost my husband, and my children lived a life characterized by stress and fear. I experienced imprisonment, life in the camps, and then exile. For women who take part in political life, there are many more difficulties than for men. We have gone through things that men will never experience.

The women who remain members of the divided Komala branches generally do not regard a separate women's movement or a women's organization within the communist parties as necessary. Azar Majedi, a spokeswoman for the Worker-Communist

Party of Iran (one of the branches of the original Komala) and the chairwoman of the Women's Liberation Organization, makes no attempt to hide her reservations about such a project:

> In our view, this idea is at best strange, and in the long run harmful to the achievement of our goal (which is the abolition of the capitalist system). We regard female segregation as irrelevant. It makes no sense for women to campaign "separately" from men. Women workers are victims of the same capitalist oppression as men, and they must fight alongside their male comrades, not on the margins. We firmly reject the principle of gender separatism in the struggle. For us, this is the only path for our struggle, and there is no intermediate way. The idea of an autonomous women's movement is really outdated as far as we are concerned. We must, once again, oppose this sexual "apartheid" within the Party and fight the battle together, men and women, hand in hand.[26]

On the other hand, some of the women who disengaged from Komala and were critical of their subordinate position within the organization have become increasingly involved in activism around women's issues. During the years of exile, reflecting on the contrast between their own subordinate position in Komala and the status of women in Europe, as well as that of women in other socio-political movements notably the Kurdish women fighters in Turkey and Syria, has made them all the more critical of their experiences within Komala. Jaleh comments with regret:

> Some of us are now disillusioned about our political experience in Komala. We did everything for the organization, we sacrificed our lives, our children, and in the end, we got nothing. The organization was, and still is, very proud to have had women in its ranks, but we women have nothing to be proud of. We have paid a heavy price, but with no reward, not even symbolic recognition. This is why some of my comrades and I decided to set up a women's association, independent of the divided branches of Komala.

Some of these women subsequently engaged with feminist politics. For Golrokh Ghobadi, this was a turning point:

> I joined various women's groups in Sweden, and as a result I became more and more focused on women's issues. I was always comparing my experience during my years of activism with other movements, and I realized that I needed to arm myself with feminism. I took courses, and I learned a lot of things, about how to see and analyze.[27]

In 2006, some of these disengaged peshmergas, both men and women, founded a Kurdish Women's Rights Association, with branches in Sweden, Norway, and England. Its manifesto states: "We seek to establish a secular and democratic society that recognizes the rights of women in all areas. We also seek to be the voice of women in the world media and, by defending Kurdish women activists in Iran, we aim to promote their emancipatory struggle."[28]

Conclusion

The same gender relations tend to prevail in activist circles as elsewhere in society, even within the most progressive groups.[1] Challenging long-established gender relations is difficult, and they can persist even through sweeping socio-political changes such as revolution, armed struggle, and militancy. As we have seen, Komala was no exception in this regard. Gender norms that shaped concepts such as "political subject," "peshmerga," "fighter," and "martyr" as exclusively masculine in character were gradually modified, but not to the point of significantly reshaping gender relations. Women activists not only broadened their scope of action by entering the armed struggle, traditionally considered a male domain, they also challenged these essentialist definitions. Dozens of women fell in battle or were killed in prison during this period. Nevertheless Komala, despite its reputation as revolutionary and avant-garde, continued to exist in a state of "back and forth"[2] between the dominant norms of society and the ruptures in those norms that it provoked.

The (re)production of social gender relations was firmly embedded in Komala. The youth of its members, their lack of organizational experience, and the outbreak of armed struggle were contributing factors. However, the organization itself also maintained prevailing gender relations, on both theoretical and practical levels. The "women's issue" was among its concerns, insofar as from 1979 to 1983 it considered women as members of the oppressed Kurdish people and after the formation of the CPI in 1983, as members of the working class, but the ideology of the organization did not develop a specific analysis of women's oppression.

From the outset, everyday practice within the organization was differentiated by gender. Women activists were subject to greater collective control by their peers over how they represented themselves and interacted with others. Moreover, the practice of assigning them work that was considered less dangerous and more general in character did not allow them to make the most of their skills. The growing number of women from rural areas and their insistence to be accepted into the armed struggle forced the organization in 1981 to bring them into its ranks as peshmergas and finally, in 1982, into the armed wing. Had women not been tenacious in their insistence to be accepted as peshmergas, the gender-based division of labor within Komala would likely have continued: men in the role of peshmergas and warriors, and women taking on roles of support.

To protect its moral reputation, Komala formalized the institution of marriage between its members, and women thus found themselves reassigned to reproductive work. The structure of the family system persisted. While peshmerga marriage deviated somewhat from the dominant patterns of the Kurdish community, marriage within the organization, and particularly the custom of women marrying more senior men, reinforced male dominance in couples. Most female peshmergas remained invisible, while the "great men" played a decisive role. At the end of the 1980s, women were faced with a double defeat: a political and military defeat at the hands of the government forces, and an internal defeat at the hands of their male comrades, who successfully monopolized the symbolic capital generated by the political struggle—the name of the organization, the acknowledgment of heroism, the official memory of the past, and recognition by the generations of revolutionaries that came after them.

The Komala organization (re)produced gender relations like most Kurdish and non-Kurdish socio-political movements, for both external and internal reasons. While differences between women in class, marital status, and level and field of activity could lead to a range of different experiences, and while some women might enjoy various temporary privileges, they generally occupied lower positions in the organization's hierarchy than men. As one peshmerga writes in her memoir:

> Although women joined the armed struggle in Komala, it was not the end of patriarchy, neither in society nor in our political movement. But it was still a very important historical step.

> Unfortunately, the traditional patriarchal culture of our society obstructed the rise and prosperity of women.[3]

The experience of the women of Komala challenges superficial, idealized representations of Kurdish women as revolutionaries, especially in the Western media—liberated, liberating, and determined.[4] Such representations fail to capture the complexity and nuances of these women's situation, either in their society or the Kurdish socio-political movements. It should not be forgotten that they suffered double discrimination, as women and as Kurds, directly linked to the discriminatory socio-economic situation in which they found themselves. While their activism represented a challenge to the sexual division of labor, gender relations are tenacious and resistant to change.

Kurdish women's political commitment is not limited to Komala, as the Kurdish political movements in Turkey and Syria demonstrate. The involvement of women in political life is a defining feature of the Kurdish struggle. However, in the absence of a systematic analysis of gender roles and relations, Kurdish activists, including women, will continue to see the transformation of the patriarchal system as only a secondary goal. From this perspective, the presence of Kurdish women activists in socio-political movements, armed or not, and the sacrifices they endured would represent only a temporary "feminization" of resistance, in the interests of the Kurdish cause or organizational aims. Women's political activism for this cause can at any time be turned against them and their specific rights. The case of Komala shows us the outcome of involving women without making the specific situation of women one of its priorities.

Appendix 1
List of Women in Komala Killed During the 1980s

	Name	Date and Place of Birth	Date of Death	Cause and Place of Death
1	Nayereh Azami		1979	Execution in prison
2	Mastoure Shahsawari		May 25, 1980	Execution in prison, Sanandaj
3	Nasrin Ka'abi		August 29, 1980	Execution in prison, Sanandaj
4	Shahla Ka'abi		August 29, 1980	Execution in prison, Sanandaj
5	Farideh Golnasab		1980	Execution in prison
6	Zarifeh Badjalani		1980	Execution in prison, Kamiaran
7	Ameneh Shabani		1980	Execution in prison
8	Khanim Khormali		1980	Execution in prison
9	Fazilat Darayie	1964	November 23, 1981	Execution in prison, Saqqez
10	Shahla Chamanara		1981	Execution in prison
11	Zahra Daneshwar		June 16, 1982	Execution in prison, Tehran
12	Farnoosh Vakilzadeh		June 1982	Execution in prison, Shiraz
13	Sadieh Karimian		1982	Execution in prison
14	Nasrin Pakniya		1982	Execution in prison
15	Fatemeh Djamshidi		1982	Execution in prison
16	Farideh Yousefi		March 17, 1983	Execution in prison, Tehran
17	Shaboo Sayed Zahedi		May 4, 1983	Suicide in prison, Marivan
18	Ameneh Hassani	1936	May 31, 1983	Torture in Urmiyeh prison
19	Fereshteh Arabian Khoshkoo	1965, Mashhad	June 14, 1983	Execution in prison, Tehran
20	Monir Hashemimahin	1954	August 13, 1983	Execution in prison, Tehran

	Name	Date and Place of Birth	Date of Death	Cause and Place of Death
21	Vahideh Vahidi		August 14, 1983	Execution in prison, Saqqez
22	Marie Taraghi	1961	1983	Execution in prison
23	Fariba Farshchi	1964	1983	Execution in prison
24	Khoshnam Ghazi Zadeh		1983	Execution in prison
25	Narmin Karimi	1966, Mahabad	1983	Execution in prison
26	Masooumeh Sarhangi	1966, Mahabad	1983	Execution in prison
27	Mahin Abdollah Zadeh		1983	Execution in prison
28	Sholeh Ebrahimi		1983	Execution in prison
29	Shahrbanoo Modaresi	1958	1983	Execution in prison
30	Iran Khaksar	1961, Tehran	October 1984	Execution in prison, Tehran
31	Safiyeh Mohammadi	1963, Mahabad	December 1984	Execution in prison, Sanandaj
32	Mehri Zamani		1984	Execution in prison, Tehran
33	Pooran Djam Pour	1953, Tehran	July 13, 1984	Execution in prison
34	Ashrafi Vaisi	1959	1984	Execution in prison
35	Latifeh Abbasi	1967	1985	Execution in prison
36	Fahimeh Taghadosi	1953, Amol (northern Iran)	July 30, 1985	Execution in prison, Tehran
37	Azizeh Nawdinian	1949	September 9, 1985	Execution in prison
38	Ameneh Parastar		July 30, 1988	Torture in prison
39	Shahla Kolahghoochi	1961, Sanandaj	September 1989	Execution in prison, Sanandaj
40	Atiyeh Sharifi	1968	September 1989	Execution in prison, Sanandaj
41	Zamaneh Ghaderi	1963	Autumn 1989	Execution in prison
42	Khorshid Dayeh		1980	In armed combat with government forces, Divandarah
43	Kalebey Azhar		1981	In armed combat with government forces, Diwandarah

	Name	Date and Place of Birth	Date of Death	Cause and Place of Death
44	Zibandeh Khalendi		1981	In armed combat with government forces, Mahabad
45	Fereshteh Hakimi	1958, Sanandaj	February 15, 1984	In armed combat with government forces, Diwandarah
46	Asmar Madjnoon		March 15, 1984	In armed combat with government forces, Mahabad
47	Fatemeh Rahmani	1966	April 10, 1984	In armed combat with government forces, Sardasht
48	Shahla Mohammadi		April 29, 1984	In armed combat with government forces, Baneh
49	Mastoure Nasseri		May 19, 1984	In armed combat with government forces, Saqqez
50	Roonak Mahmoud-zadeh		May 25, 1984	In armed combat with government forces, Piranshahr
51	Tahereh Amadji		June 24, 1984	In armed combat with government forces, Urmia
52	Fayzeh Shahabi	1964, Sanandaj	August 24, 1984	In armed combat with government forces, Mahabad, Salas Babadjani
53	Mahnaz Madani	1963, Piranshahr	October 4, 1984	In armed combat with government forces, Diwandarah
54	Fatemeh Hakimi	1965, Sanandaj	March 12, 1985	In armed combat with government forces
55	Saniyeh Bahrami	1967, Divandara	May 18, 1985	In armed combat with government forces, Divandarah
56	Mariam Sa'id Panah (Kobra Marendj)	Sanandaj	May 18, 1985	In armed combat with government forces
57	Sharifeh Talebi		September 5, 1985	In armed combat with government forces

	Name	Date and Place of Birth	Date of Death	Cause and Place of Death
58	Zahra Daneshfar		September 8, 1985	In armed combat with government forces, Baneh
59	Tooba Faizi		November 28, 1985	In armed combat with government forces, Bukan
60	Shahdokht Hoshiarian	1961	May 2, 1986	In armed combat with government forces
61	Roshanak Zangi	1967, Sanandaj	August 31, 1986	In armed combat with government forces, Marivan
62	Fatemeh Banavand	1964, Naghadah	September 1987	In armed combat with government forces
63	Zivar Rashid (Ziba)	1966	March 17, 1988	In armed combat with government forces, Iraqi Kurdistan
64	Susan Farighi	1966, Marivan	March 17, 1988	In armed combat with government forces, Iraqi Kurdistan
65	Arezoo Doustkami	1965	March 17, 1988	In armed combat with government forces, Iraqi Kurdistan
66	Azizeh Azami		March 17, 1988	In armed combat with government forces, Iraqi Kurdistan
67	Rezvan Ahmadzadeh	1962, Sanandaj	March 17, 1988	In armed combat with government forces, Iraqi Kurdistan
68	Fereshteh Moradizar	1953, Kamiaran		In armed combat with government forces, Kamiaran
69	Nazdar Hadjiji		September 1989	In armed combat with government forces

	Name	*Date and Place of Birth*	*Date of Death*	*Cause and Place of Death*
70	Mahbubeh Kurdian Targhi	1968, Sanandaj	December 19, 1983	In armed combat with KDPI, Divadareh
71	Tali'ah Aliramayi	1965, Paveh	November 16, 1984	In armed combat with KDPI, Paveh
72	Farah Adman	1965, Sanandaj	November 16, 1984	In armed combat with KDPI, Paveh
73	Djamileh Ghafari		April 6, 1984	In armed combat with KDPI, Sanandaj
74	Jila Andalibi	1959, Sanandaj	January 26, 1985	In armed combat with KDPI, Paveh
75	Sahebeh Nasseri	1965, Kamiaran	January 26, 1985	In armed combat with KDPI, Paveh
76	Nazifeh Lotfolahi	1958, Sanandaj	March 12, 1985	In armed combat with KDPI, Baneh
77	Servat Sharifi		March 12, 1985	In armed combat with KDPI, Baneh
78	Tooran Rahimi	Srdasht	March 12, 1985	In armed combat with KDPI, Baneh
79	Bashe Shokri (Bayan)	1966, Marivan	March 1985	In armed combat with KDPI
80	Azita Sharfi	1967, Sanandaj	March 31, 1985	In armed combat with KDPI
81	Naskeh Fathi		March 31, 1985	In armed combat with KDPI
82	Pirshing Rostamgorji		September 2, 1985	In armed combat with KDPI, Kamiaran
83	Homaira Basami		September 2, 1985	In armed combat with KDPI, Kamiaran
84	Miriam Zahedan		September 8, 1985	In armed combat with KDPI, Baneh
85	Khadijeh Ahmadi		November 13, 1985	In armed combat with KDPI, Urmia
86	Nasrin Hasankhali	1964, Mahabad	November 13, 1985	In armed combat with KDPI, Urmia
87	Monir Modaresi		November 14, 1985	In armed combat with KDPI, Urmia
88	Hanifeh Rezapour	1961, Bukan	October 3, 1986	In armed combat with KDPI, Sanandaj

	Name	Date and Place of Birth	Date of Death	Cause and Place of Death
89	Shahin Sa'idpanah	1967, Kamiaran	September 20, 1989	In armed combat with KDPI
90	Panahi Hossain		1984	Bombing, Sanandaj
91	Parvin Rostam Gorji	1961, Sanandaj	September 16, 1986	Bombing of Komala camps by Iraqi forces
92	Nasrin Rostam Gorji	1959, Sanandaj	September 16, 1986	Bombing of Komala camps by Iraqi forces
93	Habibeh Shirwani		February 17, 1987	Bombing by Iraqi forces, Sanandaj
94	Farangisse Shahoyi	1958, Sanandaj	May 15, 1988	Bombing of Komala camps by Iraqi forces
95	Mariam Majnoon	1963, Naghadah	May 15, 1988	Bombing of Komala camps by Iraqi forces
96	Fereshteh Rezayi		May 15, 1988	Bombing of Komala camps by Iraqi forces
97	Golriz Ghobadi	1951	March 29, 1979	Car accident
98	Faezeh Ghotbi		March 29, 1979	Car accident
99	Farideh Zakariayi		March 29, 1979	Car accident
100	Nashmile Rasoulpour	1943	1980	Car accident
101	Farakh Atlasi	1962, Sanandaj	April 1980	Car accident, Sanandaj
102	Ameneh Khaiat		September 16, 1980	Car accident, Sanandaj
103	Djamila Fathi		September 22, 1982	Illness
104	Asieh Gageli		Summer 1986	Illness
105	Hadjar Fayzi	1962, Langrood	May 22, 1984	Killed by pro-government people in a factory, Langrood
106	Badri Sharifi	1969, Bukan	1989	Not known
107	Fariba			Not known
108	Chiman Zamani	1965	1984	Suicide
109	Derakhshan Waisi		July 30, 1985	Killed by her ex-husband
110	Banafsheh Sabeti	1958	February 1984	Killed by her cousin

Appendix 2
List of Interviewees, 2014–18

	Name	*Sex*	*Age (at time of interview)*	*Socio-economic status of the family of origin*	*Country of exile*
1	Akbar	M	55	Urban disadvantaged family	Sweden
2	Ali	M	76	Urban middle-class family	France
3	Amir	M	74	Urban middle-class family	Sweden
4	Aram	M	67	Urban middle-class family	UK
5	Asrin	F	57	Urban middle-class family	Germany
6	Azita	F	64	Urban middle-class family	Germany
7	Farzaneh	F	63	Urban middle-class family	Sweden
8	Fatima	F	57	Urban disadvantaged family	Sweden
9	Galawej	F	55	Disadvantaged village family	Germany
10	Golnar	F	72	Urban disadvantaged family	Sweden
11	Hamed	M	60	Urban disadvantaged family	Sweden
12	Hamid	M	66	Urban middle-class family	Norway
13	Jaleh	F	60	Urban middle-class family	Sweden
14	Kaveh	M	70	Urban disadvantaged family	France
15	Laila	F	60	Urban middle-class family	Sweden
16	Mahine	F	60	Urban middle-class family	Sweden
17	Mahrokh	F	56	Disadvantaged village family	Sweden

	Name	*Sex*	*Age (at time of interview)*	*Socio-economic status of the family of origin*	*Country of exile*
18	Mahmoud	M	57	Disadvantaged village family	Sweden
19	Mahshid	F	67	Urban non-Kurdish disadvantaged family	UK
20	Mandana	F	55	Urban disadvantaged family	Germany
21	Mansoor	M	60	Landowner family	Germany
22	Marjan	F	62	Landowner family	Sweden
23	Mastoureh	F	63	Urban middle-class family	Sweden
24	Mehri	F	61	Urban middle-class family	Sweden
25	Miriam	F	60	Urban middle-class family	Sweden
26	Mojgan	F	63	Disadvantaged village family	Germany
27	Monireh	F	61	Urban middle-class family	Sweden
28	Narmin	F	69	Urban middle-class family	Sweden
29	Nashmin	F	59	Urban middle-class family	Germany
30	Nasrin	F	60	Urban landowner family	Sweden
31	Pershing	F	58	Urban middle-class family	France
32	Roonak	F	62	Urban middle-class family	Sweden
33	Roya	F	63	Urban middle-class family	Sweden
34	Sara	F	69	Urban middle-class family	Sweden
35	Sayran	F	68	Urban middle-class family	Sweden
36	Serveh	F	57	Urban middle-class family	Sweden
37	Shadi	F	55	Urban middle-class family	Sweden
38	Shahla	F	56	Urban middle-class family	France
39	Shaho	M	58	Disadvantaged village family	Sweden

	Name	*Sex*	*Age (at time of interview)*	*Socio-economic status of the family of origin*	*Country of exile*
40	Shilan	F	62	Urban disadvantaged family	Germany
41	Shirin	F	73	Disadvantaged village family	Sweden
42	Sohaila	F	64	Urban non-Kurdish middle-class family	Germany
43	Solmaz	F	55	Urban non-Kurdish disadvantaged family	Sweden
44	Soraya	F	55	Urban middle-class family	Sweden
45	Susan	F	69	Urban middle-class family	Sweden
46	Zara	F	61	Disadvantaged village family	Sweden
47	Zohreh	F	63	Disadvantaged village family	Sweden

Acknowledgments

This book is the result of work I did for my doctoral thesis at the School for Advanced Studies in the Social Sciences in Paris between 2013 and 2020. A number of people have contributed to its realization. First, I would like to thank my thesis supervisor, Amélie Le Renard, and my co-supervisor, Lucia Direnberger, who reread my work several times sentence by sentence and provided extremely useful advice with patience. They taught me a lot, not only about scientific research, but also about sisterhood as a real practice.

It is also a great pleasure for me to express my deepest gratitude to the Kurdish Institute of Paris, which allowed me to continue my studies in France by granting me a scholarship in January 2013, early in my work. Special thanks go to Katharine Hodgkin, Janet Biehl, Kamran Matin, Pedram Baldari, and Morteza Samanpour for their careful review of the manuscript and their valuable advice. I am particularly grateful to Golrokh Ghobadi; this study would not have been possible without her help. I appreciate her infinite patience and generosity in answering all my questions, and in sharing her knowledge and experiences about Komala and peshmerga women.

I would also like to thank Roonak Shiwani, a Kurdish writer and translator, who generously provided me with a translation of the autobiography of a Kurdish ex-combatant published in Swedish. These thanks, however, would be far from complete if I omitted to mention the presence of friends that has always been the most precious support throughout my work.

Notes

INTRODUCTION

1. Omid Barin (@barin_omid), "Mahabad, the bastion of resistance," Twitter Post, November 19, 2022, https://x.com/barin_omid/status/1593927194115338240?t=zOoIiWs9e5ZUUDOsCaVaWg&s=35.
2. Nawendi Perwerdei Komala, "Our Way of Struggle: Shaheed Helow," YouTube, February 18, 2020, www.youtube.com/watch?v=DRAkF4FXPio. Accessed March 31, 2024.
3. Farangis Ghaderi, "Jin, Jiyan, Azadi and the Historical Erasure of Kurds." *International Journal of Middle East Studies* 55, no. 4 (2023): 718–23; Somayeh Rostampour, "Jin, Jiyan, Azadi (Woman, Life, Freedom): The Genealogy of a Slogan." *CrimethInc., March.* https://crimethinc. com/2023/03/08/jin-jiyan-azadi-woman-life-freedom-the-genealogy-of-a-slogan (2023); Kurdistan Human Rights Network, "Details of 121 Kurdish People Killed During Mahsa (Jina) Amini Protests in Iran," January 11, 2023, https://kurdistanhumanrights.org/en/publications/special-reports/2023/01/11/details-of-121-kurdish-people-killed-during-mahsa-jina-amini-protests-in-iran. Accessed March 31, 2024.
4. Yann Richard, *L'Iran: Naissance d'une république islamique* (Iran: Birth of an Islamic Republic) (Paris: La Martinière, 2006).
5. Amir Hassanpour, "The (Re)production of Patriarchy in the Kurdish Language," in *Women of a Non-State Nation: The Kurds,* ed. Shahrzad Mojab (Costa Mesa, CA: Mazda, 2001), 236.
6. See Appendix 1.
7. Shahrzad Mojab, "Introduction: The Solitude of the Stateless: Kurdish Women at the Margins of Feminist Knowledge," in *Women of a Non-State Nation: The Kurds,* ed. Shahrzad Mojab (Costa Mesa, CA: Mazda, 2001), 9.
8. Olivier Grojean, "Penser l'engagement et la violence des combattantes kurdes : des femmes en armes au sein d'ordres partisans singuliers," (Thinking about the Commitment and Violence of Kurdish Female Fighters: Armed Women Within Singular Partisan Orders) in *La lutte armée, instrument d'émancipation des femmes?*(Armed Struggle,

Instrument of Women's Emancipation?) ed. Caroline Guibet Lafaye and Alexandra Frénod (Presses de l'INALCO, 2019), 186.

9. The list prepared by the organization presents 103 Komala "martyrs" who died for various reasons during the 1980s. However, data collected from my interviewees suggests that this Komala list is not very accurate. A new list was compiled as part of this study, considering as much information as possible (Appendix 1). The incomplete Komala list is cited in Bahman Saidi, *Sé Sal le gel Ebrahim Alizadeh* (Three Years with Ebrahim Alizadeh) (Sulaymaniyah: Ranj, 2009), 470–3. The Komala video is divided into three parts, available on YouTube: www.youtube.com/watch?v=gayBvjTzSug&feature=share; www.youtube.com/watch?v=x6xIMZFc488&t=1537s; www.youtube.com/watch?v=fUKhYNT35KA&t=17s. Accessed March 31, 2024.
10. Malaka Mostafa Soltani, *Sébari Qalabard La Sar Almane u Talasowar (The Shadow of the Qalabard on Almane and Talasowar)* (Sweden: 49books, 2023), 257.
11. Martin van Bruinessen, "From Adela Khanum to Leyla Zana: Women as Political Leaders in Kurdish History," in *Women of a Non-State Nation: The Kurds,* ed. Shahrzad Mojab (Costa Mesa, CA: Mazda, 2001), 105–6.
12. Hilal Alkan, "The Sexual Politics of War: Reading the Kurdish Conflict Through Images of Women," *Les cahiers du CEDREF*, no. 22 (2018): 68–92.
13. Farideh Koohi-Kamali, *The Political Development of the Kurds in Iran: Pastoral Nationalism* (New York: Palgrave Macmillan, 2003).
14. Ibid., 148.
15. See, for example, Eliz Sanasarian, *The Women's Rights Movement in Iran: Mutiny, Appeasement, and Repression from 1900 to Khomeini* (New York, Praeger, 1982).
16. Mojab, "Introduction," 11.
17. Ibid., 12.
18. The five books and autobiographies published by these former peshmerga women are: Malakeh Mostafa Soltani, *Sébari Qalabard La Sar Almane u Talasowar (The Shadow of the Qalabard on Almane and Talasowar)* (Sweden: 49books, 2023); Diana Nammi and Karen Attwood, *Girl with a Gun*, (London: Unbound, 2020); Amineh Kakabaveh and Johan Ohlson, *Amineh: inte större än en kalasjnikov: från peshmerga till riksdagsledamot* (Amineh: No Bigger Than a Kalashnikov: From Peshmerga to Member of Parliament) (Stockholm: Ordfront, 2016); Akhtar Kamangar, *Farazhayi az zendegiye Akhtare Kamangar* (Passages from the Life of Akhtar Kamangar) (Stock-

holm: Khanyeyh Farhange Shamloo, 2016); and Golrokh Ghobadi, *Shaghayg-ha bar sanglakh, zendegi u zamaneye yek zane Kurd* (Anemone on the Rock, the Life and Time of a Kurdish Woman) (Sweden: Self-published, 2015).

19. Françoise Thébaud, *Écrire l'histoire des femmes et du genre* (Writing the History of Women and Gender) (Lyons: ENS, 2007), 72.
20. From the perspective of the sociology of life stories, I follow the advice of Daniel Bertaux, who suggests that sociologists use "historical chronology" based on life-history approach to shed light on life stories and to detect in them the events in people's lives. See Daniel Bertaux, *Le récit de vie* (The Life Story) (Paris: Armand Colin, 2010).
21. Arlette Farge, "Thinking and Defining the Event in History," in *Archives of Infamy: Foucault on State Power In the Lives of Ordinary Citizens*, ed. Nancy Luxon (Minneapolis: University of Minnesota Press, 2019), 223.
22. Farge, "Thinking and Defining the Event," 216.
23. Danièle Kergoat, "Division sexuelle du travail et rapports sociaux de sexe," (Sexual Division of Labor and Social Relations of Sex) in *Genre et économie: un premier éclairage* (Gender and Economy: A First Look,), ed. Jeanne Bisilliat and Christine Verschuur (Geneva: Graduate Institute Publications, 2001), 78–88.
24. Olivier Fillieule, "Travail militant, action collective et rapports de genre," (Activist Work, Collective Action and Gender Relations) in *Le sexe du militantisme* (The Sex of Activism), ed. Olivier Fillieule and Patricia Roux (Paris: Presses de Sciences Po, 2009), 28–29.
25. Vali, *Forgotten Years of Kurdish Nationalism*, vii.
26. Bernard Hourcade et al., *L'Iran au XXe siècle : entre nationalisme, islam et mondialisation* (Iran in the Twentieth Century: Between Nationalism, Islam and Globalization) (Paris: Fayard, 2007).
27. Koohi-Kamali, *Political Development of Kurds in Iran*, 27; David Romano, *The Kurdish Nationalist Movement: Opportunity, Mobilization and Identity* (Cambridge: Cambridge University Press, 2006), 3.
28. Alam Saleh, *Ethnic Identity and the State in Iran* (New York: Palgrave Macmillan, 2013).
29. Vali, *Forgotten Years of Kurdish Nationalism*, 46.
30. Abdul Rahman Ghassemlou, "Kurdistan in Iran," in *A People Without a Country: The Kurds and Kurdistan*, ed. Gérard Chaliand, 95–121 (London: Zed Books, 1993).
31. Vali, *Forgotten Years of Kurdish Nationalism*, xi.
32. Ghassemlou, "Kurdistan in Iran," 105.

33. Tanyel B. Taysi and Kerim Yildiz, *The Kurds in Iran* (London: Pluto Press, 2007), 5.
34. Source of the map: David Romano, "A Nuclear Deal Would Help Iran 'Fund Proxy Groups, Repress Its People,' Warns Iranian Kurdish Leader Mustafa Hijri," *Arab News*, November 2, 2022.
35. Abbas Vali, *Kurds and the State in Iran: The Making of Kurdish Identity* (London: I.B. Tauris, 2011), xiv.
36. The roots of Kurdish nationalism go back to the 1920s. See Abbas Vali, "The Kurds and Their Fragmented 'Others': Fragmented Identity and Fragmented Politics," *Comparative Studies of South Asia, Africa, and the Middle East* 18, no. 2 (2002): 83.
37. Taher Khadiw, *Bazkhaniye Jonbeshe chap dar Kurdistan (1979–1990)* (Analysis of the Far-Left Movement in Kurdistan, 1970–1990), master's thesis, Tehran, University of Shahid Beheshti, 2006; Hamit Bozarslan, *La question kurde: État et minorités au Moyen-Orient* (The Kurdish Question: State and Minorities in the Middle East) (Paris: Presses de Sciences Po, 1997), 123.
38. Vali, "Kurds and Fragmented 'Others'"; Bozarslan, *La question kurde* (The Kurdish Question), 123–24.
39. Saidi, *Sé Sal le gel Ebrahim Alizadeh*, 432.
40. Khadiw, *Analysis of the Far-Left Movement in Kurdistan.*
41. Ibid.
42. Hosain Morad Baigi, *Tarikh'ë Zende : Kurdestan, Chap et Nationalism* (Living History: Kurdistan, the Left and Nationalism) (Nasim, 2004), 42.
43. David McDowall, *Modern History of the Kurds* (London: I. B. Tauris, 2004), 275; Maziar Behrooz, *Rebels with a Cause: The Failure of the Left in Iran* (London: I.B. Tauris), 131.
44. Ibid.
45. Ibid.

PART I: KURDISH WOMEN IN REVOLUTION

1. Eliz Sanasarian, *The Women's Rights Movement in Iran: Mutiny, Appeasement, and Repression from 1900 to Khomeini* (New York, Praeger, 1982); Parvin Paidar, *Women and the Political Process in Twentieth-Century Iran* (New York: Cambridge University Press, 1997).
2. Hammed Shahidian, "Women and Clandestine Politics in Iran, 1970–1985," *Feminist Studies* 23, no. 1 (1997): 7–42.
3. Vida Hadjebi Tabrizi, *Yadha* (Memoirs) (Cologne: Mortezavi, 2009), 12.

4. Maziar Behrooz, *Rebels with a Cause: The Failure of the Left in Iran* (London: I.B. Tauris), 50.
5. While the first bloody demonstrations against the Pahlavi regime began in early January 1978 in a few major cities of Iran, accounts mention the first demonstrations in the Kurdish regions on June 10 in Mahabad and July 8 in Sanandaj. See Yasin Sardashti, *Kurdistanî Éran: Lékolineweyeki méjuyi le julanewey rizgarikhwazi netewey gali kurd (1939–1979)* (The Kurdistan of Iran: A Historical Analysis of the Emancipatory Movement of the Kurdish Nation between 1939–1979) (Sulaymaniyah: Sima, 2011), 698.

CHAPTER 1: BETWEEN REPRESSION AND DEPRIVATION

1. Abbas Vali, *Kurds and the State in Iran: The Making of Kurdish Identity* (London: I.B. Tauris, 2011), 15.
2. Ervand Abrahamian, *Iran Between Two Revolutions* (Princeton, NJ: Princeton University Press, 1982), 424–41.
3. Kumari Jayawardena, *Feminism and Nationalism in the Third World* (London: Zed Books, 1986), 8–23.
4. Azadeh Kian-Thiébaut, "Mouvements de femmes en Iran: entre l'islam et l'Occident," (Women's Movements in Iran: Between Islam and the West) in *Vents d'Est, vents d'Ouest: mouvements de femmes et féminismes anticoloniaux* (East Winds, West Winds: Women's Movements and Anticolonial Feminisms), ed. Christine Verschuur (Geneva: Graduate Institute Publications, 2009), 117–28.
5. Marie Ladier-Fouladi, "Étude démographique du divorce en Iran: le cas de la ville de Shiraz en 1996," (Demographic Study of Divorce in Iran: The Case of the City of Shiraz in 1996). *Cahiers d'Études sur la Méditerranée Orientale et le monde Turco-Iranien* (Notebooks of Studies on the Eastern Mediterranean and the Turkish-Iranian World), no. 28 (1999): 287–95.
6. Farideh Farhi, "Crafting a National Identity Amidst Contentious Politics in Contemporary Iran," *Iranian Studies* 38 no. 1 (2005): 12.
7. Benedict Anderson, *Imagined Communities: Reflections on the Origin and Spread of Nationalism* (London: Verso, 1991), 6.
8. Stephanie Cronin, ed., *Anti-veiling Campaigns in the Muslim World: Gender, Modernism and the Politics of Dress* (New York: Routledge, 2014); Azadeh Kian, "La fabrique du genre, des corps et des sexualités en Iran. Entre nationalisme et islamisme," (The Making of Gender, Bodies and Sexualities in Iran. Between Nationalism and Islamism) in *État-nation et fabrique du genre, des corps et des sexualités: Iran,*

Turquie, Afghanistan (Nation-State and the Making of Gender, Bodies and Sexualities: Iran, Turkey, Afghanistan), ed. Lucia Direnberger and Azadeh Kian (Presses universitaires de Provence, 2019), 28–29; Houchang E. Chehabi, "Staging the Emperor's New Clothes: Dress Codes and Nation-Building under Reza Shah," *Iranian Studies* 26, no. 3/4 (1993): 209–29.

9. Houchang E. Chehabi, "Staging the Emperor's New Clothes: Dress Codes and Nation-Building under Reza Shah", *Iranian Studies*, no. 3/4, vol. 26, 1993, 209–29.
10. Afsaneh Najmabadi, "Authority and Agency: Revisiting Women's Activism During Reza Shah's Period," in *The State and the Subaltern. Modernization, Society and the State in Turkey and Iran*, ed. Touraj Atabakim, 159–78 (London: I.B. Tauris, 2007).
11. Jasmin Rostam-Kolayi and Afshin Martin-Asgari, "Unveiling Ambiguities: Revisiting 1930s Iran's *kashf-i hijab* Campaign," in Cronin, *Anti-veiling Campaigns*, 121–48; Hamideh Sedghi, *Women and Politics in Iran: Veiling, Unveiling, and Reveiling* (New York: Cambridge University Press, 2007), 87.
12. Kian, "La fabrique du genre," 28–29.
13. This information was obtained during my contact with Kobra Azimi, a 92-year-old woman from Mahabad.
14. Kobra Azimi, *The Meaning of My Life (Manay Jiyanim)*, collected and edited by Simin Eftekhari (Sweden: Kitab-i Arzan), 63–64.
15. Azadeh Kian-Thiébaut, "Making of Gender, Bodies and Sexualities in Iran," 75.
16. Mojab, "Introduction," 7.
17. Eliz Sanasarian, *Religious Minorities in Iran* (Cambridge: Cambridge University Press, 2000), 5.
18. Mohamad Tavakoli-Targhi, "Refashioning Iran: Language and Culture During the Constitutional Revolution," *Iranian Studies* 23, no. 1 (1990): 77–101.
19. Amir Hassanpour, *Nationalism and Language in Kurdistan, 1918–1985* (San Francisco: Mellen Research University Press, 1992), 126.
20. Ibid.
21. Anne-Marie Thiesse, *La création des identités nationales, Europe XVIIIe–XXe siècle* (The Creation of National Identities, Europe 18th–20th Centuries) (Paris: Le Seuil, 1999), 237.
22. On the role of the school in the Pahlavi era, see Rudi Matthee, "Transforming Dangerous Nomads into Useful Artisans, Technicians, Agriculturalists: Education in the Reza Shah Period," in *The*

Making of Modern Iran: State and Society Under Riza Shah, 1921–1941, ed. Stephanie Cronin, 123–45 (New York, Routledge, 2003).

23. Diana Nammi and Karen Attwood, *Girl with a Gun*, (London: Unbound, 2020), 13.
24. Fathali M. Moghaddam and David S. Crystal, "Revolutions, Samurai, and Reductions: The Paradoxes of Change and Continuity in Iran and Japan," *Political Psychology* 18, no. 2 (1997): 355–84.
25. Homa Katouzian, *The Political Economy of Modern Iran, 1926–1979* (New York: New York University Press, 1981), 192–93, 197.
26. Ali Mirsepassi, *Intellectual Discourse and the Politics of Modernization: Negotiating Modernity in Iran* (Cambridge: Cambridge University Press, 2000), 61.
27. Richard W. Cottam, *Nationalism in Iran* (Pittsburgh: University of Pittsburgh Press, 1964), 8; Joseph M. Upton, *The History of Modern Iran: An Interpretation* (Cambridge, MA: Harvard University Press, 1960), 29.
28. Kaveh Bayat, "Riza Shah and the Tribes: an Overview," in *The Making of Modern Iran: State and Society Under Riza Shah, 1921–1941*, ed. Stephanie Cronin, 213–19 (New York: Routledge, 2003); Farideh Koohi-Kamali, *The Political Development of the Kurds in Iran: Pastoral Nationalism* (New York: Palgrave Macmillan, 2003), 41.
29. Donald Newton Wilber, *Iran Past and Present: From Monarchy to Islamic Republic*, 9th ed. (Princeton, NJ: Princeton University Press, 1981), 153.
30. Manizheh Zavareei, "Dependent Capitalist Development in Iran and the Mass Uprising of 1979," in *Research in Political Economy: A Research Manual*, ed. Paul Zarembka (Jai Pr, 1984), 152.
31. Amnesty International, *Annual Report 1974–1975*, quoted in Mahmood Delkhasteh, *Islamic Discourses of Power and Freedom in the Iranian Revolution, 1979–81*, Ph.D. thesis (London: School of Economics and Political Science, 2007), 71.
32. One of the revolts of this period was an 18-month armed struggle led by a fringe of the DPKI in 1967–68, which government forces brutally suppressed by massacring its members. See Martin van Bruinessen, *Agha, Shaikh and State: The Social and Political Structures of Kurdistan* (London: Zed Books, 1992), 35.
33. Taifur Bathai, *Safare Khiyal* (The Voyage of the Spirit) (Khaniyeh honar va adabiyat, 2012), 43.
34. Mohammed Amjad, *Iran: From Royal Dictatorship to Theocracy* (London: Greenwood Press, 1989), 30.
35. Koohi-Kamali, *Political Development of Kurds in Iran*, 156.

36. Farhad Kazemi, *Poverty and Revolution in Iran: The Migrant Poor, Urban Marginality and Politics* (New York, New York University Press, 1980), 35; Akbar Aghajanian, "Ethnic Inequality in Iran: An Overview," *International Journal of Middle East Studies* 15, no. 2 (1983): 220–21.
37. Jamshid Amouzegar, "Administrative Barriers to Economic Development in Iran," *Middle East Economic*, no 11 (1964): 5–7.
38. Ervand Abrahamian, *Iran Between Two Revolutions* (Princeton, NJ: Princeton University Press, 1982), 120, 427, 529, 535.
39. Said Lailaz, *Nowsazi ameraneh dar Iran* (Imposed modernization in Iran) (Tehran: Niloofar, 1398 [2019]), 416–17.
40. Azar Tabari, "The Enigma of Veiled Iranian Women," *Feminist Review*, no. 5 (1980): 21.
41. Erica Friedl, "Women and the Division of Labour in an Iranian Village," *MERIP Report*, no. 95 (1981): 17.
42. Azam Kamgouyan, "Gozareshi az kar u zendegi zanane kargare khanegi ghalibaf dar Kurdistan" (A Report on the Work and Life of Women Domestic Carpet Weavers in Kurdistan), *Communiste*, no. 28, (1986): 32–33.
43. Tabari, "Enigma of Veiled Iranian Women."
44. Kamgouyan, "Work and Life of Women Domestic Carpet Weavers."
45. Parvin Paidar, *Women and the Political Process in Twentieth-Century Iran* (New York: Cambridge University Press, 1997), 162–63.
46. Maria O'Shea, "Medic, Mystic or Magic? Women's Health Choices in a Kurdish City," in *Women of a Non-State Nation: The Kurds*, ed. Shahrzad Mojab (Costa Mesa, CA: Mazda, 2001), 161–79.
47. Aghajanian, "Ethnic Inequality in Iran," 216.
48. Amineh Kakabaveh and Johan Ohlson, *Amineh: inte större än en kalasjnikov: från peshmerga till riksdagsledamot* (Amineh: No Bigger Than a Kalashnikov: From Peshmerga to Member of Parliament) (Stockholm: Ordfront, 2016), 23.

CHAPTER 2: WOMEN'S SUBORDINATION IN KURDISH SOCIETY

1. Ogburn quoted in Luis Guay et al., *Mouvements sociaux et changements institutionnels* (Social Movements and Institutional Changes) (Québec: Université du Québec, 2005), 398 ; Amin Banani, *The Modernization of Iran,(1921–1941* (Stanford, CA: Stanford University Press, 1961), 119–29.

2. Azadeh Kian-Thiébaut, "Mouvements de femmes en Iran: entre l'islam et l'Occident," (Women's Movements in Iran: Between Islam and the West) in *Vents d'Est, vents d'Ouest: Mouvements de femmes et féminismes anticoloniaux* (East Winds, West Winds: Women's Movements and Anticolonial Feminisms), ed. Christine Verschuur (Geneva: Graduate Institute Publications, 2009), 117–28.
3. Afsaneh Najmabadi, "Hazards of Modernity and Morality: Women, State and Ideology in Contemporary Iran," in *Women, Islam and State*, ed. Deniz Kandiyoti (London: Macmillan, 1991), 65.
4. Marie Ladier-Fouladi, *Iran, un monde de paradoxes (Iran, a World of Paradoxes)* (Nantes: Atalante, 2009), 27.
5. Amir Hassanpour, "The (Re)Production of Patriarchy in the Kurdish Language," in *Women of a Non-State Nation: The Kurds*, ed. Shahrzad Mojab (Costa Mesa, CA: Mazda, 2001), 238–39.
6. Thomas Bois, *Connaissance des Kurdes* (Beirut: Khayats, 1956), 44.
7. Martin van Bruinessen, *Agha, Shaikh and State: The Social and Political Structures of Kurdistan* (London: Zed Books, 1992), 72.
8. While in Tehran, 53.8 percent of marriages were between maternal cross-cousins, the figure for rural areas was 38.5 percent. See Vida Nassehi-Behnam, "Change and the Iranian Family," *Current Anthropology* 26, no. 5 (1985): 557–62.
9. Van Bruinessen, *Agha, Shaikh and State*, 72.
10. Hassanpour, "(Re)production of Patriarchy," 241.
11. Ibid., 243.
12. Ibid., 244.
13. The divorce rate in Iran in the 1960s was between 17.2 and 22.25, the highest among most Muslim countries at the time. This figure was 6.6 percent in Algeria in 1960–1964, 14.9 percent in Iraq and 9.8 percent in Syria. Quoted in Marie Ladier-Fouladi, "Étude démographique du divorce en Iran: le cas de la ville de Shiraz en 1996," (Demographic Study of Divorce in Iran: The Case of the City of Shiraz in 1996). *Cahiers d'Études sur la Méditerranée Orientale et le monde Turco-Iranien* (Notebooks of Studies on the Eastern Mediterranean and the Turkish-Iranian World), no. 28 (1999): 287–95.
14. Leila Enayatzadeh, "Baz tajarode zanan" (The New Celibacy of Women), *Djamei'a shenasan* (Tehran), 1397 (2017): 151.
15. Ibid., 187–201.
16. Marie Ladier-Fouladi, "La transition de la fécondité en Iran (The Fertility Transition in Iran), *Population* 51, no. 6 (1996): 1101–27.
17. Azadeh Kian, "La fabrique du genre, des corps et des sexualités en Iran. Entre nationalisme et islamisme," in *État-nation et fabrique*

du genre, des corps et des sexualités: Iran, Turquie, Afghanistan (The Making of Gender, Bodies and Sexualities in Iran. Between Nationalism and Islamism) in *État-nation et fabrique du genre, des corps et des sexualités : Iran, Turquie, Afghanistan* (Nation-State and the Making of Gender, Bodies and Sexualities: Iran, Turkey, Afghanistan), ed. Lucia Direnberger and Azadeh Kian (Presses universitaires de Provence, 2019), 34.

18. Rosemary Gillespie, "When No Means No: Disbelief, Disregard and Deviance as Discourses of Voluntary Childlessness," *Women's Studies International Forum* 23, no. 2 (2000): 223.
19. Françoise Héritier, *Masculin, féminin. La pensée de la différence* (Masculine, Feminine. The Thought of Difference) (Paris: O. Jacob, 1996), 79.
20. Somayeh Rostampour, *Vakaviye jami'a shenakhtiye mafhume namus: Kurdistan* (Analysis of the Concept of Namûs Among the Kurds), master's thesis (Tehran: University of Tehran, 2012), 120–26.
21. Fatemeh Karimi, *Chand hamsari, shiweh zist va payamadhaye an dar Iran* (Polygamy, Lifestyle and Its Outcomes in the Kurdish Society of Iran) (London: H & S Media, 2014), 109–18.
22. Bois, *Connaissance des Kurdes,* 56.
23. Karimi, *Polygamy in Kurdish Society.*
24. Bois, *Connaissance des Kurdes,* 56.
25. Karimi, *Polygamy in Kurdish Society,* 117.
26. Maria O'Shea, "Medic, Mystic or Magic? Women's Health Choices in a Kurdish City," in *Women of a Non-State Nation: The Kurds,* ed. Shahrzad Mojab (Costa Mesa, CA: Mazda, 2001), 165.
27. Bois, *Connaissance des Kurdes,* 27–28.
28. Hassanpour, "(Re)production of Patriarchy," 235–36.
29. Christine Allison, "Folklore and Fantasy: The Presentation of Women in Kurdish Oral Tradition," in *Women of a Non-State Nation: The Kurds,* ed. Shahrzad Mojab (Costa Mesa, CA: Mazda, 2001), 184.
30. Ibid., 187.
31. Bois, *Connaissance des Kurdes,* 58.
32. Rostampour, *Analysis of the Concept of Namûs,* 276.
33. Karimi, *Polygamy in Kurdish Society,* 124–5.
34. Lila Abu-Lughod, "Do Muslim Women Really Need Saving? Anthropological Reflections on Cultural Relativism and Its Others," *American Anthropologist* 104, no. 3 (2002): 783–90.
35. Nazand Begikhani and Gill Hague, "'Honour'-Based Violence: Moving Towards Action and Change in Iraqi Kurdistan," *Copernicus Journal of Political Studies* 2, no. 4 (2013): 215.

36. Diana Nammi and Karen Attwood, *Girl with a Gun*, (London: Unbound, 2020), xiii–xiv.
37. Nazand Begikhani and Gill Hague, "'Honour'-Based Violence," 215.
38. Hassanpour, "(Re)production of Patriarchy," 239.
39. Christiane Chaulet-Achour, *Autobiographies d'Algériennes sur l'autre rive: se définir entre mémoire et rupture* (Biographies of Algerian Women on the Other Sid : Defining Oneself Between Memory and Rupture) (Paris: L'Harmattan, 1994), 291.
40. Nadine Puechguirbal, *Le genre entre guerre et paix* (Gender Between War and Peace) (Paris: Dalloz, 2007), 29.

PART II: MILITANT TRAJECTORIES WITHIN KOMALA

1. Farideh Koohi-Kamali, *The Political Development of the Kurds in Iran: Pastoral Nationalism* (New York: Palgrave Macmillan, 2003), 172.
2. Nikki R. Keddie, *Modern Iran: Roots and Results of Revolution* (New Haven, CT: Yale University Press, 2003), 313.
3. Koohi-Kamali, *Political Development of Kurds in Iran,* 179–86.
4. Ali Ezzatyar, *The last mufti of Iranian Kurdistan: ethnic and religious implications in the greater Middle East* (New York: Palgrave Macmillan, 2016), 135.
5. Ibid., 185–6.
6. Ibid., 185.
7. Abbas Vali, "The Kurds and Their Fragmented 'Others': Fragmented Identity and Fragmented Politics," *Comparative Studies of South Asia, Africa, and the Middle East* 18, no. 2 (2002): 91.
8. David McDowall, *A Modern History of the Kurds* (London: I.B. Tauris, 2004), 270.
9. Martin van Bruinessen, *Agha, Shaikh and State: The Social and Political Structures of Kurdistan* (London: Zed Books, 1992), 373.

CHAPTER 3: THE ERUPTION OF KURDISH WOMEN INTO ORGANIZED POLITICAL LIFE

1. Shahrzad Mojab, "Women and Nationalism in the Kurdish Republic of 1946," in *Women of a Non-State Nation: The Kurds,* ed. Shahrzad Mojab (Costa Mesa, CA: Mazda, 2001), 71–91.
2. David Romano, *The Kurdish Nationalist Movement: Opportunity, Mobilization and Identity* (Cambridge: Cambridge University Press, 2006), 235.

3. David McDowall, *A Modern History of the Kurds* (London: I.B. Tauris, 2004), 270.
4. Golrokh Ghobadi, *Shaghayg-ha bar sanglakh, zendegi u zamaneye yek zane Kurd* (Anemone on the Rock, the Life and Time of a Kurdish Woman) (Sweden: Autoédition, 2015), 205.
5. Simona de Simoni, "La 'vie quotidienne' : une analyse féministe" (Everyday Life: A Feminist Analysis), *Revue période* (2014), http://revueperiode.net/la-vie-quotidienne-une-analyse-feministe/. Accessed March 31, 2014.
6. *Barname-i Komala baray-i Khudmukhtari-i Kurdistan* (Komala's Program for the Autonomy of Kurdistan), a publication of the Fourth Congress of the Kurdish Organization of the Communist Party of Iran (1983), https://cpiran.org/ketabkhane/asnad/pdf/bkbx.pdf. Accessed March 31, 2024.
7. Ibid.
8. Amineh Kakabaveh and Johan Ohlson, *Amineh: inte större än en kalasjnikov: från peshmerga till riksdagsledamot* (Amineh: No Bigger Than a Kalashnikov: From Peshmerga to Member of Parliament) (Stockholm: Ordfront, 2016), 42.
9. De Simoni, "La 'vie quotidienne.'"
10. Kakabaveh and Ohlson, *Amineh,* 47.
11. Danièle Amrane-Minne, "Les femmes face à la violence dans la guerre de libération" (Women Facing Violence in the War of Liberation)," *Confluences Méditerranée,* no. 17 (1996): 90.
12. According to Montezeri, one of Ayatollah Khomeini's close associates: "Women are mostly misguided. . . . Most of them do not have the power of discernment and have therefore been influenced. They should be sentenced to imprisonment so that they realize their folly, and then be released." Quoted in Hossain Ali Montezeri, *Khterate Ayatollah Montezeri* (Memoir of the Ayatollah Montezeri), Etehadiye Nasherane Irani Dar Uruopa (Baran: Khavaran, Nima), 1379 (2000), 344–5.
13. F. Peshko, "Be Ser Hat" (Fate), *Peshang,* no. 9 (1989): 75–83.
14. Olivier Fillieulle and Patricia Roux, *Le Sexe du militantisme* (The Sex of Activism), (Lausanne: Sciences Po, 2009), 21–72.
15. Christine Delphy, "Pour une théorie générale de l'exploitation. Deuxième partie: repartir du bon pied" (Toward a General Theory of Exploitation. Part Two: Getting Back on the Right Foot), *Mouvements* 1, no. 31 (2004): 97–106.
16. Laetitia Bucaille, "Louisette et Dipuo, combattantes du FLN et de l'ANC: engagement et transgression," (FLN and ANC fighters:

Commitment and Transgression) in *La lutte armée, instrument d'émancipation des femmes?* (Armed Struggle, an Instrument for Women's Emancipation?), ed. Caroline Guibet Lafaye and Alexandra Frénod (Presses de l'INALCO, 2019), 83–101.

17. Jalil Muin Afshar, *Jamal Khompareh* (Jamil's Memories), Ya Leyl [Khaterate jamil, Jamal khompareh, Ya Leyl] (2015), 57–8, https://tinyurl.com/26efpenc. Accessed March 17, 2018.
18. Marie Ladier-Fouladi, *Iran, un monde de paradoxes (Iran, a World of Paradoxes)* (Nantes: Atalante, 2009), 85–91.

CHAPTER 4: THE OBSTACLES TO WOMEN'S POLITICAL PARTICIPATION

1. Gail Pheterson, *Le prisme de la prostitution (The Prism of Prostitution)* (Paris: L'Harmattan, 2001), 56.
2. Caroline Fayolle, "La 'femme monstre'. La citoyenneté à l'épreuve de la peur de la confusion des sexes," (The 'Monster Woman': Citizenship Tested by the Fear of Gender Confusion) in *La citoyenneté républicaine à l'épreuve des peurs* (Republican Citizenship Tested by Fears), ed. Lisa Bogani, Julien Bouchet, Philippe Bourdin, and Jean-Claude Caron (Rennes: PUR, 2016), 109–18.
3. Hosain Morad Baigi, *Tarikh'é Zende: Kurdestan, Chap et Nationalism* (Living History: Kurdistan, the Left and Nationalism) (Nasim, 2004), 133.
4. Christine Delphy, "Pour une théorie générale de l'exploitation. Deuxième partie: repartir du bon pied" (Toward a General Theory of Exploitation. Part Two: Getting Back on the Right Foot), *Mouvements* 1, no. 31 (2004): 97–106.
5. Jules Falquet, "Division sexuelle du travail révolutionnaire : Réflexions à partir de l'expérience salvadorienne (1970–1994)" (Sexual Division of Revolutionary Labor: Reflections from the Salvadoran Experience (1970–1994), *Cahiers des Amériques latines,* no. 40 (2013): 109–28.
6. Golrokh Ghobadi, *Shaghayg-ha bar sanglakh, zendegi u zamaneye yek zane Kurd* (Anemone on the Rock, the Life and Time of a Kurdish Woman) (Sweden: Self-published, 2015), 218.
7. Geneviève Pruvost says, "Behind-the-scenes activities are not only essential for neophytes learning the ropes; they are part of the career-building elements of the job, especially when professional ascent works by co-option." Geneviève Pruvost, "Le hors-travail au travail dans la police et l'intérim, Approches interactionnistes des coulisses" (Out-of-Work at Work in the Police and Temporary Work,

Interactionist Approaches Behind the Scenes), *Communications,* no 89, vol. 2 (2011), 184.

8. Ghobadi, *Anemone on the Rock,* 195.
9. Naser Mohadjer's interview with Golrokh Ghobadi in Naser Mohadjer and Mahnaz Matin, *Khizeshĕ Zanan dar Esfandĕ 1357* (The Women's Revolt in March 1979) (Cologne: Ghatreh, 2013), 1:456–79.
10. Ghobadi, *Anemone on the Rock,* 111.
11. Malekeh Mostafa Soltani and Sa'ad Vatandoost, eds., *Mabahese Kongrey Awale Komala* (Proceedings of the First Komala Congress) (Rebazi Komala, 2018), 59.

CHAPTER 5: THE SOCIO-POLITICAL ACTIVITIES OF FEMALE MILITANTS

1. Quoted in Golrokh Ghobadi, *Shaghayg-ha bar sanglakh, zendegi u zamaneye yek zane Kurd* (Anemone on the Rock, the Life and Time of a Kurdish Woman) (Sweden: Self-published, 2015), 219–20.
2. Ibid., 219.
3. Naser Mohadjer and Mahnaz Matin, *Khizeshĕ Zanan dar Esfandĕ 1357* (The Women's Revolt in March 1979) (Cologne: Ghatreh, 2013), 1:473.
4. Ibid.
5. On the politicization of the life network, see Temma Kaplan, "Female Consciousness and Collective Action : The Case of Barcelona (1910–1918)," *Signs* 7, no. 3 (1982): 545–66.
6. Ghobadi, *Anemone on the Rock,* 204.
7. Quoted in Mohadjer and Matin, *The Women's Revolt,* 357.
8. Sheila Rowbotham, *Women, Resistance and Revolution* (New York, Vintage Books, 1974), 12.
9. According to *Kayhan* (March 31, 1979), these three women were Golriz Ghobadi, Faezeh Gotbi, and Farideh Zakaryai.
10. One of the most important of these organizations, prominently featured during this period in Kurdish regions, was the Islamic Revolutionary Guard Corps (IRGC), officially organized by order of Ayatollah Khomeini on May 6, 1979. See Farhad Khosrokhavar, *L'utopie sacrifiée* (The Sacrificed Utopia) (Paris: Presses of the National Foundation of Political Sciences, 1993), 86, 175; Ervand Abrahamian, *Iran Between Two Revolutions* (Princeton, NJ: Princeton University Press, 1982), 526.
11. Rashad Mostafa Soltani, "*Kak Foad: the leader, the politician, and the political scholar.*" *[Kak Foad: Rébar, siyasat madar u Zanayeki siyasi] (Rojhelat,* 2006), 366.

12. *Tehran Mosavar* magazine, July 21, 1979.
13. *Tehran Mosavar* magazine, July 21, 1979, cited in Ghobadi, A*nemone on the Rock*, 261.
14. Elizabeth Ferris, *Women, War and Peace: An Issue Paper* (Uppsala: Life and Peace Institute, 1992), 6.
15. Ghobadi, *Anemone on the Rock*, 315.
16. Ibid., 298.
17. Ibid., 202.
18. Ibid., 370–1.
19. *Kayhan*, April 26, 1979.
20. Vahid Abedi, *Baznegari-e Komala Dar Masir-e Tarikh* (Review of Komala Throughout History) (Rebazi Komala, 2012), 9.
21. Ghobadi, *Anemone on the Rock*, 442–3.
22. Yassaman Saadatmand, "Separate and Unequal Women in Islamic Republic of Iran," *Journal of South Asian and Middle Eastern Studies* 18, no. 4 (1995): 21.
23. Vida Hajebi Tabrizi, *Yadha* (Memoirs) (Cologne: Mortezavi, 2009), 184.
24. Haleh Safarzadeh, *Sayre Mobarezate Zanane irani dar dahayeh 50 shamsi* (The Course of Iranian Women's Struggles in the 1970s) 1398 (2019), 73, https://persianbooks2.blogspot.com/2020/03/blog-post_10.html. Accessed April 15, 2019.

CHAPTER 6: BECOMING A PESHMERGA UNDER STATE REPRESSION

1. Golrokh Ghobadi, *Shaghayg-ha bar sanglakh, zendegi u zamaneye yek zane Kurd* (Anemone on the Rock, the Life and Time of a Kurdish Woman) (Sweden: Self-published, 2015), 359.
2. Ibid., 437.
3. Jean-François Revel, *L'Express*, July 5–11, 1980, 74.
4. Ibid.
5. Ghobadi, *Anemone on the Rock*, 454.
6. Photos of these three executed women were taken from Facebook: www.facebook.com/ukkomala/posts/2320108904778727/. Accessed March 31, 2024.
7. Lætitia Bucaille, "Femmes à la guerre. Égalité, sexe et violence," *Critique internationale* 3, no. 60 (2013), 11.
8. Shadi Sadr and Shadi Amin, *Crime and Impunity Sexual Torture of Women in Islamic Republic Prisons* (Justice for Iran, 2012), 54.
9. Ibid.
10. Marouf Ka'abi, *Dashti Daré* (Plain of Daré) (Aweneh, 2010), 68.

11. Amir Hassanpour, "The (Re)production of Patriarchy in the Kurdish Language," in *Women of a Non-State Nation: The Kurds,* ed. Shahrzad Mojab (Costa Mesa, CA: Mazda, 2001), 239.
12. Christine Guionnet and Erik Neveu, *Féminins/Masculins* (Female/Male) (Paris: Armand Colin, 2004), 203.
13. Sadr and Amin, *Crime and Impunity,* 117.
14. Ibid., 115.
15. Ibid., 217.
16. Kobra Bane'i, a Kurdish woman, quoted in Sadr and Amin, *Crime and Impunity,* 143.
17. Ghobadi, *Anemone on the Rock,* 510.
18. Cynthia H. Enloe, *Does Khaki Become You? The Militarization of Women's Lives* (London: Pluto Press, 1983), 10.
19. Ghobadi, *Anemone on the Rock,* 471–2.
20. Ibid., 547.

PART III: PATRIARCHY IN THE LIVES OF THE KOMALA PESHMERGA

1. Farideh Koohi-Kamali, *The Political Development of the Kurds in Iran: Pastoral Nationalism* (New York: Palgrave Macmillan, 2003), 179.
2. https://tinyurl.com/d9xbhhn4. Accessed January 20, 2025.
3. Suzanne Maloney, "Identity and Change in Iran's Foreign Policy," in *Identity and Foreign Policy in the Middle East,* ed. Shibley Telhami and Michael N. Barnett (Ithaca, NY: Cornell University Press, 2002), 106.
4. David McDowall, *A Modern History of the Kurds* (London: I.B. Tauris, 2004), 275.
5. Taifur Bathai, *Safare Khiyal* (The Voyage of the Spirit) (Khaniyeh honar va adabiyat, 2012), 168.
6. Koohi-Kamali, *Political Development of Kurds in Iran,* 190.
7. Hamit Bozarslan, *La question kurde: État et minorités au Moyen-Orient* (The Kurdish Question: State and Minorities in the Middle East), (Paris: Presses de Sciences Po, 1997), 201–2.
8. This information was given to me by Golrokh Ghobadi.

CHAPTER 7: PESHMERGA WOMEN AND THE PROBLEMS OF INTEGRATION

1. Manuel Cervera-Marzal, "Domination masculine dans le militantisme" (Male Domination in Activism), *Sociologies,* May 26, 2015, https://doi.org/10.4000/sociologies.5116.

2. Christine Bard, *Les filles de Marianne, histoire des féminismes 1914–1940* (Marianne's Daughters: History of Feminism 1914–1940) (Paris: Fayard, 1995).
3. Jules Falquet, "Division sexuelle du travail révolutionnaire : Réflexions à partir de l'expérience salvadorienne (1970–1994)" (Sexual Division of Revolutionary Labor: Reflections from the Salvadoran Experience (1970–1994)), *Cahiers des Amériques latines*, no. 40 (2013): 109–28.
4. On the importance of Komala medical centers in Kurdish rural areas, Amineh Kakabaveh writes: "There were already no medical centers in Kurdish rural areas. That was why the medical area of Komala had been receiving dozens of sick village women every day free of charge." Amineh Kakabaveh and Johan Ohlson, *Amineh: inte större än en kalasjnikov: från peshmerga till riksdagsledamot* (Amineh: No Bigger Than a Kalashnikov: From Peshmerga to Member of Parliament) (Stockholm: Ordfront, 2016), 98.
5. Nicole-Claude Mathieu, "Homme-culture et femme-nature ?," (Man-Culture and Woman-Nature?) *L'Homme* 13, no. 3 (1973): 101–13.
6. Sonia Dayan-Herzbrun, "La mixité dans la politique," (Gender Diversity in Politics) in *Genre et politique: débats et perspectives* (Gender and Politics: Debates and Perspectives), ed. Thanh-Huyen Ballmer-Cao, Véronique Mottier and Léa Sgier (Paris: Gallimard, 2000), 292.
7. Bahman Saidi, *Sé Sal le gel Ebrahim Alizadeh* (Three Years with Ebrahim Alizadeh) (Sulaymaniyah: Ranj, 2009), 81.
8. Yadi az Zanan'é Mobareze Kordestan (A Memorial to the Fighting Women of Kurdistan) Facebook page, www.facebook.com/pg/112830855470735-یادی-از-زنان-مبارز-کردستان. Accessed March 31, 2024.
9. Mostafa Amin Noshirwan, "Keshey afratan u bezutnewey jinan le newan wahm u waqeyiyetde" (Women's Issues and the Women's Movement Between Reality and Illusion), in *Diyalog le gal bashek le roshanbir u siyasatmadar u halsurawi bezutnaway jinan la mar keshe w bezutnaway afratan* (Dialogue with Some Intellectuals, Politicians and Activists of the Women's Movement on the Issue of Women), ed. Hama Ali Salar (Sulaymaniyah, 2008), 28.
10. Videos of the ceremony are available on YouTube: www.youtube.com/watch?v=gayBvjTzSug&t=448s; www.youtube.com/watch?v=x6xIMZFc488&t=511s; www.youtube.com/watch?v=fUKhYNT35KA. Accessed March 31, 2024.
11. Golrokh Ghobadi, *Shaghayg-ha bar sanglakh, zendegi u zamaneye yek zane Kurd* (Anemone on the Rock, the Life and Time of a Kurdish Woman) (Sweden: Self-published, 2015), 563.

12. Sruch Khani, photo, www.facebook.com/pg/112830855470735 ادی-از-زنان-مبارز-کردستان- (A Memorial to the Fighting Women of Kurdistan). Accessed March 31, 2024.
13. "Gozareshi az amuzeshgahaye peshmergayatiye Komala" (A Report from the Komala Peshmerga Training Centers), *Peshro*, no. 12 (1986).
14. Ghobadi, *Anemone on the Rock*, 559.
15. Saidi, *Three Years with Ebrahim Alizadeh*, 80–1.
16. Ibid., 81.
17. "Gozareshi az amuzeshgahaye peshmergayatiye Komala" (A Report from the Komala Peshmerga Training Centers), *Peshro*, no. 12 (1986).
18. "Commemoration of March 8," *Peshro*, no. 6 (1985).
19. Saidi, *Three Years with Ebrahim Alizadeh*, 470–3.
20. Marouf Ka'abi, *Dashti Daré* (Plain of Daré) (Aweneh, 2010), 198.
21. Ibid., 83.
22. On women fighters' unequal access to tools and weapons, see Paola Tabet, "Les Mains, les outils, les armes," (Hands, Tools, Weapons) *L'Homme* 19, no. 3/4 (1979): 5–61.
23. Neither the author of the poem nor its original language are not specified in the party journal, *Peshang*, See "Kiçe peshmerga" (The Peshmerga Young Woman), translated by Rebwar. J. Rebwar *Peshang*, no. 13 (1989): 58–9.
24. Ahmad Bazgar, "Sirenjek le shiri Bayan" (A Glance at Bayan's Poem), *Peshang*, no. 9 (1989): 119–32.

CHAPTER 8: BODILY DISCIPLINE AND THE PESHMERGA

1. Olivier Grojean, "Penser l'engagement et la violence des combattantes kurdes: des femmes en armes au sein d'ordres partisans singuliers," (Thinking about the Commitment and Violence of Kurdish Women Fighters: Armed Women Within Singular Partisan Orders) in *La lutte armée, instrument d'émancipation des femmes?*(Armed Struggle, an Instrument for the Emancipation of Women?), ed. Caroline Guibet Lafaye and Alexandra Frénod (Presses de l'INALCO, 2019).
2. Luca Greco, "Exhumer le corps du placard. Pour une linguistique queer du corps king," (Exhuming the Body from the Closet. For a Queer Linguistics of the King Body) in *Ecritures du corps. Nouvelles perspectives* (Writings of the Body. New Perspectives), ed. Pierre Zoberman, Anne Tomiche and William J. Spurlin (Paris: Classiques Garnier, 2013), 275.
3. Eric John Hobsbawm, "Revolution Is Puritan," in *The New Eroticism: Theories, Vogues and Canons*, ed. Philip Nobile (New York: Random House, 1970), 40.

4. Laurent Gayer, "Militariser les femmes. Doctrines, pratiques et critiques du féminisme martial en Asie du Sud," (Militarizing Women. Doctrines, Practices, and Critiques of Martial Feminism in South Asia) in *La lutte armée, instrument d'émancipation des femmes?* (Armed Struggle: An Instrument of Women's Emancipation?), ed. Caroline Guibet Lafaye and Alexandra Frénod (Paris: Presses de l'INALCO, 2019).
5. When Komala fighters discovered the presence of alcoholic beverages in an armed base of the KDPI, their Kurdish rival in the region, they did not hesitate to instrumentalize the event so as to spread the idea that the KDPI was in a bourgeois party. See Hatam Menbari, *Azar u Azimun* (Concern and Experience) (Sweden: Self-published, 2011), 238.
6. Marouf Ka'abi, *Dashti Daré* (Plain of Daré) (Aweneh, 2010), 62.
7. Hammed Shahidian, "Women and Clandestine Politics in Iran, 1970–1985," *Feminist Studies* 23, no. 1 (1997): 7–42
8. Bahman Saidi, *Sé Sal le gel Ebrahim Alizadeh* (Three Years with Ebrahim Alizadeh) (Sulaymaniyah: Ranj, 2009), 233.
9. Haideh Moghissi, *Populism and Feminism In Iran: Women's Struggle in a Male-Defined Revolutionary Movement* (New York: St. Martin's Press, 1994), 74.
10. Saidi, *Three Years with Ebrahim Alizadeh,* 81.
11. Laila Danesh, "Hijab" [Hijab], *Communist,* no. 32 (1987): 44.
12. Diana Nammi and Karen Attwood, *Girl with a Gun*, (London: Unbound, 2020), 144–5.
13. Mohammad Jafari, *Roshanak* (Shanbeh, 2005), 107.
14. Khaled Ali Panah, *Fulad'é Ab Dideh* (Frozen Steel) (Self-published, 2009), 20–1.
15. List of Komala martyrs in the 1980s from Saidi, *Three Years with Ebrahim Alizadeh,* 470–3.
16. Ibid., 233.
17. Golrokh Ghobadi, *Shaghayg-ha bar sanglakh, zendegi u zamaneye yek zane Kurd* (Anemone on the Rock, the Life and Time of a Kurdish Woman) (Sweden: Autoédition, 2015), 536.
18. Jafari, *Roshanak,* 107.
19. Taken from Golrokh's personal archive.
20. Hatam Menbari, *Azar u Azimun* (Concern and Experience) (Sweden: Self-published, 2011), 254.
21. Jafari, *Roshanak,* 122.

CHAPTER 9: FAMILY LIFE WITHIN THE ORGANIZATION

1. Golrokh Ghobadi, *Shaghayg-ha bar sanglakh, zendegi u zamaneye yek zane Kurd* (Anemone on the Rock, the Life and Time of a Kurdish Woman) (Sweden: Self-published, 2015), 492.
2. Ibid., 522.
3. Mohammad Jafari, *Roshanak* (Shanbeh, 2005), 108.
4. Ibid.
5. List of martyrs of Komala cited in Bahman Saidi, *Sé Sal le gel Ebrahim Alizadeh* (Three Years with Ebrahim Alizadeh) (Sulaymaniyah: Ranj, 2009), 470–3.
6. Testenoire Armelle, "Carrière féminine, résistances masculines: couples à hypogamie féminine," (Female Careers, Male Resistance: Couples with Female Hypogamy) in *L'inversion du genre. Quand les métiers masculins se déclinent au féminin... et réciproquement* (Gender Inversion. When Male Professions are Declined in the Feminine... and Vice Versa), ed. Danièle Kergoat, Yvonne Guichard-Claudic, and Alain Vilbrod (Rennes: PUR, 2005), 385–96.
7. Azar Majedi, *Komonist'ha va Masely'é Zanan* (Communism and the Women's Question), 1983, hezbe_komonist-hezbe_komonist_masleye_zanan.pdf. Accessed April 10, 2014.
8. Ibid., 9.
9. Ghobadi, *Anemone on the Rock*, 572.
10. Akhtar Kamangar, *Farazhayi az zendegiye Akhtare Kamangar* (Passages from the Life of Akhtar Kamangar) (Stockholm: Khanyeyh Farhange Shamloo, 2016), 112, 143.
11. Ghobadi, *Anemone on the Rock*, 592.
12. Ibid., 591–2.
13. Galewej Rostami, "Nameyi daykek" (A Mother's Letter), *Pehang*, no. 10 (1989): 109.
14. Kamangar, *Passages from the Life of Kamangar*, 165.
15. Adrienne Rich, *Of Woman Born: Motherhood as Experience and Institution* (New York, Norton, 1976).
16. Personal archive of peshmerga woman Zobaydeh Zabihi.
17. Cited in *Peshro* no. 7 (1985).
18. Iraj Azine, "Tudeh gir shodene Aghayede komonisti yek vazifiyeh tablighate mast" (It is our duty to spread communist ideas in masse), *Peshro*, no. 2 (1984).
19. Diana Nammi and Karen Attwood, Girl with a Gun, (London: Unbound, 2020), 168–170.

CHAPTER 10: THE DISAPPEARANCE OF PESHMERGA WOMEN

1. Danièle Amrane-Minne, "Les femmes face à la violence dans la guerre de libération" (Women Facing Violence in the War of Liberation), *Confluences Méditerranée*, no. 17 (1996): 89.
2. Hamed Shahidian, "The Iranian Left and the 'Woman Question' in the Revolution of 1978–79," *International Journal of Middle East Studies* 26, no. 2 (1994): 223–47.
3. Malekeh Mostafa Soltani and Sa'ad Vatandoost, eds., *Mabahese Kongrey Awale Komala* (Proceedings of the First Komala Congress) (Rebazi Komala, 2018), 93.
4. Mansoor Hekmat, "Mobarezeye mosalahaneh dar Kordestan" (The Armed Struggle in Kurdistan), *Communist*, no. 60 (1991): 3–11.
5. Report "Payané nokhostin dowreye madreseyeh hezbi'é Oktobr" (The End of the First Period of the October School of the Party), *Peshro*, no. 2 (1984).
6. Ibid.
7. Christine Guionnet and Erik Neveu, *Féminins/Masculins* (Female/Male) (Paris: Armand Colin, 2004), 186.
8. Michelle Perrot, *Les femmes ou les silences de l'histoire* (Women or the Silences of History) (Paris: Champs Flammarion, 1988, 18.
9. Laura Fournier-Finocchiaro, ed., "Les mères de la Patrie. Représentations et construction d'une figure nationale" (Mothers of the Fatherland. Representations and Construction of a National Figure), *Cahiers de la MRSH*, no. 45 (2006), 9.
10. According to the list of Komala martyrs in the 1980s, among 110 women, 96 were martyred in prison, in combat or during the bombing (Appendix 1).
11. The names of these "martyred" women (Fayezeh Shahabi, Fatemeh Hakimi, Mahnaz Lotfolahi, Bashi Shokri, Saniyeh Ebrahimi, Ameneh Hassani) were mentioned in issues no. 5, 6, 7, 10 and 12 of *Peshro* magazine, published between January 25, 1985 and February 1, 1986.
12. *Peshro*, no. 6 (1985).
13. Ghobadi, *Anemone on the Rock*, 607.
14. *Peshro*, no. 26 (1988), 22.
15. Bahman Saidi, *Sé Sal le gel Ebrahim Alizadeh* (Three Years with Ebrahim Alizadeh) (Sulaymaniyah: Ranj, 2009), 456–68.
16. Ghobadi, *Anemone on the Rock*, 613.
17. Ibid.

18. Akhtar Kamangar, *Farazhayi az zendegiye Akhtare Kamangar* (Passages from the Life of Akhtar Kamangar) (Stockholm: Khanyeyh Farhange Shamloo, 2016), 200.
19. Malakeh Mostafa Soltani, *Sébari Qalabard La Sar Almane u Talasowar (The Shadow of the Qalabard on Almane and Talasowar)* (Sweden: 49books, 2023), 257.
20. Lucia Bargel, "La socialisation politique sexuée : apprentissage des pratiques politiques et normes de genre chez les jeunes militantes" (Gendered Political Socialization: Learning Political Practices and Gender Norms Among Young Female Activists), *Nouvelles Questions Féministes,* no 3, vol. 24 (2005), 36–49.
21. Jules Falquet, "Division sexuelle du travail révolutionnaire : Réflexions à partir de l'expérience salvadorienne (1970–1994), (Sexual Division of Revolutionary Labor: Reflections from the Salvadoran Experience (1970–1994)), *Cahiers des Amériques latines,* no. 40 (2013): 109–28.
22. Cited in Geneviève Dermenjian and Dominique Loiseau, "Itinéraires de femmes communistes," (Itineraries of Communist Women) in *Le sexe du militantisme* (The Sex of Militancy), ed. Olivier Fillieule and Patricia Roux (Paris: Presses de Sciences Po, 2009), 93–113.
23. Philippe Gottraux, *Socialisme ou Barbarie. Un engagement politique et intellectuel dans la France de l'après-guerre* (Socialism or Barbarism. A Political and Intellectual Commitment in Post-War France) (*Lausanne: Payot,* 1997), 174.
24. Ghobadi, *Anemone on the Rock,* 621.
25. Ibid., 627.
26. Azar Majedi, "Independent Organization of Working Women and the Generalization of Sexual Apartheid to the Labor Movement" [Tashakolé Mostaghele Zanane Kargar Ta'amime Apartaidé Jensi be Jonbeshe Kargari], 2013: www.mobarez-k.com/arshiv. Accessed January 6, 2014.
27. Ghobadi, *Anemone on the Rock,* 628, 637.
28. Ibid., 639.

CONCLUSION

1. Olivier Fillieule, "Travail militant, action collective et rapports de genre," (Activist Work, Collective Action and Gender Relations) in *Le sexe du militantisme* (The Sex of Activism), ed. Olivier Fillieule and Patricia Roux (Paris: Presses de Sciences Po, 2009), 28–9; Lucie Bargel, *Jeunes socialistes, jeunes UMP. Lieux et processus de socialisation politique* (Young Socialists, Young UMP [Union for a Popular

Movement]. Places and Processes of Political Socialization), (Paris: Dalloz, 2009).

2. Jules Falquet, "Entre rupture et reproduction: femmes salvadoriennes dans la guerre révolutionnaire (1981–1992)," (Between Rupture and Reproduction: Salvadoran Women in the Revolutionary War (1981–1992), *Nouvelles questions féministes* (New Feminist Questions), 17, no. 2 (1996): 20.
3. Akhtar Kamangar, *Farazhayi az zendegiye Akhtare Kamangar* (Passages from the life of Akhtar Kamangar) (Stockholm: Khanyeyh Farhange Shamloo, 2016), 209.
4. Hilal Alkan, "The Sexual Politics of War: Reading the Kurdish Conflict Through Images of Women," *Les cahiers du CEDREF*, no. 22 (2018): 68–92.

Index

The Pluto Press Newsletter

Hello friend of Pluto!

Want to stay on top of the best radical books we publish?

Then sign up to be the first to hear about our new books, as well as special events, podcasts and videos.

You'll also get 50% off your first order with us when you sign up.

Come and join us!

Go to bit.ly/PlutoNewsletter